FROM CIVIL RIGHTS TO BLACK LIBERATION

Malcolm X and the Organization of Afro-American Unity

William W. Sales, Jr.

South End Press
Boston, Massachusetts

Cover design by Wen-Ti Tsen
Cover photo by Robert Parent, Pathfinder Press, taken at a press conference in Kennedy Airport, November 24, 1964
All inside photos by Robert Parent, courtesy of Pathfinder Press
Text design and production by South End Press collective
Printed in the U.S.A.

Library of Congress Cataloging-in-Publication Data

Sales, Jr., William W.
From Civil Rights to Black Liberation: Malcolm X and the Organization of Afro-American Unity/William W. Sales, Jr.
p. cm.
Includes bibliographic references and index
1. X, Malcolm, 1925-1965. 2. Organization of Afro-American Unity.
I. Title. BP223. Z8L5772 1994 94-8691
320 5'4'092—DC20 CIP
ISBN 0-89608-480-9:$14.00 paper
ISBN 0-89608-481-7:$30.00 cloth

South End Press, 116 Saint Botolph Street, Boston, MA 02115

99 98 97 96 95 94   2 3 4 5 6 7 8 9

*Dedicated to the memory of
Ellen Parker Sales and William Sales, Sr., my parents.*

CONTENTS

Acknowledgements

This book is an outgrowth of the activities of the Malcolm X Work Group of the Cooperative Research Network in Black Studies (CRN). It is part of a larger effort to establish a data base for research on Malcolm X. My particular thanks are extended to the members of the Malcolm X Work Group, in particular its co-founder Abdul Alkalimat, James Cone, and Gloria Joseph. Their commentary and support have been invaluable in supporting my research. My thanks are extended also to the widow of Malcolm X, Dr. Betty Shabazz, who graciously received us and encouraged our work from the outset.

I have received valuable institutional support from the Africana Studies Department at Queens College, City University of New York (CUNY), Alem Habtu, director. Dr. Joseph Murphy, former chancellor of CUNY, with the help of his indefatigable aide, David Fields, provided needed financial support without which important aspects of this research could not have gone forward.

Seton Hall University extended a needed sabbatical, which, together with a fellowship from the Revson Foundation, supported the initial year of my research on Malcolm X.

My research was greatly facilitated by David Garrow, who provided me with his copies of the FBI's Muslim Mosque, Inc. file, the FBI's Organization of Afro-American Unity file, and the FBI's record of telephone tap logs on Malcolm X's personal phone. The Schomburg Center for Research in Black Culture provided valuable assistance in locating additional materials concerning Malcolm X and Harlem-based Black nationalism.

A special thanks is due to Dr. Charles V. Hamilton of the Political Science Department of Columbia University. His encouragement and sound advice facilitated my writing during difficult stages. The comments of Dr. Tony Marx were crucial in sharpening my insights on several of the more important questions addressed in this study. Drs. Hollis Lynch and Eric Foner also shared important insights on the historical context of this study.

I am happy to extend heartfelt thanks to the friends and associates of Malcolm X, too numerous to mention here, who helped me along the way. Representative of this group is my friend from childhood, Akbar

Muhammed Ahmed (aka Max Stanford), and Harlem's own Yuri Kochi-yama.

My wife, Aishah, was a special inspiration through it all. She kept the homefront in order but also provided necessary editorial help and in many different ways helped me to make this book happen.

My thanks to my editor, Dionne Brooks, and all of the other members of the South End Collective, whose commitment and persistence contributed immeasurably to the final product.

I thank all of the ordinary folks who shared their experiences of Malcolm X with me. I hope my effort here has done justice to the truth and their hope to see Malcolm X established in his rightful place as a seminal thinker of this century. Nevertheless, I bear full responsibility for the conclusions herein. I hope that my research effort does justice to the integrity and nobility of El Hajj Malik El Shabazz, the "Black Shining Prince" of African American manhood.

Preface

This book represents a detailed description and analysis of the Organization of Afro-American Unity (OAAU). Such an analysis is necessary to do justice to the content of Malcolm's life and his politics. Such a description and analysis, based on interviews with OAAU members, FBI surveillance files, previously published accounts, and OAAU documents has never before been done. The legacy of Malcolm X cannot be appreciated without a clear and detailed exposure to the OAAU. In addition, the hostility of the U.S. government toward Malcolm X is logical in the context of his OAAU activities. Spike Lee's film biography of Malcolm X does not in any way present or discuss the OAAU, its process of creation, or Malcolm X's activities in Africa or the United States on its behalf. The CBS documentary on Malcolm X which aired on December 3, 1992 and was hosted by Dan Rather also skirted any substantive description of the OAAU or Malcolm's activities in Africa. In fact, on this show Mike Wallace asserted that in Malcolm X's last months he was a man without a following, a constituency, or a plan. Substituted for the significance of the OAAU is a thoroughly unwarranted argument that the most important development in Malcolm X's life at this point was his trip to Mecca and his changing pro-integrationist stance on White people. This is a thread common to both the Spike Lee film and the Dan Rather special. If this approach is sustainable, it leads directly to the conclusion that Malcolm X is not a revolutionary but rather a tragic figure in the mold of Shakespeare's Hamlet. Another more liberal but equally deceptive perspective suggested by these treatments is that Malcolm X was a misunderstood African American Horatio Alger. Psycho-historian Bruce Perry's controversial biography of Malcolm X has almost nothing to say about this most important period in Malcolm's life.

Information from the OAAU period will refute these erroneous images of Malcolm X. This refutation starts with the process of the organization's creation. Domestic and international developments meshed to produce the OAAU. In creating the OAAU, Malcolm X in the last eleven months of his life cultivated three groups: a united front composed of progressive segments of the Black middle-class and working-class activists in Harlem united around a community-based agenda of and struggle against the common forms of ghetto exploitation; allies in Africa and the Third World who could get international recognition for his organization; and friends in the Civil Rights movement who supported Malcolm's desire for reconciliation. The OAAU concept was particularly successful among the youth wing of the Civil Rights movement. This group also gave Malcolm access to the radicalized White students. As it turned out, the OAAU found that its allies in the White community came most readily from among White students.

Most importantly, I will argue that the OAAU represented a compelling experience of Pan-Africanism for the inner circle of that organization and more generally for the most radicalized as well as the youngest segments of the Civil Rights movement. This is crucial in evaluating the OAAU because it explains why the influence of the organization actually grew and became widespread *after* the death of Malcolm X. The activities of Malcolm X and the OAAU created in the minds of the leadership of African nations and that of the Afro-Asian bloc the sense that the U.S. Civil Rights struggle possessed the qualities of a Pan-Africanist national liberation movement.

1

THE YEAR THEY RE- DISCOVERED MALCOLM

Giving a Brother His Due

The Malcolm X resurgence matured in 1990, which marked the sixty-fifth anniversary of his birth and the twenty-fifth anniversary of Malcolm's assassination. These two occasions gave rise to unprecedented scholarly activity and serious commemorative efforts. So much new activity was initiated around the recognition and examination of Malcolm X that Preston Wilcox of AFRAM Associates was able to establish a national Malcolm X Lovers Network which provided information and coordination for these numerous efforts. The Malcolm X Work Group initiated several research projects with scholars like James Cone and Abdul Alkalimat. In addition, it joined with the Cooperative Research Network in Black Studies and the City University of New York to co-sponsor the first international conference on Malcolm X, which took place in New York City in November 1990. Earlier in that same year, members of the Malcolm X Work Group participated with about twenty-five other African American scholars and activists in the symposium "Malcolm X Speaks to the 1990s," which took place in Havana, Cuba.[1] The interest in Malcolm X, initiated in the 1990 commemorations, gave rise to about twenty-five new books on Malcolm which are presently or will soon be published.

Mrs. Rowena Moore established the Malcolm X Foundation and succeeded in having Malcolm X's birthplace in Omaha, Nebraska declared a national and state landmark. African American scholars and activists led by Ron Daniels established a commission to make Malcolm X's birthday a national holiday. Throughout the Black communities of this country, streets, schools, and community centers have been renamed after Malcolm X. One of the most significant and successful efforts in this regard was waged by the New Afrikan Peoples Organization (NAPO) and coordinated by Ahmed Obafemi. NAPO succeeded in getting Harlem's Lenox Avenue renamed Malcolm X Boulevard.

Re-discovered in the Marketplace

While the efforts just cited represent a serious and lasting commitment to Malcolm X led by long-established scholars and activists, it is also important to recognize that Malcolm X has become an icon for an increasingly assertive African American youth generation. In the '90s, Malcolm's image graces numerous T-shirts and sweat shirts. The omnipresent baseball caps with the X logo come in all colors and sizes. They grace the coiffures of Black males and females alike and not a few of their White counterparts. The "X" has even appeared as the logo of a new brand of potato chips. Strident quotations from Malcolm's *Autobiography* and his more well-known speeches call out from the speakers of "beat boxes" in every ghetto community. "By any means necessary" is for African American youth the slogan of the 1990s, assuming the same significance as the slogans "Black Power," "Black is beautiful," and "I'm Black and I'm proud" for the generation of the 1960s. The canonization of Malcolm reached its peak with the premiere of film maker Spike Lee's three hour and twenty-one minute larger-than-life film biography, *X*. It was preceded by $35 million in production costs and an unprecedented $10 million advanced publicity campaign. The commercial possibilities of Malcolm's image and the X logo have initiated an increasingly bitter struggle for control of these properties. Dr. Betty Shabazz, Malcolm's widow, has retained counsel and initiated several court actions to protect her interests in the many products which attempt to exploit Malcolm's name and legacy.

The Struggle to Define Malcolm

There has been intense competition for the image of Malcolm X not only in the marketplace but in the ideological and political arena as well. In this regard the treatment of Malcolm X parallels that of leaders like Marcus Garvey and Nelson Mandela. Once the image of these leaders can no longer be suppressed or ignored, their value and their significance is distorted, often by being reduced to slogans, which satisfy temporarily but whose superficiality masks the deeper meaning of the issues and analysis these leaders tried to convey. Television has been a very important medium in bringing Malcolm X to African American youth. The electronic media has left its imprint on the popular conception and treatment of Malcolm X. The sound bite and the popular preoccupation with news as entertainment have made Malcolm an icon but threatened to subvert the need to study and evaluate Malcolm as a thinker, a leader, and a role model. CBS initiated some of the media's fascination with Malcolm X. In 1959, the Mike Wallace documentary *The Hate That Hate Produced*, made Malcolm X famous. On December 3, 1992, CBS anchor Dan Rather closed the electronic media circle with a primetime one-hour documentary treatment of Malcolm X which emphasized the pop culture, iconographic aspects of Malcolm's life. It had much of the flavor of the popular television exposé *Current Affair*, and much of *Current Affair*'s superficiality and sensationalism. Nevertheless, it has been through the medium of television and its music

4

videos like *Sun City,* and rap group Arrested Development's soundtrack to Spike Lee's movie that Malcolm's image and words have reached large numbers of African American youth. Malcolm X was among the first African Americans who seriously discussed the possibility of the revolutionary option for Black people. In this sense he was somewhat ahead of his time and scared many of his peers initially. Today's youth generation, out of the desperate conditions of its existence, is much less shocked by Malcolm's rhetoric and seeks to embrace his revolutionary speech and example.

Rap Music Finds Malcolm

The U.S. ruling class has presented Black youth with a coopted image of Dr. Martin Luther Dr. King, Jr. Thus, Dr. King's "dream" does not resonate as much with the '90s generation, and many have chosen Malcolm instead. Unlike Dr. King, Malcolm was a product of the urban ghetto and always spoke to the "nightmare" of its reality, a reality which is very much still with the rap generation.

The artistic expression of today's Black youth, rap music, owes a particular debt to Malcolm X. It is through rap music that this youth generation speaks to the world. Malcolm X helped this generation find its voice. Dennis O'Neill has written about the striking parallels between the life of Malcolm X and the thematic content of rap: the hustler bravado, the ever-present threat of jail, the transformative effect of Islam, the condemnation of Black-on-Black violence, and the reconciliation with Africa. O'Neill pinpoints the connection between rap and Malcolm X:

> ...the rhythms of Malcolm's voice are the rhythms of rap itself in a very real sense...the emphasis on the words—their content—rather than the emotion that can be wrung from them or even injected into them by the passion of the performer—this is Malcolm and this is rap.[2]

Malcolm's image as well as his words have been prominently featured in rap videos, an image of youth, of armed defiance, and of grace and power. As Malcolm spoke, he punctuated the air and struck down imaginary enemies in a style which anticipates the performance style of today's rap artists. In rap videos, Malcolm is often featured as an icon hovering in the background and looking down upon the mass of his following. In film-star Eddie Murphy's recent video, Malcolm's image opens the festivities by miraculously emerging out of the depths of the sea.[3]

Being Black in the United States

If anything, today's African American youth and their counterparts in the Third World urban ghettos and reservations inside the United States are in much more jeopardy than the "lost generation" of Malcolm's era. Malcolm X lived in a nation with a rising standard of living for its White population. The persistent poverty of African Americans stood in glaring contradiction to the still widely believed myth of equal opportunity. Today, the United States is a declining economic power, unable to shake a persistent recession which has eroded the living standards of middle-class and working-class Whites and exacerbated genocidal conditions inside urban ghettos. In 1991, the United States was the industrial nation with "the greatest amount of economic inequality."[4] The top 1 percent of earners had collectively almost as much after-tax income as the bottom 40 percent. Most families earned less in 1990 than they had in 1973. The United States' economic decline tore at the social fabric of the African American community. In 1991, African Americans experienced a poverty rate three times that of their White counterparts. Almost one in every three African Americans lived in poverty. Poverty particularly victimized the very young and the very old in the Black community. Half of all African American children under age six lived in poverty. During the decade of the 1980s, Black children living in hyperpoverty (in families whose incomes were less than half the official poverty level) increased by 52 percent.[5] Over half of the female-headed households in Black communities are impoverished.[6] Since 1970, the proportion of all African Americans living in female-headed families has risen from 30 percent to 45 percent. During the same period, 2.35 million African Americans living in these households have joined the ranks of the poor.[7]

Employment rates for Black males declined sharply during the 1970s and 1980s.[8] African American teenagers were particularly hard hit with only one in four finding any meaningful work in the economy during the quarter century since Malcolm X's death.[9] They were over twice as likely as their White counterparts to be unemployed.[10]

African American women for the last two decades have attempted to take up the slack by entering the labor market in greater numbers. After initial gains in the 1970s, these women have seen their position deteriorate relative to White women in the 1980s and 1990s.[11] Black economist, Barbara Jones, has recognized that Black women have always constituted a large proportion of the reservoir of potential workers who could be tapped when necessary by the private sector. For most of the history of this country, Black women have been denied entrance to all but the most menial of jobs. Their recent inclusion into other positions in the labor force, primarily as service and clerical workers, has been a function of the need of corporations to keep labor costs down and far below the rates that would prevail if men or White women continued to have exclusive access to these jobs. In an era of prolonged economic decline, more than any other category of the labor force, African American women are "the last hired and the first fired." As more and more African American families and youths are dependent on the earning power of the female heads of their households, the economic status of Black women is an accurate mirror of the chronic depression facing the whole community. The figures for Black male and female employment and unemployment understate the severity of the predicament because these figures ignore those who are discouraged workers and those who, while employed, cannot earn a decent wage.

Relative to their White counterparts, African Americans own little significant wealth, occupy the lowest rungs of the occupational ladder, and have less education.[12]

Too many young African Americans in urban ghettos have mistakenly perceived, as did Malcolm X in his teenage years, that the only available route to material gain is through hustling, petty crime, and drug dealing. There are several factors which have contributed to this development. First, with the success of the Civil Rights movement in improving access to integrated housing for middle-class African Americans, the older inner-city communities have fewer middle-class role models for their youth. Second, fiscal crises in these older municipalities have accelerated the decay of inner-city institutions like the public schools, the parks and recreation facilities, and the settlement houses. Traditionally, workers and professionals in these institutions often resided in the community and provided role models for the youth. At the same time, these institutions provided whatever training and socialization the society was prepared to extend to African Americans. Moreover, they often were the base of operations of progressive individuals and organizations which pushed these institutions to levels of community service far beyond the intentions of their originators. Third, the Black churches have been less able to provide leadership and financial resources as their congregations shrink while the needs of their communities grow. Ironically, many of the biggest and most affluent African American congregations remain located in inner cities, but the majority of their parishioners no longer live in the old neighborhoods. While some of these churches have been doing excellent work in the area of social welfare, too many of them reflect the lack of interest of their "expatriate" parishioners in the welfare of the communities that surround them. This phenomenon contributes to the cynicism that is characteristic of many of today's ghetto youth. Last but most important, there is no Black Liberation movement in our communities as there was in the 1960s. The feeling of power that such a movement creates in a community, the orientation toward collective values, and the discipline and accountability that flow from the movement's existence are all absent today in our inner-city neighborhoods.

Materialism and Our Youth

The bankruptcy of the economy and the nihilism of popular culture are the sources of the distorted values and internalized violence of ghetto youth. Today the entire society is ensnared in the worship of material culture. Manhood is defined in terms of how much you have, not how well you care for others. This occurs side-by-side with an increasing inclination to smear the ghetto poor as an underclass and blame them for their own poverty. This material deprivation, and the lack of status and respect in U.S. society, create a desperate situation for African American youth and other youth of color. In the ghetto, with the failure of education and the job market, the available avenues for youth to accumulate goods are concentrated in hustling and criminal activities. Similarly, U.S. culture today has not abandoned its worship of the values of the frontier and rugged individualism. With few available legitimate options to exercise power and control over their lives, Black youth often turn to an exaggerated commitment to a macho lifestyle. The role models fabricated by the make-believe world of the electronic media, sports, and Hollywood appear to our youth to be the only ones relevant to their lives.

Too often, these media role models are romantic stereotypes and caricatures of the all-too-real anti-social elements who populate the narcotics trade and plague our streets. The entertainers, sports figures and rappers so popular with African American youth too often present a style of dress, a mode of speech, and a manner of carriage which is rooted in the criminal culture of the ghetto. The image of the Black man here is one of outrageous macho aggression and self-destruction. Our youth play out against each other the fantasies and orgies of violence seen in the pop culture of movies and television.

Those who start down this road often end up with no lasting rewards but a life-threatening drug dependency. In the last decade, drug dependency, poor housing and nutrition, and little or nonexistent health care for inner-city youth have contributed to an AIDS epidemic from which disproportionate numbers of African American and Latino youths, especially young women and their babies, are dying. Close on the heels of the AIDS epidemic, previously controlled diseases like tuberculosis are again out of control.[13] Life expectancy for Black males in Harlem is lower than for that of males in Bangladesh. Likewise, infant mortality in this same community is greater than in the United States' nemesis, Cuba. Tens of thousands of African Americans, Latinos, and poor White people can find no housing in the United States, a country which is still the wealthiest economy on Earth.

Racism and the "Underclass"

These contemporary social realities, however, explain only a part of the predicament of Black people in the United States. African Americans suffer from the legacy of slavery and continued racial discrimination in all aspects of life in the United States.[14] Through their own untiring efforts and those of their allies, African Americans mounted a social movement in the 1960s, the Civil Rights movement, which forced important concessions from the U.S. ruling class. Nevertheless, as Margaret Burnham has written, the "War on Poverty" and the "Great Society" initiatives of Presidents Kennedy and Johnson, respectively, were "only bits and pieces...representing a piecemeal rather than a systematic approach."[15] Nothing approaching the sums and institutions necessary to eradicate poverty and racism was ever committed by the government. Not withstanding this, Burnham is insightful in recognizing that the benefits of the "Great Society" programs, while leaving the "Black masses (and others of the poor) far from redeemed, also left them less inclined to abandon hope that the mythic American promises extended to Black people too."[16]

Since the Civil Rights era, however, racism has reemerged in a new garb and with novel justifications. Our youth have been socially isolated from sympathetic public sentiment and stigmatized beneath the weight of a post-liberal designation as the "underclass." Michael Katz, in his review of the literature on the underclass, notes that "two groups—Black teenage mothers and Black jobless youths—dominate the images of the underclass."[17] Katz cites *Time* magazine's cover story of August 19, 1977, "The American Underclass":

> Behind [the ghetto's] crumbling walls lives a large group of people who are more intractable, more socially alien and more hostile than almost anyone had imagined. They are the unreachables: the American underclass...Their bleak environment nurtures values that are

often at odds with those of the majority—even the majority of the poor. Thus the underclass produces a highly disproportionate number of the nation's juvenile delinquents, school dropouts, drug addicts and welfare mothers, and much adult crime, family disruption, urban decay, and demand for social expenditures.[18]

Katz concludes that *Time* defines the underclass "primarily by its values and behavior, which [it argued] differed sharply from those of other Americans."[19] Quite accurately, Katz emphasizes that the identification of the "menacing" underclass with unmarried Black women and other popular stereotypes "distracted casual readers from the imprecision, contradictions and weak evidence" offered in support of this ideological concept.[20]

The Reagan-Bush Era

What has the government done as the conditions confronting African Americans have deteriorated? The administration of President Ronald Reagan dashed the hopes of African Americans beneath a full-scale onslaught against domestic social programs. In 1982 Reagan slashed $44 billion in social spending and in the succeeding year lopped off another $19 billion.[21] Under President Bush there was no reversal in this orientation toward the destruction of public social welfare programs.

In his first campaign for president, George Bush appealed to the base, racist instincts and fears of Whites to overcome an early Dukakis lead. The Willie Horton ad, a television spot implying that Dukakis's release from jail of a convicted Black rapist on a pass led to the rape of a young White woman, set the tone for the entire Bush campaign. President Bush vetoed the 1990 Civil Rights Act. Along with Ronald Reagan, he packed the Supreme Court with neoconservative jurists who are prepared to undermine the constitutional basis of the gains achieved since the Civil Rights movement.

The ascension of Judge Clarence Thomas to the Supreme Court in 1992 completed the process of transforming the liberal Warren Court into its conservative opposite. Ironically, all of the retrograde trends associated with the nomination of Judge Thomas—Black neoconservatism, the subversion of the Supreme Court, and sexual harassment—came together in the brutal persecution of Anita Hill, a fellow Republican neoconservative, before a nationwide television audience. The spectacle exposed the Far Right's perception of women and women's rights, the male-dominated bipartisan consensus on this issue as demonstrated by the spineless behavior of the Democratic members of the Senate Judiciary Committee, and the opportunism of White middle-class feminists who rushed to the defense of Anita Hill but who had no previous profile on issues and struggles related to poor Black women.[22] The Clinton administration, unfortunately, has continued this trend with its cavalier treatment of the potential nomination for government posts of Spelman College President Johnnetta Cole and the withdrawal of the nomination of Civil Rights attorney and University of Pennsylvania law professor Lani Guinier.

Ironically, as the conditions African Americans face become worse and worse, the political and business leadership of the nation speaks less and less about this crisis confronting the race. Both Johnnetta Cole and Lani Guinier were rejected because they refused to pursue what the political scientists call a politics of "deracialization." One popular sense of "deracialization" simply means that it is considered politically expedient not to talk about the problems of African Americans because White people feel uncomfortable with that topic and because the topic is "divisive."[23]

The Criminalization of Black Youth

In the face of chronic economic stagnation and recession, the lack of an adequate government "security net" has had a devastating impact on African Americans, especially the youth. Nevertheless, the Bush administration was best only at building jails in response to chronic social problems. Its "Weed and Seed" anti-drug program and its "Violence Initiative" had genocidal implications for ghetto dwellers. Black youth have been criminalized in the popular mind. With this public mood of vindictiveness toward our youth, it might not be surprising that 23 percent of all Black men aged twenty to twenty-nine either are in jail, on probation, or on parole.[24] Rates of incarceration in the United States exceed those in every other Western industrial democracy and are rivaled only by those of South Africa.[25]

The previous Republican administration was joined by prominent Democrats in a bipartisan attack on the welfare and image of African American youth. New York's governor Mario Cuomo, known for his liberal credentials and intellectual bearing, is in fact setting new records for prison construction in upstate New York. Democratic President, Bill Clinton, when governor of Arkansas, endorsed the execution of a mental incompetent. Clinton did not campaign as a strong advocate of the rights of ghetto dwellers and the victims of racism. He is president because of

Bush's failure to resolve chronic depression in the nation's economy. Clinton rapidly reversed his campaign pledges on Haiti and willingly continued Bush's policy of using violence against peoples of color abroad, as evidenced by the continued attacks on Iraq.

The Fire This Time

The victimization of young people of color has legitimized racist attitudes which have increased in White communities undergoing severe economic recession. Overt acts of bigotry, hate, and crime have multiplied. Right-wing racist and lunatic fringe groups like the Ku Kux Klan, the Nazi Party, and the National Association for the Advancement of White People and their candidate, David Duke, have gained respectability and widespread media exposure.[26]

This growing insensitivity to the plight of Black America was glaringly reflected in the acquittal in April 1992 of the policemen responsible for the vicious beating of Rodney King, a Black motorist, in Los Angeles. Subsequently, two of the four police officers acquitted by state courts were convicted of the federal crime of violating Rodney King's civil rights. Unfortunately, this favorable decision does not reflect a national trend, as deaths of African Americans while in police custody continue unabated. In the very year of his death, 1965, Malcolm X had warned of a very hot summer for America, which in fact culminated in the Los Angeles Watts rebellion.[27] Twenty-seven years later, Malcolm's warning remained unheeded, and East Central Los Angeles exploded in unprecedented fury, its shock waves flowing over the Los Angeles metropolitan area and reaching far afield into San Francisco, Seattle, and Atlanta, among other places. The rebellion in Los Angeles was unique in that it was not solely or possibly even primarily a Black riot. Rather it included significant participation from a host of Los Angeles' communities of color and even from some poor Whites.

In recent years in Los Angeles, the color of the clothing and baseball caps of ghetto youth have symbolized their division into hostile fighting gangs. The response of these same forces to the Rodney King verdict was to pull together and attempt to go beyond these violent divisions. This process achieved a national dimension with the successful "gang summit" convention held in Kansas City in May of 1993. Those involved in the process, however, feel that the police are making every effort to subvert it. In Los Angeles, leaders of the gang truce have found themselves subject to police harassment and arrest.

In Los Angeles as in other cities, the X emblem of Malcolm was seen everywhere on the T-shirts and caps of youth who previously were wearing only their gang colors. For Malcolm X, the X stood for the original African name that every African American lost in the middle passage and slavery, but it is rapidly coming to represent a new identity, unity, and pride in this generation of Black youth.

Malcolm X Speaks to the 1990s

Economic depression, stagnation, and the lack of an effective government response have endangered the very social fabric of Black America. The departure or closing of businesses which are never replaced, continuing layoffs, and a lack of jobs have permanently detached too many inner-city residents from any meaningful relationship to the job market. Crucial Black institutions like the family are subjected to intense forces which threaten to break them up and destroy them. Important personal relationships like those between man and woman, children and adults are destabilized. The real danger, however, is not material want alone but something more profound.

Cornel West, former chairperson of the African American Studies Department at Princeton University, makes a good attempt at getting at this deeper danger. He argued in a recent article:

> The proper starting point for the crucial debate about the prospects for Black America is the nihilism that increasingly pervades Black communities. *Nihilism is to be understood here not as a philosophic doctrine that there are no rational grounds for legitimate standards or authority; it is, far more, the lived experience of coping with a life of horrifying meaninglessness, hopelessness, and (most important) lovelessness.* This usually results in a numbing detachment from others and a self-destructive disposition toward the world. Life without meaning, hope, and love breeds a coldhearted, mean spirited outlook that destroys both the individual and others [emphasis in the original].[28]

I would sharpen West's focus to those factors which are unique to the present situation that he has described as nihilism. African Americans have previously experienced periods of intense material poverty and racial ostracism. Never before, however, has there been such a threat to our sense of self-worth, our optimism about the future, and our confidence that others in our community would stick by us throughout our hardship. In this climate, too many of our young people are seeking refuge in a rugged individualism and a conspicuous consumption of goods, no matter what the costs to others. The consequences of this behavior go beyond unprecedented individual suffering. They constitute a threat to the survival of African Americans as a people.

Malcolm's Message

Malcolm X knew and lived this material and spiritual deprivation as Malcolm Little, the child, and Detroit Red, the teenager. This kind of deprivation has become the reality of too many of our young people today, especially those in the most at-risk group, aged sixteen to twenty-four. But they are beginning to find their way out of this dead end with the help of Malcolm's words and the example of his life. To return to Dennis O'Neill's perceptive discussion of rap culture and Malcolm X, he pinpoints the basis for Malcolm's contemporary popularity.

> Part of why the connection is so strong is that Malcolm came out of the urban ghetto and spoke to and for its people. His experience, his life are recapitulated in rap because they are recapitulated in the daily lives of millions of young Black people every day. Things in the ghetto have changed, if at all, for the worse since his day. So his message, like the style in which it was delivered, remains fresh...This makes Malcolm an iconic figure in the growing resurgence of national consciousness in the African American community and in its reflection in rap.[29]

O'Neill recognizes that "rap hasn't yet been the vehicle to bring Malcolm's full and real message to African American youth." He feels that young people need Malcolm X as more than just a Black icon.[30] Presently he is an icon of the anger of young Black people. He can be much more, a source of critical thought and teaching on the art and science of individual redemption and social transformation. Our Black youth are reading more as a by-product of the Malcolm craze. Almost everywhere that you can get an X hat or Malcolm T-shirt you can also get popular and scholarly books on Malcolm X. In addition, our youth are not on the periphery but right at the center of the debate now raging on the content of Malcolm X's teaching and its message for us today. What a refreshing change for this generation to be enticed away from the television and the movies to be engaged with other flesh and blood human beings in a debate about Malcolm's real teachings and their relevance for the struggle ahead.

Cornel West, in an important article in *The Village Voice*, has argued that Malcolm's relevance may be more limited than that of Dr. Martin Luther King, Jr. or Elijah Muhammad.[31] In comparing the three African American leadership figures of the 1960s, West observed that:

> Elijah Muhammad and Martin Luther King, Jr. understood one fundamental truth about Black rage: It must be neither ignored nor ignited. This is what separates them from the great Malcolm X. Malcolm indeed articulated Black rage in an unprecedented manner in American history; yet his broad Black nationalist platforms were too vague to give this Black rage any concrete direction. Elijah and Martin knew how to work with Black rage in a constructive manner: shape it through moral discipline, channel it into political organization, and guide it by visionary leadership.[32]

As sensitive and insightful as Cornel West can be, his analysis of Malcolm X unfortunately reflects the media image of Malcolm in his Nation of Islam period. Even here this image is not an accurate reflection of the basis of Malcolm's leadership. Moreover, it speaks not at all to the obvious development of Malcolm X's Black nationalism into Pan-African internationalism in the last year of his life. Dr. King's plan was successful in defeating legal discrimination. He engineered a monumental victory for African Americans. Unfortunately, Dr. King's model does not achieve the same success in channeling the rage of today's African American youth in a positive direction. Elijah Muhammad achieved notable success in developing a model for helping the most downtrodden Black people rehabilitate themselves. Nevertheless, his model achieved widespread popularity in the Black community only under Malcolm's day-to-day leadership. In order to achieve such popularity, Malcolm X introduced significant modifications into the Black religious nationalism of Elijah Muhammad. These modifications will be discussed in more detail in subsequent chapters. Today's youth are actually learning about the Nation of Islam not in its original presentation but as reflected and modified by the speeches and presentations of Malcolm X. This later form, however, is more popular with today's youth than the original version. Malcolm X was not simply the biblical John the Baptist crying in the wilderness for one greater than he.

The Roots of the Malcolm X Resurgence

A closer look at the origins of Malcolm X's renewed popularity will reveal much about its basis. As early as 1976, the potential for the politicization of Black youth culture became evident. The Soweto Uprising of June 16, 1976 was largely led by the youth of South Africa. It was a ghetto township uprising, and martyred student and Black Consciousness leader Stephen Bantu Biko was its icon. Soweto gave rise to sympathy demonstrations in the United States in which young African American youth were prominently featured. The date June 16 subsequently became a day of worldwide commemoration of the struggle of South African youth against apartheid. In the major U.S. urban centers Black youth were involved in demonstrations and commemorative activities in subsequent years. These anti-apartheid activities were organized by the remnants of the activists from the 1960s like New York's Blacks in Solidarity With Southern African Liberation (BISSAL) and Black Liberation Press. In Chicago, anti-apartheid activities were sponsored by the Peoples College Collective among others, and the splintered African Liberation Support Committee aligned with Kwame Toure's (Stokely Carmichael) All Afrikan Peoples Revolutionary Party (AAPRP), which committed itself to preserving the commemoration of African Liberation Day each May.

In reaction to this motion at the grassroots, the African American petty bourgeoisie was energized to join the anti-apartheid movement. TransAfrica, the African American lobby on Africa, undertook to lead Black notables and celebrities in highly symbolic demonstrations with orchestrated arrests. These activities garnered considerable media attention by the 1980s, but the energizing motion of the grassroots African American community in this period is too often overlooked. It was from the Soweto Uprising that a new anti-apartheid movement gradually reconstructed itself to become a major force through the actions of high school and college youth in the mid-1980s.

In 1980 African American youth gave a preview of their heightened frustration and anger, and of the considerable potential for massive social disruption contained therein. In response to an obvious travesty of police brutality, Miami youth rebelled and set fire to the city's Black neighborhoods. While nowhere near the scale of the 1960s disturbances, this uprising indicated that Black youth would not remain quiet in the face of rapidly escalating poverty and abuse. It was from this event that Jesse Jackson began to develop a program and an electoral political strategy which climaxed in the emergence of the Rainbow Coalition in 1984.

In Search of a Movement

By the early 1980s, the rage of the so-called Black underclass sought positive as well as negative outlets. Our young people were objectively in search of the Black Liberation movement. Initially they found it not so much at home but in the events associated with the dynamic and changing international environment of the 1980s.

African American youth found the image of their rage in the political demonstrations of their counterparts in South Africa against the constitutional revisions that the apartheid government introduced through the 1984 referendum. Children of the electronic media experienced the fusing of South African news media images with the rap culture of urban rebellion through late 1984 and on into 1985. Our youth were served nightly doses of their counterparts in South Africa channeling their rage in a disciplined and revolutionary freedom struggle. Shouting, dancing, protesting in the streets, heroically throwing stones against the apartheid government's armored vehicles, policemen and regular army units, African youth taught their elders new ways of fighting back and led them to a new level of resistance.

The living hero of the young South African freedom fighters was Nelson Mandela, imprisoned but uncompromising for over twenty years. Our youth also drew strength and a new sense of hope and power from the youth of South Africa and from the examples of their martyred compatriots, Stephen Biko, and Nelson Mandela. Young African American women found particular pride in the magnificent image of resistance and defiance that was Winnie Mandela.

African American youth sought ways of relating to this struggle in South Africa. On college campuses they joined the anti-apartheid divestment movement, disrupting the halls of ivy and when necessary going to jail. Through this process a new generation of activist-intellectuals was born; nurtured by veteran activists waiting to welcome new blood into a previously moribund Black Liberation movement. Leaders of the cultural boycott of South Africa recruited rap artists and popular Black entertainers. They made a video against performers appearing in "Sun City" (a large South African entertainment complex). Rap, reggae, music videos, and South African township music were potent political channels to express the youths' rage and frustration. The images and sounds of South African youths defying oppression infused the consciousness of the so-called American underclass. This generation of African American youth for the first time asked the question, "Could it happen here?" Was there an African American who could emulate the heroic symbol of uncompromising resistance represented in South Africa by Nelson Mandela?

Through anti-apartheid work and grassroots mobilization, veteran African American activists were able to introduce Malcolm X to a new generation of youth. Organizations like Peoples College in Chicago, the Patrice Lumumba Coalition in Harlem, and the New Afrikan Peoples Organization nationally kept Malcolm's image and message in the forefront of a resurgent youth generation. This work stood in stark contrast to the bourgeois-led anti-apartheid movement of organizations like TransAfrica, which too often erred by reducing the South African liberation struggle to a struggle for civil rights. These groups raised the philosophy of nonviolence and the image of Dr. King in the face of a South African freedom struggle which had affirmed the inherent right to pursue liberation "by any means necessary." Therefore, of all the recent African American leadership figures, our youth felt Malcolm X could best fulfill the inspirational role they first saw in Nelson Mandela.

The sense of their ability to have an impact on societal conditions has grown in our youth as the decade of the 1980s ended. The end of the 1970s provided excellent examples of revolutionary movements with charismatic youthful leadership overcoming considerable odds to assume state power. In Central America, the Sandinistas prevailed in 1979. In the Caribbean, they were joined by the New Jewel Movement in Grenada under the leadership of Maurice Bishop. It is important to recognize that these movements were not unknown in the birthplace of rap and break dancing, New York City. Daniel Ortega toured the Bronx ghetto neighborhoods, and Maurice Bishop addressed youth at Hunter College and later received New York high school students who came to Grenada to work for the revolution there. Throughout the world and especially in Eastern Europe and the former Soviet Union, youth have had a disproportionate impact on bringing down long-established governments and systems. The image of mobilized youth dominated the scene at the Berlin Wall's destruction, during the Baltic states' independence struggle, in Red Square during the abortive Soviet coup, and in China's Tiananmen Square. Cuba harnessed this youthful idealism and energy in the fighting forces it sent to aid the Angolans and the Namibians to resist South African military intervention. Through their excellent example of sacrifice, the great victory over South Africa at Quito Carneval was won, creating irreversible momentum to free Namibia and unban the African National Congress (ANC).

A Spiritual Mentor to Black Youth

The example of Malcolm X has also become a very important recruiting device for the orthodox branch of Islam (called Sunni Islam) to reach African American youth. In their rejection of a Eurocentric orientation in U.S. education and culture, African American youth have increasingly been attracted to a rising form of Islamic fundamentalism now visible in Black communities in the United States. This process has extended beyond Sunni Islam itself to other branches of Islam like the Sufis, which are experiencing a more thoroughgoing turn toward fundamentalism. The renewed interest in Malcolm X has also led many Black youth who are not familiar with the history of Malcolm's relationship with the Nation of Islam(NOI) back to the various offshoots of the old NOI and most prominently to its new leader, Louis Farakkhan.

The Significance of Malcolm X Today

Today it is apparent that the tremendous energy of our youth, in search of a politics of liberation, has firmly established Malcolm X as an icon equal to Dr. King in the pantheon of Black heroes. Rekindling the movement for Black liberation requires that Malcolm X must be much more than an icon in the quest for a new Black Liberation movement. The central thesis of this work will demonstrate that Malcolm X's ultimate value to the Black Liberation movement today is as a thinker who returned the movement to a radical Pan-Africanist tradition—as represented in the Organization of Afro-American Unity (OAAU)—and identified and grappled with crucial questions that still confront our movement today.

Learning All that Malcolm Has to Teach Us

Frantz Fanon, the Martiniquan-born psychiatrist and theorist of the Algerian revolution, said that "every generation rises from relative obscurity and either fulfills its historic mission or betrays it."[33] For each generation, however, the identification of its historic mission is no easy task. In fact, every generation is bequeathed by the previous one unfinished business which must be attended to. In the activity of both the African American street youth and the African American political tycoons, like Jesse Jackson and the Reverend Al Sharpton, there is still a lack of understanding of the African American nationalist tradition and the context within which it reemerged in the 1960s. Little is known or understood about the important integrationist-nationalist debate of this same period. If this generation of African American youths is to be oriented toward revolutionary options, it must deepen its understanding of the African American protest tradition and the ideological and programmatic alternatives between which they must choose.

How the 1960s Can Speak to the 1990s

We need to understand the African American social upheaval of the 1960s. The agenda which it sought to address, achievement of the full range of fundamental human rights for African Americans, has yet to be achieved. In pursuit of this human rights agenda, important questions were raised about organization, tactics and strategy, and the appropriate guiding ideas which have yet to be accurately and comprehensively answered. Today the African American people need these answers if we are going to rebuild our movement for liberation. An accurate understanding of Malcolm X and the issues with which he grappled is crucial to understanding the 1960s. The various weaknesses and errors in our understanding of Malcolm X also distort our understanding of the 1960s. There is a pronounced tendency in the current revival of Malcolm X to ignore his significance as a thinker and a theorist. The prevailing view of Malcolm X as an icon of Black rage facilitates the possibility of a ruling class cooptation of this erroneous image. Equally problematic is the common desire to meld Dr. King's stance and that of Malcolm X. It is easy to embrace both leaders as heroes. It is more difficult to embrace them equally at the level of tactics and strategy. Can a person at one and the same time be unconditionally nonviolent while reserving the right to self-defense by any means necessary? It is, therefore, just as important to understand the basic differences between Dr. King and Malcolm X and the significance of those differences in a program for Black liberation. One of the important tasks in this book is to draw out and clarify these differences. The questions that confronted Dr. King, Malcolm X, and the movement in the 1960s still confront those who seek to rebuild the Black Liberation movement today. Dr. King *and* Malcolm X must be seriously studied if the lessons of the decade of the 1960s are to inform the human rights struggle which must be waged in the decade of the 1990s and beyond.

The Importance of Afro-American Unity

Much attention has been paid to the integrationist phase of the Civil Rights movement. But in its later Black Power phase, this mobilization took on many of the characteristics of a modern nationalist insurgency, like the struggles against colonialism and imperialism in the Third World. Black Power demands were no longer advanced in the Civil Rights format, which claimed only the individual rights of citizenship. These demands were now communicated in the language of collective rights of peoples and nations, such as the right to self-determination. This emphasis on the collective identity of those petitioning the government and the collective nature of their demands and proposed remedies gave a renewed importance to ethnicity in the U.S.[34] Yet our understanding of the role nationalism played in the social mobilization of African Americans is limited. The African American nationalism of the later 1960s has often been defined in the literature as an abnormality, a residue from the spent Civil Rights mobilization. I do not accept this interpretation. It is one of the important reasons why Malcolm X's impact on the 1960s has been until recently undervalued.

Nationalist ideology became a major force at a transition stage in the development of the Civil Rights movement: the stage requiring the accelerated institutionalization of formal movement organizations, the transformation of a regional movement into a truly national one, and the integration of previously inactive classes and social groups into the ongoing mobilization. If these organizational requirements were not met, the social movement faced dissolution. To meet these organizational requirements, however, difficult tactical and strategic choices had to be made between programs of reform or revolution. Doug McAdam, in an important work on the Civil Rights movement, *Political Process and the Development of Insurgency*, recognized that both options presented dilemmas. Reform strategies might have limited the ability to broaden the mobilization, while revolutionary strategies invited repression. African American nationalism emerged as a major ideological force in the Civil Rights movement because it offered a plan of action to overcome the dilemma of cooptation or repression.

Malcolm X evolved in his thinking from Black nationalism to Pan-African internationalism and created the Organization of Afro-American Unity (OAAU) in order to address this dilemma that confronted the further development of the Civil Rights movement at the end of its first decade, the crucial period of 1963–65. It is impossible to summarize the social mobilization of African Americans in the 1960s without significantly improving our knowledge of Malcolm X and the role that Pan-African internationalism and the OAAU played in his thinking and actions.

The OAAU represented the first major attempt in the 1960s to create an African American united front based on nationalist ideology. It was based in a northern urban ghetto, and its leadership and membership reflected the social classes mobilized during this late phase of the Civil Rights movement.

Who Must Tell Malcolm's Story?

I feel that it is particularly important that someone of my generation and position in the African American community undertake this project on Malcolm X. Who am I to tell Malcolm's story? I am an intellectual-activist who experienced firsthand the turmoil of the 1960s. I came to activism as a leader of a student NAACP chapter on an Ivy League campus. I was very much committed to Dr. King's Dream. It was on that same campus that I first encountered Malcolm in 1962. He spoke thoughts, feelings, and ideas which were deep within me as a first-generation African American urbanite but which had as yet not been uttered. These were ideas that I and many in my generation and class were afraid of. In that sense we were also afraid of Malcolm X. I did not accept Malcolm X with open arms, but I, for the first time, openly debated his notions of Black identity and racial mission. Malcolm had dared to give voice to what had previously been deemed unspeakable.

Malcolm X was not to be absorbed in a vacuum; the spirit of the decade of the 1960s was composed of a mosaic of ideas and searches in open interaction and confrontation. I experienced Malcolm's Black nationalism while learning also of the nonviolent direct action philosophy of the Congress of Racial Equality (CORE) and its director James Farmer, while debating the merits of Black culture with one of the founders of the Black Arts movement, the poet Larry Neal, and while walking my first picket line in support of the Revolutionary Action Movement's (RAM) Robert Williams.

The year Malcolm X was assassinated, I was broadening my education, trying to read Franz Fanon in French, learning of my ancient African roots from associates of Malcolm like the historians Dr. John Henrik Clarke, Keith Baird, and James Campbell, the founder and Director of the OAAU's Liberation School. I defended Malcolm X's relevance to confused Black Ivy Leaguers who were struggling to find a Black identity. In 1968, those same students were able to seize the main administration building of Columbia College, renaming it Nat Turner Hall of Malcolm X Liberation University. Thus started the Columbia University student uprising of 1968. Later my intellectual-activism took me into the open enrollment struggles in the City University of New York and later into over a decade of struggle in the African liberation support movement. All the while, my work was informed by Malcolm's image of an OAAU with its internationalist-oriented Pan-Africanism. By the early 1970s, Malcolm's OAAU was reborn in the activities of the Pan-African Solidarity Committee, Pan-African Skills Project, the African Liberation Support Committee, Malcolm X Liberation University, and numerous other contemporary efforts.

I moved into middle age fighting for decent housing and education in Harlem, Malcolm X's base for his most formative years and my home for over a decade. Coming out of the 1970s, it was clear to me and a number of other 1960s activists that the younger generation behind us did not know Malcolm X. We saw that generation as a potentially lost generation if we did not bring them to the knowledge of Malcolm. I was working with the Harlem-based Black New York Action Committee (BNYAC). In this organization, I joined with established Harlem activists like Bill Epton and older community residents, some like "Harlem's barber," John Guerrant, who were actually members of the OAAU while Malcolm lived. BNYAC's community-based political education programs and forums featured Malcolm X's life and thought prominently. Throughout this period we cooperated closely with other organizations attempting to rekindle Malcolm's flame, most notably the New Afrikan Peoples Organization, coordinated in New York at that time by Ahmed Obafemi, and Harlem's Patrice Lumumba Coalition, led by Elombe Brath. We were closely associated with Peoples College Press in Chicago, which in 1985 produced a popular *Black Liberation Month News* devoted entirely to Malcolm X and his legacy. Out of the Black New York Action Committee-Peoples College cooperation came the Malcolm X Work Group, a project of the Cooperative Research Network in Black Studies. The Malcolm X Work Group identified scholars who were doing work for publication on Malcolm X and established some ongoing process of cooperation and review among them. The present work is one of several which have benefited from the existence of the Malcolm X Work Group.

Fanon was right in emphasizing the historic mission of each generation. In the United States, it has always been important for the older generation of radical intellectual-activists to make sure that an accurate analysis of the experiences of that generation be passed down. Never is this responsibility as important as now. W.E.B. Du Bois, writing about the history of the American Reconstruction period, warned that the history of African Americans in that period had been ignored, distorted, or destroyed.[35] While my generation of middle-aged activists need not be concerned with the possibility of Malcolm X being ignored, the main danger today is that he will be destroyed through distortion of his real witness and what he stood for. Whether this will happen or not is really not solely in the hands of the mass media and the educational system. It is as much in the hands of those of us who knew and studied Malcolm X. We must tell his truth while we still have the breath to do so.

Why Another Book on Malcolm?

This book discusses things about the experience and thinking of Malcolm X which are necessary to take Malcolm's legacy beyond the stage of hero worship. Chapter Two will tell us who Malcolm X was and what kind of a world he lived in.

Chapter Three will focus on the nature of the crisis facing the Civil Rights movement when Malcolm actively entered it. The specific content of Malcolm X's political thought, highlighting elements of continuity and change in Malcolm's nationalism, is the focus of Chapter Four. It will summarize and analyze Malcolm X's political thought within the Black nationalist tradition and tell us what Malcolm X was trying to do when he intervened in that great social movement.

Chapters Five and Six represent a detailed study of the last eleven months of Malcolm X's life and his efforts during that period to concretize his Pan-African internationalism in the Organization of Afro-American Unity (OAAU). These chapters also analyze Malcolm's successes and failures in that effort and the role of conflict within the Nation of Islam and of government repression in ending his life. Chapter Seven, Eight, and Nine examine and evaluate the legacy of Malcolm X. They seek to establish the relevance of Malcolm's political legacy in rebuilding the movement for Black liberation almost thirty years after his assassination.

2

THE
GESTATION
OF A
REVOLUTIONARY

The Significance of Malcolm X in the 1960s

Malcolm X was one of two preeminent leadership figures in the African American social upheaval of the 1950s and '60s. In this same period, the Black nationalism of Malcolm X emerged as the major alternative to Dr. King's nonviolent integrationist philosophy. While still in the Nation of Islam (NOI), Malcolm pushed the development of the Civil Rights movement forward while standing apart and outside of it. The nationalism of the NOI represented a scathing critique of the established Civil Rights movement, although it provided little or no guide to anti-racist activism. When the Civil Rights movement entered its period of crisis, between 1963 and 1965, Malcolm X broke with the NOI. By so doing, he was able to expand his critique of the Civil Rights movement, and also actively join it in trying to change it from a domestic mobilization focused on civil rights to a movement for human rights with a recognized international stature. In addition, Malcolm was able to inject into the movement the kind of revolutionary nationalism that had deep roots in the African American radical tradition. He infused this nationalism into what was at the time an assimilationist-integrationist movement. Moreover, in the last eleven months of his life, Malcolm X's revolutionary nationalism restored Pan-Africanism to its traditional place of preeminence in Black radical thinking.

Malcolm X emerged as a leader in the African American freedom struggle because poor and working-class African Americans joined the movement and were projected to center stage. Malcolm X taught Black working-class and street people the tradition of Black nationalism in a language and style that they could understand. Reintroducing the intellectual tradition of Black nationalism was an important ideological intervention in the Civil Rights movement. C.E. Wilson observed that a space was created within the movement for this newly emergent group to articulate its mood and agenda with Malcolm X as its spokesperson.[1] This made Black working people the most dynamic part of the Black population and established Malcolm as one of the most important African American leaders of the 1960s.

Malcolm Little: A "New Negro"

The publication of Malcolm X's *Autobiography* in 1965 after his death allowed his charismatic leadership example to transcend his assassination.[2] The autobiography became one of the most read and important works of 20th-century U.S. literature. Its immediate impact was to make available to millions of Black street youths, inmates, and activists the model of Malcolm's self-emancipation. Because of the publication of the *Autobiography*,

> Malcolm X set the standard for a generation of activists and intellectuals and young people as he was a role model of how one can transform oneself through self emancipation and one's brothers in the struggle for social liberation.[3]

The four periods in the autobiographical transformation of Malcolm X are a model of the social transformation of African Americans in the 1960s. This point has been made previously by writer and activist Abdul Alkalimat, who characterized these four periods under the rubric of Malcolm Little: the Exploited; Detroit Red: the Exploiter; Malcolm X: the Self-Emancipator; and El Hajj Malik El Shabazz: the Social Liberator.[4]

Malcolm X was born in Omaha, Nebraska on May 19, 1925. By the time of his father's death Malcolm had lived in a number of midwestern industrial areas including Milwaukee and Lansing, Michigan. He was born into the first generation of African Americans completely sired in the northern urban industrial order.

The out-migration of African Americans to northern and later western cities was to have the most profound impact on the development of the African American community and more generally on U.S. society. Technological improvements in industrial production and assembly line methods combined with wartime levels of labor demand pulled rural African Americans into the northern and western cities. This trend was exacerbated by the disruption and ultimately drastic curtailment of European immigration. Consequently, a permanent place in the nation's economy was established for an African American industrial working class.

Omaha was an important rail head, granary, and meat-processing center. Its White working class was angered by the importation of large numbers of southern Blacks into that city by the captains of industry. Black sharecroppers were used as strikebreakers and scabs to enforce labor discipline and undermine the efforts to organize White labor. Eight years before Malcolm's birth, Omaha had exploded in a vicious race riot, one unfortunately typical of race relations in the U.S. industrial heartland in the period immediately surrounding World War I. Interracial class solidarity was difficult and often impossible to achieve during and after World War I because the United States was a racist society and the working classes of both races had entered the urban industrial order at widely separate times. White labor feared the competition of Black labor and thus became easy prey for the divide-and-conquer tactics of capitalists. Black sharecroppers resented the racism of White workers and had no extensive experience of class solidarity across racial lines. In northern cities these two segments of the U.S. working class fought it out for jobs, living spaces, recognition, and respect.

The southern, rural, sharecropping social order was not yet dead. It would remain alive for several more decades only to be finally put to rest by the Civil Rights movement. But Malcolm's generation grew to maturity in another reality. This new generation of African Americans was remade as a super-exploited pool of super-abundant, surplus labor. It was to perform the hot, dirty, and dangerous "shit work" no one else wanted. It would be "the last hired and the first fired." There was, however, another side to the accession of African Americans to the U.S. industrial working class. For the first time in great numbers, Black workers would be in direct competition with White workers for jobs, housing, education, and social services. They would also be working together in factories and other workplaces, cooperating in production in ways not previously possible.

Crowded into cities, African Americans would begin to develop a more cosmopolitan consciousness of the world. They would begin to sense their potential as a people to better the conditions of their existence. More and more Black people would become what Alain Locke, the intellectual mentor of the Harlem Renaissance, called the "New Negro."[5] This "New Negro" was filled with the sense of racial awakening, of the quest for a racial tradition and African historical and cultural roots. This "New Negro" had also fought in World War I and had seen White men defeated by Black men in arms. An offspring of the emerging Black urban ghetto, the "New Negro" no longer felt the powerlessness which came from legally sanctioned discrimination and segregation on isolated rural farms or in small southern communities. In numbers there is power, even if crowded into ghetto conditions.

Not every African American of this period was a New Negro. In fact, most were not. The generalization of this mental orientation would parallel Malcolm's lifetime and the maturation of African Americans inside of the urban industrial order. This process would take almost half a century. But it had already started shortly before Malcolm's birth and it had advanced enough even then to evoke a strong response in fearful White people.

Malcolm X was born in the era of the so-called Second Ku Klux Klan. This Klan resurgence particularly targeted Catholics, immigrants, and Jews but retained its antipathy for African Americans. It was a truly national phenomenon with particular strength in the Midwest. For a short time it achieved political respectability, its members or sympathizers winning governorships, mayoralties and other important positions in western and midwestern states as well as the South.

One student of the Second Klan described the historical continuity in Klan thinking on the race question:

> White supremacy had always been a tenet in the Klan's creed. In the wake of Black migration to the North, kleagles exploited White fears of a "new Negro" emerging from World War I demanding political, economic, and social equality. They even spread rumors that Black leaders advocated intermarriage with whites. Citing the Bible and "scientific evidence" of Black mental inferiority inherited from "savage ancestors, of jungle environment," Klansmen stood ready to battle for the purity of the white race.[6]

Born into a family headed by "New Negroes," Malcolm grew up in a Garveyite family. Both parents were active in the Universal Negro Improvement Association (UNIA), the largest 20th-century mass-based Black nationalist organization, which was created in 1914 by the charismatic Jamaican Marcus Garvey. Malcolm's father, Earl Little, a Baptist minister, headed UNIA chapters in midwestern cities like Omaha, Milwaukee, and Lansing.[7] His mother was a corresponding secretary for these chapters, filing detailed reports of chapter activities with Garvey's international headquarters in New York.[8] Malcolm's sister, Ella Collins, reported that Malcolm X was present at these chapter meetings almost from birth.[9] When his father died Malcolm was seven years old, and his teenage years were spent in Boston with Ella Collins, who retained her father's orientation to Garveyism.[10]

Malcolm's family was unusual in that it made the transition from the southern rural countryside to the northern urban city intact and started out as the nuclear family of the American Dream. It was not a "broken family" at the beginning. His family possessed two strong leadership figures with consciousness and politics. We should take special note of the role Malcolm's mother played both in the family and in the UNIA. The "New Negro" concept embodied a new view of the role of Black women in social change. It represented a further development of themes first seen in the Negro women's club movement at the turn of the century. Malcolm's mother was following a model of Black womanhood popularized at this time by Ida B. Wells Barnett, a founder of the Niagara Movement and one of Garvey's most important supporters.

Malcolm X's family represented a threat to White supremacy, and it was targeted for destruction. Driven into poverty by worsening economic conditions and White chicanery, Malcolm's father died under suspicious conditions, and his mother could not maintain her sanity in the harsh Depression era to which her children were subsequently subjected.

Detroit Red: The Descent into Criminality

Malcolm's sister, Ella Collins, a strong and politically conscious Black nationalist, rescued him from the welfare system. She helped him as a teenager, during the Depression, to find a place in the U.S. working class. Malcolm X entered the service sector of the working class, first as a dishwasher, then as a shoeshine boy, a soda jerk, and a busboy. Later he found work as a Pullman porter, and thereby joined the largest and most autonomous organization of Black workers at this time.[11] He loaded trains, worked as a "fourth cook" and a sandwich man. Malcolm also worked as a waiter in Harlem and briefly washed dishes in a Harlem speakeasy.

His teenage years were filled with the emerging urban culture of Black America. Malcolm's rooting in the U.S. working class was incomplete. Riding the rails as a porter and later established in Harlem, the cultural capital of the Black world, Malcolm X developed a deep, if only partly conscious, sense of the peoplehood of the African American. But no Black man at this time could be easily and unequivocally rooted in the working class. The particular positioning of Black labor as a super-exploited pool of surplus labor meant that full-time, year-round, decent-paying jobs were rarely achieved by most African Americans. While speaking of a later period of ghetto life, economist Bennet Harrison recognized that the economy of the ghetto fuctioned like those of the Third World "periphery" in which Black labor migrated between a weak secondary labor market and several other sources of support, including an "irregular" sector of hustling and petty crime.[12] With slight modification, this model is valid for many Black workers of Malcolm's teenage years. For many young African Americans in the late '30s and early war years, the choice of legitimate or illegitimate pursuits was not an option. One had to choose both whenever the opportunity arose. Harrison describes this predicament:

> While all irregular activity is not illegal, it is the latter type of work which is undoubtedly the most controversial—and the most lucrative

(although the high risk associated with narcotics distribution, grand theft, and other serious criminal activities probably induces the same kind of discontinuous work patterns found elsewhere in the periphery of the economy with the result that annual income is still relatively low for all but a very few professional criminals).[13]

Malcolm's descent into criminality was the result of the normal operation of the capitalist system upon the labor market conditions facing Black workers. To be super-exploited means that available employment in the market for Black labor will not over the long run support a worker and his or her family at a livable wage. Income must be found, therefore, through a second job, hustling, or in illicit activity. In Malcolm's young working years this trend was new and not fully developed. The wartime years were years of boom and the aftermath of World War II saw the U.S. economy unchallenged and dynamic. Today, the U.S. economy is stagnating, and it faces strong competition. What Malcolm experienced has become the norm for inner-city youth. The mechanism described above is now the typical means by which inner-city youth are both exploited and marginalized in the urban labor market.

Even though World War II had already started and was helping to lift many White workers out of the 1930s Depression, for several years the wartime economy had little impact on African Americans, especially those like Malcolm X. It took the threat of the March on Washington movement of A. Philip Randolph to get President Roosevelt to issue Executive Order 8802, which opened up defense industries to Black workers. This came too late for Malcolm X. The wartime experience which saw so many African Americans improve their employment and living conditions saw Malcolm X sink out of the working class and descend into the criminal element.

Malcolm in Prison: The Self-Emancipator

In January 1946, Malcolm X was sentenced to ten years in prison for breaking and entering. He first entered the Charlestown State Prison in Massachusetts, later moving successively to the Concord State Reformatory and the Norfolk Prison Colony.[14] His criminal and prison experience paralleled that of so many African Americans in the urban industrial order. The prisons, along with the military and the welfare systems, are institutions where the relative surplus of working-class Blacks are "warehoused" until an expanding capitalism again needs their presence in the job market. Malcolm X, however, was not merely "warehoused" in these prisons; he was transformed.

> After more than seven years in prison and after his conversion to the NOI in the late 1940s while behind bars, Malcolm's view of work had changed, but not his view of prison or military service. He was now willing to "work hard" in industry rather than taking a "soft" job in the low paying service sector where he had worked in the early 1940s.[15]

In prison, Malcolm worked in the machine shop making license plates, in a coal warehouse, and in the woodworking shop.[16] Upon his release from prison, Malcolm worked briefly as a salesman in a furniture store before returning to industrial labor. In 1953 he worked on the automobile assembly lines in and around Detroit. He worked at the Gar Wood factory in Detroit, where large garbage truck bodies were made and briefly at the Ford Motor company's Wayne assembly plant.[17] By 1954, he had embarked upon his ministry in the NOI but still supported himself by seeking work on the waterfront of Philadelphia as a longshoreman.[18]

Ferrucio Gambino notes that prison offered Malcolm the opportunity to "pause and reflect on the sense of his life."[19] It was in prison that Malcolm learned to respect the intellectual disciplines: reading, writing, and being articulate. Moreover, he came to respect the tasks and responsibilities of the intellectual: to think and to analyze as a basis for action. The jailhouse savant, Bimbi, taught him to respect these skills and to reconstruct his life and his reputation around their mastery.

It was in jail that Malcolm X found religion and the role model of the Honorable Elijah Muhammad. Through his new-found religion, he cleaned himself up, and gained self-respect, discipline, and a mission in life. Malcolm X learned how to help others and organized them to stand up for their rights. He learned the importance of using the skills Bimbi taught him to advocate for the rights of the dispossessed. Malcolm led the struggle of Muslim prisoners to get their religious and dietary needs respected. He wrote for the prison newspaper and made it a forum for the rights of prisoners.[20] It was in prison that Malcolm begins to use some of the skills which later are so powerfully evident in his founding and editing of *Muhammad Speaks*, the official newspaper of the NOI.

Malcolm's Changing World

While Malcolm was in jail, sweeping changes in the international and domestic order had altered the consciousness of Black people. The experience of World War II and its aftermath required the reorganization of the international system. Openly colonial relationships and power relationships based on racial superiority were delegitimized. The breaking up of the old European colonial system greatly expanded the number of nations in the postwar international arena, especially from the non-Western parts of the globe. The dominant characteristic of the new arrangement was the grouping of the old nations around two hostile, competitive, and ideologically exclusive superpowers, the United States and the Soviet Union. Under an umbrella of nuclear "balance of terror," superpower competition for newly emergent nations shifted into the ideological arena. Amid heightened ideological competition, traditional distinctions between domestic affairs and international concerns eroded. The treatment of domestic racial minorities by the superpowers was one area of growing international scrutiny, especially by the newly emergent nations of the Third World. This development was eventful for African Americans because it forced the federal government to reconsider the "home rule" which had been granted to the South on the race question. This concession, to allow southern politicians free rein over Black sharecroppers without interference from the national government, had been an essential part of domestic policy since the Compromise of 1877.

The post-World War II U.S. economy was in the forefront of fundamental changes in the structure of international economic activity.[21] Economic interdependence confounded traditional conceptions of state sovereignty. The primary unit of production and finance increasingly became the transnational corporation. Easy and uninterrupted accessibility to international markets became the basis for economic growth. New nations wanted to develop, and this desire in the Third World was politicized in the context of the ideologically exclusive models of development offered by the United States and the USSR.

Moreover, the importance of underdeveloped regions within the advanced countries impressed itself upon corporate leaders. The economic basis for the southern system of racial domination began to erode in the 20th century. African Americans were pushed out of southern agriculture and pulled into urban areas, first in the South, then later in the North and West. Transformations in production and profound changes in the domestic and international markets in cotton and other southern staple crops drastically increased the economically repetitive

34

population in southern agriculture. These changes had the most impact on the lowest layer of the rural population, agricultural day laborers and sharecroppers, the layer in which African Americans were disproportionately represented. Urbanization and industrialization in the South absorbed an increasing proportion of this repetitive population even under conditions of the color bar in employment. With the coming of the New Deal, public relief payments and allotments were much more equitably delivered to African Americans in the urban as opposed to the rural context, and this attracted large numbers of African Americans to southern cities.[22]

The economic development of the South promised to rival international investment as a source of raw materials, cheap labor, and new markets. The existing political and social realities of the South, however, had been fashioned to support a local elite whose power position and outlook on life stood in the way of the agendas of transnational corporate leadership to transform this region economically. As Malcolm X spent his last years in jail, African Americans in the South were moving to the center of an emerging coalition and movement which was to sweep this anachronistic remnant of the slaveocracy from power.[23]

In the post-World War II period, the urbanization process created a "critical mass" in the African American community, which became the social base of the Civil Rights movement. Political scientist Doug McAdam identified three areas of transformation which created conditions for the emergence of the southern protest movement. First, the size and budget of urban-based African American churches increased markedly over their rural counterparts. Their ministers were more highly educated and higher-paid than rural Black preachers. Second, legal challenges to the separate-but-equal doctrine stimulated southern states to invest more in public, segregated higher education for Black people. African Americans who graduated from these institutions contributed to the rapid expansion of the urban-based African American middle class. Third, urbanization and the growth of the African American middle class stimulated the development of Civil Rights organizations in the South with a manifold increase of the southern chapters of the National Association for the Advancement of Colored People (NAACP).[24]

While these changes identified by McAdam constituted the necessary conditions for the emergence of Civil Rights protests, sociologist Aldon Morris assigned equal importance to the emergence of a young, itinerant leadership within an expanded and revitalized urban Black church. This young leadership came together with the Black church, the NAACP, and other Civil Rights organizational traditions in what Morris called the "Movement Center." The formation of movement centers constituted the sufficient condition for the flowering of the modern Civil Rights movement.[25] These movement centers were based on a young southern Black working class not completely proletarianized and still attached to the church. They were staffed by cadres of women and lead by a newly emergent middle-class leadership pursuing objectives which ultimately would disproportionately benefit the Black "bourgeoisie." At this same time Malcolm X was being prepared for leadership in a northern prison.

Muslim Minister in the Nation of Islam

Malcolm left prison, joined the industrial working class, and took up the Muslim ministry of the NOI. In the latter half of the 1950s, he became the national spokesperson for the Honorable Elijah Muhammad, the NOI's founder. Under Malcolm's direction, more than 200 additional NOI temples were organized. During his stewardship, the NOI grew in size and prestige and was noted for its ability to reach and transform the lives of the most anti-social Black people, including those incarcerated in prison. By 1959, the whole nation was made aware of the presence of the NOI as Malcolm X appeared on nationwide TV openly advocating racial separation.[26]

Between 1958 and his 1964 break with the NOI, Malcolm X became the alter ego of the Civil Rights movement. His staunchly nationalist and rejectionist stance made him the *bete noire* (no pun intended) of U.S. liberal discourse. Nevertheless, he understood and articulated the rage of those in the northern Black ghettos. Malcolm X gave this group of street people its voice and a public persona. During this same period, Malcolm was being systematically reintroduced to the Black nationalism and Garveyism of his parents. He developed a profound concern for Africa and the Third World, and reinstituted a sense of peoplehood and interna-tionalism into the African American community. Most important, he wanted to establish an activist, nationalist presence within the Civil Rights movement, using the NOI as his base. This desire brought Malcolm into conflict with the leadership of the NOI and ultimately convinced him to leave the organization in order to pursue his political agenda.

El Hajj Malik El Shabazz: Pan-African Internationalist

In this period, Malcolm X terminated his membership in the NOI, recognized his ideology as Black nationalism, and made a conscious decision to join the Civil Rights movement in order to transform it into a "human rights" movement. Malcolm's efforts gained international and diplomatic status for his leadership and that of his organization, the Organization of Afro-American Unity (OAAU). His OAAU concept was an attempt to give the previously domestically based Civil Rights movement more of the form, content, and personality of a legitimate national liberation movement.

Malcolm X made the *hajj* to Mecca in the spring of 1964. He effected a link between African American Muslims and their co-religionists within Sunni Islam. Malcolm X believed that Sunni Islam was an attractive religion because it provided answers to the moral degradation into which Black people had fallen while at the same time recognizing the right of the dispossessed to rebel. We must also understand Malcolm's shift toward Sunni Islam as the beginning of an African American critique of Eurocentrism, which has become one of the most visible aspects of the Islamic fundamentalism which has swept the Muslim world in the last two decades.

In two trips to Africa in the spring and summer of 1964, Malcolm X became the first major African American leader to go to Africa and present a detailed description and explanation of racism in the United States. It was Malcolm who attempted to unite the African unity movement, which reached its high point with the creation of the Organization of African Unity (OAU) in May 1963, with the human rights thrust of African-descended communities in the diaspora. It was Malcolm X's intention to garner the support of Africans everywhere behind the struggle of the African American and to take the United States before the international bar of justice for violating the human rights of African Americans. On July 2, 1964, J. Edgar Hoover, then director of the Federal Bureau of Investigation (FBI), defined Malcolm X and his OAAU as a threat to the security of the United States and committed his organization to the destruction of Malcolm X and all he represented.[27] On February 21, 1965, Malcolm X was assassinated in New York's Audubon Ballroom. Muslim gunmen pulled the trigger, but the available record, including government documents, strongly suggests that Malcolm X was the victim of a government-inspired political assassination.

Malcolm X became a revolutionary force in the Civil Rights movement due to the intersection of his own personal biography with the larger

forces transforming the African American community from a rural peasantry into an urban proletariat. As a role model he quintessentially
represented the possibilities of individual redemption and transformation
resident in the newly activated social group composed of urban ghetto
workers and street people. Malcolm was accorded the mantle of leadership
by these same people because he both taught them self-knowledge and
gave them a voice to debate the strategies and tactics of Black liberation.
The nationalism of Malcolm X—taught to him by his parents, Elijah
Muhammad, and the political and cultural environment of Harlem—reso-
nated with the mood of this newly emergent social force and gave to it the
beginnings of a new conceptual framework for answering the question,
"Which way toward Black liberation?" This new conceptual framework
allowed for the reformulation of Black nationalism in a more internationalist, Pan-African, and revolutionary manner and thus facilitated the
linking of the Civil Rights movement with the movement toward continental African unity and the world revolutionary process. Chapter Three
will elaborate on the intellectual and ideological impasse which confronted Malcolm and the Civil Rights movement during 1963–65.

3

A
New Model
in the
Civil Rights Movement

Black Nationalism Revisited

Malcolm X's thought represents a conceptual framework useful in analyzing the Civil Rights decade not so much for the answers it provides as for the questions it asks and for which it seeks answers. The questions first articulated by Malcolm X in the last eleven months of his life became the ones which the movement was to take up for the remainder of the 1960s and beyond. Even Dr. King was primarily involved in responding to those questions thrown up by the struggle in transition which were first recognized and articulated by Malcolm X. The significance of Malcolm X is misunderstood. He was not then and has not yet been accorded respect as a major thinker of Black liberation.

Some contemporary scholars of Black nationalism and Malcolm X saw the Black nationalism of the 1960s as an unfortunate and irrational departure from the mainstream of the struggle. This is understandable for two reasons. First, Black nationalism reemerged in the early 1960s in the millenarian, non-rational theology of the Nation of Islam (NOI). Second, this nationalism sought legitimation not within the U.S. national mythology but as an alternative to it. It represented a 180-degree turn away from the thrust of a half-century of enlightened, liberal, anti-racist scholarship. Integrationist scholars were suddenly put on the defensive, and their efforts at analysis often reflected an unfortunate polemical quality.[1] They viewed Black nationalism as a pathological development, a result of the frustration and alienation associated with the entry of the northern urban ghetto "street" element into the struggle.

Malcolm X was viewed as an example of the pathological personalities thrown up out of the dispossessed urban ghetto. His leadership was indicted by these social scientists as demagogic, motivated by blind hatred of White people, and lacking the serious reflection of a rational thinker.

They assumed that collective mass action, especially rebellion, was a reflection of alienated behavior and essentially pathological. Their theories, most of which came from the discipline of social psychology, reflected a pronounced bias toward legitimating the status quo.[2] This was certainly true of the scholarly response to Black nationalism in the first half of the 1960s.

Another View of Black Rebellion

Resource mobilizaton theory, which succeeded theories originating in social psychology, at least saw urban rebellions as rationally motivated political behavior. This theory explained Black insurgency as the ability of African Americans to mobilize resources and disrupt the normal operation of society. Some scholars assigned a central role to resources controlled by disaffected members of the elite and made available to Black people. Others argued that African Americans had sufficient internal resources to initiate and sustain a movement through its formative period.[3]

Two such theorists, Richard Cloward and Frances Fox Piven, argued that insurgents had to go outside of their traditional institutions of advocacy to generate a movement.[4] Doug McAdam is representative of those who argued that insurgents use their traditional institutions in new and different ways. Aspects of the experience of both the integrationists and nationalists in the Civil Rights movement provide confirmation for both positions.

Malcolm X made the NOI a powerful nationalist organization by recruiting many of his Muslim ministers out of the ranks of the Baptist ministry. The ritual of the NOI leaned more heavily on the traditions of the Black church than on those of orthodox Sunni Islam. Martin Luther King's Southern Christian Leadership Conference (SCLC) was constructed upon the existing Black churches in the South. While the existing institutional structure supported the early period of the Black insurgency, as the movement matured the existing institutional and organizational structures were inadequate to the new tasks at hand. Both men recognized that the further development of the movement required new organizational forms and for their supporters to relate to each other in new and different ways. King's "Poor People's Campaign" represented this search while Malcolm X created the OAAU.

Resource mobilization theorists and major students of the Civil Rights movement like Piven and Cloward, McAdam, and Morris do not assign ideology a major role and therefore tend to minimize the positive role played by Black nationalism in the development of the Civil Rights movement. Neither in McAdam's work nor Morris' was there an explicit discussion of ideology or the function of Blacks in the 1960s. There is no detailed treatment of its nationalist phase or of Malcolm X and the OAAU.[5]

The nationalist phase of the Civil Rights movement has no studies comparable to those of McAdam and Morris. To the extent that the resource mobilization school and its corollaries emphasize, as does McAdam, rebellion as a political process, the nationalist phase of the Civil Rights era is seen merely as a period of movement dissolution in terms of its command of resources.[6]

The OAAU was tiny compared to Dr. King's organization. Once separated from the NOI, Malcolm X had no large independent Black institution around which he could mobilize his followers into an organized movement. In terms of his ability to reward his supporters materially and punish his enemies, Malcolm was quite limited. Malcolm's contribution is overlooked and minimized by resource mobilization theorists because the resources he mobilized were not only material but intellectual and emotional. Ideology is an important organizational resource in creating a social movement.[7]

The Role of Ideas in Oppression and Resistance

Oppression is not merely imposed by force. It is most firmly instituted when those in power have established their self-serving ideas as the "common sense" of the society. Italian marxist intellectual Antonio Gramsci argued that when oppression is firmly entrenched, those in power are able to define the frame of reference and the terms of debate of every social problem.[8] They can do this through their control of the educational system, through the media, and through the manipulation of official symbols of power and legitimacy associated with the nation and patriotism.[9] Individuals or groups among the oppressed who attempt to establish a different definition of social problems or a different frame of reference for the debate are defined as illegitimate or dangerous. They often find themselves under physical as well as intellectual attack.[10]

Under these circumstances, the oppressed find it difficult to erect a conceptual framework for understanding the methods by which they are oppressed or the means to be employed for ending oppression. In addition, one scholar has recognized that it is usually easier for those in power, a small minority, to arrive at agreement on how to maintain oppression than it is for the large number of oppressed people to reach a consensus on what is to be done.[11] The sociologist Max Weber recognized that social movements are necessary because they provide the strong emotional support necessary to make the initial break with the dominance of oppressive ideas over the thinking of the exploited. Once that break is made, organizational development seems to accelerate.[12]

Malcolm X devoted a large part of his message toward making African Americans aware of the confusion and inaction which resulted from the internalization of the racist ruling class's view of the world. This he did not only at the level of individual identity but more importantly, at the level of conceiving a new direction for the Civil Rights movement.

The Civil Rights Movement in Crisis

The Civil Rights movement emerged in the decade when the transformation of the African American community from a rural peasantry to an urban proletariat was being completed. Thus the characteristic feature of Black oppression had already substantially shifted away from legal discrimination to *de facto* segregation. Therefore, at the point of its greatest achievements, the movement was in crisis.

The 1963–65 period was critical for the changes taking place in several crucial factors affecting the African American social mobilization. Economically, the indicators of racial advancement for the period 1960–63 described urban recession and stagnation.[13] Northern urban ghettos swelled with "street people" and many African Americans were forced into the marginal sectors of a racially divided labor market. The decline in their standard of living offset the substantial but one-shot gains achieved by the final generation of Black people making the transition from southern rural life to the urban ghettoized Black people.[14] For Black people long resident in northern cities, little or no perceivable progress was made in the economic dimension of racial inequality. Some urban inhabitants responded to this obstacle by rebelling violently against ghetto conditions.

Support at the federal level began to change with the emergence of the White "backlash." The Vietnam War made policymakers doubt that they could afford racial democracy at home while funding major military efforts abroad. The monopoly of the nation's attention enjoyed by the Civil Rights movement disappeared as rival movements emerged around opposition to the war, feminism, and student power issues.

Organizational strength was affected by the dramatic growth in membership and the geographic diffusion of the Civil Rights movement. As previously inactive classes and groups attempted to establish a relationship with the movement, old organizational forms, agendas, and leadership styles proved inadequate to the new demands placed upon them. Major Civil Rights leaders disagreed over whether full access to political power had been achieved. Finally, the federal government implemented plans to discredit the movement and its more radical leadership.[15]

Crisis in the Movement: The Need for a New Model

The emerging stalemate had an ideological as well as an economic and political dimension. The traditional middle-class leadership of the Civil Rights forces judged the performance of U.S. society in race relations using the framework of ideas provided by the U.S. ruling class. It identified and exploited every inconsistency and hypocrisy between the behavior of Whites with power and their professed values. Nevertheless, this leadership professed its commitment to the "American Creed" and pursued the "American Dream." Civil Rights thinkers never exposed the ideology of the ruling class itself to critical scrutiny. Behind the facade of racial equality, African Americans were frozen at the bottom of the political, economic, and social pyramid even though the structure of legal segregation and discrimination was being dismantled. In addition, economic and social welfare rights for the poor and disadvantaged received the weakest guarantees in the American Creed.[16] Consequently, under northern urban conditions the demand for equality was transformed into one of revolutionary dimensions.

The transformation of the Civil Rights movement to a truly national one and its rooting in northern urban ghettos introduced into its ideological framework revolutionary, 20th-century notions of equality.[17] This latter sense of equality stood outside of the model of hegemonic ideology and in contradiction to it. Herein was one of the most important sources of the White backlash and emergence of symbolic racism: the feeling of Whites that there was something basically unfair, unwarranted and un-American about Black Power demands.

While the opportunity to participate in nonviolent direct action was an important part of the process of psychologically redeeming southern Blacks, the Civil Rights movement generated no specific demands relevant to the protection and enhancement of the cultural identity of the African American. In fact, the American Dream had always been identified with Anglo-conformity and therefore it clashed with what author E.U.Essien-Udom identified as the nationalist mood of the Black masses.[18]

Howard Brotz, one of the more insightful students of Black nationalism in the 1960s, felt that this mood grew out of the sentiment that so long as Black people "accepted the definition of themselves as a mere race, they could never feel an inward equality with whites." "This is so," he observed, "because they are admitting through this conception of themselves that they had no culture of their own," and are dependent upon whites for this. He concluded that the Black masses desired not only a legal equality between the races, but the "subjective fortification [that could] only come from having one's own culture, conceived as a national identity, religion and language."[19]

White Backlash: Compromising the Dream of Dr. King

Dr. King consciously embraced the American Dream, which he understood to be part of the U.S. liberal democratic tradition as embodied in the secular documents—the Declaration of Independence and the Constitution—and in the religious tradition of the Protestant variants of Old and New Testament Christianity. Thus his criticism was not of the conception of the dream itself but the hypocritical and selective way that Whites implemented the Dream.[20] As James Cone put it, King believed that the federal government, southern moderates, northern liberals, and the White religious community had both the material resources and moral capacity to extend the dream to Black folks. One simply had to challenge the moral sensibility of these constituencies to live out the content of their creed.[21]

King attempted to formulate the concept of the nonviolent revolution, a method of creative disruption which would maintain the moral high ground while forcing the federal government to play the role of agent of revolutionary social change. King saw nonviolence as creating a moral climate that would "make progress possible." Acts of violence, he felt, would dissipate that climate, as would threats of violence "verbalized by those who equate it with militancy." King distrusted the violent impulses of the Black masses not only because of his Christian pacifist orientation but also because he feared they had violent predispositions. He saw such predispositions of the Black masses as reflecting their alienation in the ghetto, not as a rational choice between available means to achieve political goals. But how did King's strategy provide for the protection of protesters from racist violence?[22]

In analyzing the ideological structure of King's nonviolent direct action philosophy, author David Garrow observed that King felt that

> a love ethic could work well in direct relationships, but in the larger social setting coercive power was necessary to increase social justice...'...men are controlled by power not mind alone.'[23]

King did not accept that this power could be morally justified when it took the form of individual or collective acts of retributive violence. Coercive force was the legitimate prerogative of the federal government alone. In this vein King considered the federal courts and the executive an ally of the movement and avoided confrontation with federal power.[24]

By 1963 it was clear that the federal government was either unable or unwilling to play this role, especially in Mississippi and Alabama, the center of gravity for the Student Nonviolent Coordinating Committee's (SNCC) voter registration activities. Around that same time SNCC began to receive an infusion of field workers whose secular backgrounds differed notably from the earlier leadership centered in southern divinity students.[25]

In the arena of operations of SNCC, the concept of nonviolence as a way of life was challenged by the traditional southern Black orientation to protect the homestead from White supremacist nightriders. Armed self-defense advocate Robert Williams had given formal recognition to this traditional Black institution in Monroe, North Carolina, and it was strong in the areas of Mississippi and Alabama where SNCC rooted itself in the 1961–63 period.[26]

For the new urban groups joining the movement, especially those in the North, the Black church and its religious ideas were much less central to their daily lives than to their southern counterparts. In addition, they had been exposed to a host of ideological currents, all of which legitimized the right of self-defense or rebellion for the dispossessed.

There were, all along, aspects of the American creed which compromised King's nonviolent direct action strategy. The American Creed values incremental and marginal change rather than the decisive and fundamental change needed by racial minorities in the U.S. The political system with its separation of powers, checks and balances, and two-party politics was structured to discourage rapid fundamental change. The system was viewed by its creators as making adequate provision for the correction of all social problems through compromise and without recourse to violence.[27] Thus protest raised outside of normal channels and as civil disobedience was often emotionally rejected as an act of violence. According to the etiquette of race relations, any visible challenge to the racial status quo was perceived as violence. In this sense many northerners as well as southerners reacted to the occurrence of mass nonviolent demonstrations as if they were being physically attacked. It was the mass character of the demonstrations, not the orientation of the participants, which determined whether they would be perceived as violent. King might have benefited from the later studies of Charles Tilly, which demonstrated that in modern Western Civilization violence in revolutionary situations was invariably initiated by the agents of the state in order to suppress the voicing of the legitimate grievances of the people.[28]

King had to contend with the reality about which his close friend and adviser Stanley Levison spoke in the spring 1965:

> ...it is poor tactics to present to the nation a prospect of choosing between equality and freedom for Negroes with the revolutionary alteration of our society, or to maintain the status quo with discrimination. The people are not inclined to change their society in order to free the Negro. They are ready to undertake some and perhaps major reforms, but not to make a major revolution.[29]

Additionally, King could have benefited from Wagley and Harris' observation that "the operation of ethnocentrism makes it very easy for the boundaries of the in-group to become the boundaries of adherence to group values."[30] Perchance it was not hypocrisy that motivated the behavior of those in power. As the movement's arena of struggle moved away from the southern region to more secularly inclined areas of the nation, it moved toward a White mass which saw no contradiction between the use of force to suppress Black people and their American Creed mandate to settle conflicts peacefully without recourse to violence. The new demands of the movement were seen as illegitimate and un-American.[31]

Malcolm X: In Pursuit of a New Way of Thinking

The crisis described above caused Black people to question not only the performance and orientation of the federal government between 1954 and 1963, but the fundamental character of the U.S. state itself. Was this state a racist state in conception and structure? If so how was a numerical minority to successfully transform it? How was the prestige and the coercive power of this state to be dealt with? The problem confronting the Civil Rights movement in the 1963-65 period was not responsive to integrationist-assimilationist ideas. Black nationalism in its Pan-African variant reemerged in the political thought of Malcolm X as part of the process of constructing a new model for the analysis of race relations in the United States.

Founding meeting of the OAAU. June 28, 1964,
Audubon Ball Room, Harlem.

4

THE
POLITICAL
THOUGHT
OF MALCOLM X
IN TRANSITION

The Search for a New Paradigm of Black Liberation

When you control a man's thinking you do not have to worry about his actions. You do not have to tell him not to stand here or go yonder. He will find his 'proper place' and will stay in it. You do not need to send him to the back door. He will go without being told. In fact, if there is no back door, he will cut one for his special benefit.

—Carter G. Woodson[1]

This type of so-called Negro, by being intoxicated over the White man, he never sees beyond the White man. He never sees beyond America. He never looks at himself or where he fits into things on the world stage. He only can see himself here in America, on the American stage or the White stage, where the White man is in the majority, where the White man is the boss. So this type of Negro always feels like he's outnumbered or he's the underdog or he's a minority. And it puts him in the role of a beggar...

Malcolm X[2]

As a precondition for developing an effective movement for Black liberation, Malcolm X insisted that Black people rethink their entire experience in the United States. Therefore, his most important contribution was an ideological one. It is easy to miss the significance of ideological innovation in the success of a social movement, but the ideological struggle is as important as the physical struggle. If the physical struggle is not guided by an accurate analysis of goals and objectives and the appropriate means for their achievement, the people, through ignorance, may stop short of achievable victory. They may be incapable of differentiating friends from enemies and might give back to their oppressors with one hand what they have seized with the other. The Black Civil Rights leadership had internalized the worldview of their oppressors, a worldview that Malcolm thought would never define self-determination for Black people as a desirable end, and thus had to be purged. Malcolm X's political thought was pushed forward by two things: his unswerving commitment to history as the ultimate determinant of truth or falsity: and his willingness to subject to critical scrutiny and revision all things which he accepted as true. Malcolm told the OAAU:

When you deal with the past, you're dealing with history, you're dealing actually with the origin of a thing. When you know the origin, you know the cause. If you don't know the origin, you don't know the cause. And if you don't know the cause, you don't know the reason, you're just cut off, you're left standing in mid-air...That's why I say it is so important for you and me to spend time today learning something about the past so that we can better understand the present, analyze it, and then do something about it.[3]

In fact, Malcolm expressed his feelings on the role that criticism had to play in the movement for Black liberation in this way:

I think all of us should be critics of each other. Whenever you can't stand criticism you can never grow. I don't think that it serves any purpose for the leaders of our people to waste their time fighting each other needlessly...But on the other hand, I don't think that we should be above criticism. I don't think that anyone should be above criticism.[4]

Malcolm's political thought had its roots not only in the period of his membership in the Nation of Islam (NOI) but also as far back as his experiences in prison in Massachusetts. Even before coming under the influence of Elijah Muhammad, Malcolm learned the basic tools of the intellectual's discipline. The jailhouse savant Bimbi opened Malcolm's eyes to the world outside of his immediate experience. Bimbi opened Malcolm's eyes to the importance of language and literacy.[5] It was during the prison period that Malcolm learned the value of extensive and copious reading. By the time of his conversion to the religion of the Nation of Islam, Malcolm had already read ancient and modern history extensively, especially for one who was incarcerated. Malcolm was attracted to Elijah Muhammad because he offered a theoretical framework within which the historical record of the White man's treatment of Black people made sense. Malcolm continued to read and study historical and contemporary race relations throughout his sojourn in the Nation of Islam. Even as a religious leader, Malcolm's appeal was to the intellect of the potential convert, not merely to his emotions. For Malcolm, conversion to the beliefs of the Nation of Islam was not a function of "grace through faith" but rather an awakening from spiritual death through exposure to the true historical record of race relations. While in the Nation of Islam, Malcolm accepted Elijah Muhammad's description of the devil nature of Whites only because he believed it to be confirmed by the historical record of the rise and decline of Europe.

Malcolm developed a profound respect for the facts. For him, facts would reveal the truth and expose the White man as a liar. One had to marshal the facts, Malcolm observed, in order to engage the opposition from an informed position. In his autobiography Malcolm said:

Ten guards and the warden couldn't have torn me out of those books. Not even Elijah Muhammad could have been more eloquent than those books were in providing indisputable proof that the collective white man had acted like a devil in virtually every contact he had with the world's collective non-white man.[6]

In a letter from prison, Malcolm continued in this vein: "This truth is so strong and clear that not even the white man himself will deny it once he knows we know..."[7]

Malcolm read voraciously. Reading was the basis of his intellectual development throughout his latter period. He kept copious notes from his readings and daily meetings and used them in his preparation for future discussions. Malcolm extended his discipline to all of his associates, requiring them to reflect his commitment to study, hard work, and excellence. In his weekly leadership classes in the temple, Benjamin Karim reported that

> Malcolm X ran the Public Speaking class for brothers who wanted to be ministers. The curriculum was ancient history broken down into the Hittites, the Egyptians, the Assyrians, Babylonians all the way up through the Persians and Rome, the Crusades and the Moors in Spain. We had to read every newspaper, the N.Y. Times, the U.S. News and World Report, the Chinese Peking Review, London Times. Every week we had to keep abreast and see historically how everything came to this point, the history of slavery...This was the class that he set up. There is no college class, calculus, trigonometry that was as rough as that Public Speaking class.[8]

It was on this basis that Malcolm almost single-handedly transformed the Nation of Islam from a small isolated sect into a national force in the African American community. He was responsible for establishing over 200 temples for the Nation of Islam.[9]

Malcolm's Historical Method

Malcolm X's political thought by 1963–64 was governed by a secular-materialist approach to questions of social change. This means that he looked for verification of the truth in the facts of history and not through divine revelation. He followed the sentiments of one of the fathers of Black nationalism, Martin Robison Delany, who asserted:

> God's means are laws—fixed laws of nature, a part of His own being, and as immutable, as unchangeable as Himself. Nothing can be

accomplished but through the medium of, and conformable to these laws…That which is Spiritual can only be accomplished through the medium of the Spiritual law; that which is Moral, through the medium of the Moral law; and that which is Physical, through the medium of the Physical law…Does a person want a spiritual blessing, he must apply through the medium of the Spiritual law—*pray* for it in order to obtain it. If they desire to do a moral good, they must apply through the medium of the Moral law—exercise their sense and feeling of *right* and *justice*, in order to effect it. Do they want to attain a Physical end, they can only do so through the medium of the physical law—go to *work* with muscles, hands, limbs, might and strength, and this, and nothing else will attain it.[10]

Delany saw the process of revolutionary social change as being in the domain of the physical law, and the political theorist of revolution, he felt, was the one who discovered the "means of elevation," the physical laws governing the liberation of oppressed people.[11]

For Malcolm X, as for Delany and Marx, these laws were discoverable through the study and analysis of history. Malcolm X rooted his knowledge in history. He did not approach history as an unconnected and unique sequence of facts. Rather he saw history as a means by which contemporary problems could be analyzed by revealing the causes which created them. By studying the history of contemporary oppression, Malcolm said that its origins would be exposed, contemporary problems diagnosed, and solutions advanced.[12]

Malcolm X was familiar with the histories of the American Revolution, the Russian Revolution, and the Chinese Revolution. His historical studies taught him that ordinary people could change society for the better and that revolution was possible for Black people. These lessons of history seemed to be confirmed by the momentous events of his day: the Civil Rights movement, the anti-colonial revolutions in Africa and Asia, and the emergence of the Third World after the Bandung Conference.

Malcolm X: Testing the Lessons of History

Malcolm X respected the written word and the power of books, but he also knew that true knowledge did not come exclusively or even essentially from books. Malcolm X validated the "truth" both from the pages of history and through testing his insights and conclusions against a broad cross-section of his street constituency. Written facts had to be validated against the lessons of his own experience and that of the people he led and influenced. This was necessary because African Americans' experiences and perspectives differed markedly from the experiences of those who wrote most of the books about history.

Malcolm's Method and Leadership

Because of its history as a dual society and the consequent impact that this reality has had on the consciousness of African Americans, the United States does not possess a unitary political culture. Milton Morris, a student of Black politics, reinforces this point:

> Where there are identifiable segments of a society sharing political attitudes and values distinct from that of the rest of society we say a 'political subculture' exists. Often these subcultures are products of deep cleavages in a society resulting from discontinuities in the level of economic development, religious, racial, or linguistic differences, or even geographic isolation.[13]

Malcolm X took advantage of the traditional ways in which Black people communicated political attitudes. He understood the importance of apparently informal encounters in influencing people's politics. Malcolm's leadership style allowed him to form personal relationships with many people who were in a position both to feed him information about the mood and condition of the ghetto masses and to react to his analysis of what was going on in the community, the country, and the world. There is a very definite relationship between the leadership style of Malcolm X and his method of testing his ideas. People believed and followed Malcolm X not out of an emotional attachment to his charisma. The basis of his leadership was that he gave back to his followers, in a more highly refined and clarified form, ideas and insights which in fact were rooted in their experiences. In contrast to the opportunities available to mainstream politicians today, Malcolm X could not depend on extensive public opinion polls to tell him of the desires of his constituency. On weekends, especially Sunday afternoons, promenading the avenues of Harlem and the side streets with one's family and friends was an old Black tradition used to meet friends and renew old acquaintances. Malcolm "fished" for converts and opinions in this manner. He visited homes on Sunday afternoons, the traditional open-house time in the Black community. He held court around a meal with its aura of personal intimacy. In fact, Malcolm's charisma and leadership were based on a very low-keyed method of personal contact and one-on-one encounters with the Black masses.

A considerable number of people revealed to me their personal encounters with Malcolm X. These unsolicited responses came from, among others, my mother-in-law, who was visited several times by Malcolm X. She remembered that he would visit the house after speaking on street corners in Brooklyn, New York. He would engage her in discussion and debate about the issues of the day and the Muslim program to confront these issues. Her impression of him was one of a decent and engaging fellow.

My first cousin first met Malcolm X in Detroit in 1952 when they were both workers in the automobile industry. He remembered that Malcolm made a special effort to get to know the workers. He would invite them to the Muslim restaurant for a meal and further informal conversation. Later, after moving to Philadelphia, my cousin encountered Malcolm X in the street. Surprisingly, Malcolm recognized him immediately and extended an invitation to lunch at the Muslim restaurant. My cousin's recollection was that Malcolm was that way with everyone he encountered.

Sociologist Alphonso Pinkney, who studied Black nationalism, met Malcolm X for the first time over a meal in the Muslim restaurant on Lenox Avenue. Yuri Kochiyama, a long-time Harlem activist, remembered Malcolm holding court over banana splits in Thomford's Ice Cream Parlor in Harlem, where she for many years was a waitress. She got to know Malcolm very well through his frequent visits there, and later their friendship grew into a political alliance. Malcolm visited her home, meeting with OAAU supporters back from Africa and admirers of his from Japan. Akbar Muhammad Ahmed (aka Max Stanford) of the Revolutionary Action Movement(RAM) remembers that his most important meetings with Malcolm X were held in Harlem's 22 West Restaurant. While these examples are anecdotal, I have been struck by how many people of my generation had meaningful personal encounters with Malcolm X. In an era of media image-making, Malcolm retained the ability to use older more traditional methods to reach and move people.

Malcolm defined history not just as what was in the books but also as that which could be validated by the collective experiences of Black people. In fact, I would argue that if Malcolm X had any particular genius regarding leadership, it was his ability as a public figure to meet so many ordinary people in situations that allowed for some measure of personal interaction. Malcolm's charisma was not based solely on a carefully crafted image to be viewed from afar, and thus it was somewhat impervious to manipulation by the mass media in relation to his core constituency.

None of this should suggest that Malcolm X had an idyllic relationship with his devotees. Today, we tend to forget how unsettling a person Malcolm X was even for his own followers. He articulated realities which many African Americans of his time had repressed and previously had refused to come to grips with.

Black Nationalism and Pan-Africanism

The development of Malcolm X's political thought was also advanced by his exposure to Black nationalism. Black nationalism can appear complex and contradictory. Any generalization about it can be subject to exception. Nevertheless, there are several excellent definitions in the literature; the best is that of Alphonso Pinkney. Pinkney observed that

> African-American nationalism is an expression of a desire for some degree of political, social, cultural, and economic autonomy. It is a movement for self determination brought about by centuries of oppression...As a movement Black nationalism has evolved through various forms...However, throughout its long history the ideology of Black nationalism has contained a common core of features.[14]

The basic components of African American nationalism according to Pinkney are the notions of unity and solidarity. It is a feeling of pride in cultural heritage, and Black consciousness. Finally, Black nationalist ideology believes some degree of autonomy from the larger society is essential.[15]

Black nationalism is a legitimate protest tradition indigenous to the African American community. That tradition was handed down to Malcolm both as a youth and as an adult. He was immersed in Black nationalism for his entire life. The form and content of that nationalism, however, changed at crucial points in Malcolm's life. His rhetoric reflected an activist style that was a product of the macho orientation of Black street culture, the "university of the penitentiary," and the themes of the quest for manhood and rebellion that were an essential element of Black political culture.[16]

As an adult, Malcolm received formal exposure to Black nationalism as it was reflected in the theology of Elijah Muhammad. It was tempered and altered in the political culture of Harlem with its street corner debaters, orators, and radical intellectuals.

The Pan-Africanist orientation of the OAAU was no doubt also a product of the street corner ideological debates around Africa Square (125th Street and Adam Clayton Powell, Jr. Blvd.).The late Hassan Washington remembered the geography of these debates. The Nationalists vs. Malcolm debates were "dogfights," he recalled, between the likes of Elombe Brath, Ahmed Basheer, Carlos Cooks, George Reed, and others. Ahmed Basheer held court outside the Broadway Bar at 126th Street and 7th Avenue. George Reed took on all comers outside the Optimal Cigar Store on the northwest corner of the intersection of 125th Street and 7th Avenue. On the corner occupied by the State Office Building today, Carlos Cooks and Josef Ben Jochanan held sway. The area in front of the Hotel Theresa was the stage for James Lawson and Eddie "Pork Chop" Davis.[17] Malcolm debated the legacy of Garvey with the likes of Carlos Cooks and his African Nationalist Pioneer Movement and the last of the street corner orators, Eddie "Pork Chop" Davis.[18] These latter sources reinforced links with the Garveyite tradition Malcolm inherited from his parents and reinforced by his sister Ella Collins and several of his paternal aunts.[19]

.The creation of the OAAU reflected the impact of Malcolm X's first trip to Africa in 1964, the impact of Julian Mayfield and other Pan-Africanists of the Afro-American expatriate community in Ghana, and the Pan-Africanism of the radical "Casablanca" powers (Ghana, Guinea, Egypt, Algeria, and Mali), the influence of Harlem-based intelligentsia, most notably John Henrik Clarke, and others like Sylvester Leaks and the Harlem Writers Guild of John Oliver Killens.[20]

Changing Perspectives in Malcolm's Thought

It is important to recognize in Malcolm X's political thought that ideas which flowered in subsequent periods were present in some manner and strength from the beginning. The periods in the development of his thinking are not set off so much by the emergence of new ideas as by the redefinition and changing emphasis placed on ideas already present (of course, some ideas of earlier periods were subsequently discarded).

We can identify three periods in the development of the political thought of Malcolm X. The first period, from 1952 through most of 1962, was characterized by the theology of the Nation of Islam. Black nationalism's renewed popularity owed much to the Nation of Islam, which offered a scathing critique of White America. It was in the Nation of Islam that Malcolm X returned to aspects of the Black nationalism of his childhood. Sometime in 1962, Malcolm X initiated the transition to the second period, secular Black nationalism. This second period in his thinking reached its highest development with the creation of the Muslim Mosque, Inc. and the speeches of the spring of 1964. With his trip to the Middle East and Africa in late April and early May 1964, Malcolm X ushered in the final period in the development of his thinking, the period of Pan-African internationalism. While the ideology and program of the Nation of Islam can be credited with the major role in launching Malcolm X upon the nationalist road, by 1962 they also represented the major barriers to the further intellectual and activist development of Malcolm. For this reason it is fruitful to take a look at the NOI's religion and program as well as its contradictory tendencies. This analysis will give greater clarity to Malcolm's break with Elijah Muhammad.

The Theology of Elijah Muhammad[21]

The Nation of Islam's conception of man was divided along the racial dimension. Western civilization was the product of White "devil-men," themselves the creation of an evil scientist 6,000 years ago. Whites were described as "devil-men," mutants from the original Black man, who controlled Black people through systematically denying them their true history and culture and physically separating them from their true home-land. White men ruled through the application of divide-and-conquer tactics using middle-class "Negro" leadership to advance the false doctrine of integration while separating the Black man from any conception of his true Asiatic origins as original man. In this way the Black man became a "so-called Negro." It was on the basis of the lack of consciousness of the "dead Negro" that the White man constructed a society based not on the divine precepts of justice and equality but on injustice, inequality, deprivation, and terror. According to the Nation of Islam this was the mortal sin of the White race. The religion of these "devils" was Christianity, and their domination would come to an end six thousand years after their creation. Islam was the "natural" religion of the Black man, the original man.

For the followers of Elijah Muhammad, the Negro was a dead man, in the sense of being a people without a real self-consciousness and therefore without a knowledge of history. An awakened Negro, an alive Negro, was a Black man who knew the meaning of history, his role in it, and the role of the White man. Psychologically, the "Negro" had to be awakened to his true status as a Black man. The awakened Black man would shed the immoral behavior characteristic of the ghetto subculture and the mentality of the "dead" and assume a morally correct stance. Such

61

an awakened Black person would recognize and uphold family and community responsibilities and demand justice and equality before the law. If denied justice and equality, the Black man should be prepared to "do for self," to take care of himself and his family through policies of economic and social self-sufficiency. Followers of Elijah Muhammad were encouraged to be law-abiding and to respect the U.S. Constitution. Racist terror was to be resisted by self-defense which was seen as not only a legal right, but as a natural and inalienable right Black people were prepared to exercise as the basic confirmation of their manhood.

The Nation of Islam's Program

The theology of the Nation of Islam created a mission of racial redemption for its followers primarily defined in terms of psychological rehabilitation from self-hatred and its corresponding anti-social behavior.[22] The long-term solution to Black oppression was in the hands of Allah, who would execute "God's judgment of White America" in the fullness of time. Allah would restore the Black man to his rightful place by separating him from the decadent West and reuniting him with the Asiatic world in a society based on justice and equality. Thus the meaning of history in this schema was no more than the progressive unfolding of God's plan to restore his people to their past glory and restore the conditions which existed in a past "golden age." The right of self-defense was claimed for the Black man, but it was seen as an individual right more than a group strategy for liberation.

The exclusive agent for social change in the world was God, Allah. Man, whether Black or White, would have no direct hand in initiating Armageddon. Nevertheless, the NOI's worldview projected an expectation of the appropriate behavior of Blacks and Whites.

Racist oppression was to be met in the economic realm by economic nationalist policies of community self-sufficiency and in the political realm by the demand for physical separation from the United States. The Nation of Islam had plans for national programs in the economic realm and made some attempts to establish colonies in the rural South as the beginnings of a separate NOI society. Part of the NOI's sense of mission was quite similar to that of Booker T. Washington's and the conservative strain in Black nationalism associated with emphasizing economic strategies and avoiding political agitation. Its separatist orientation required a very large following for viability. This latter need fostered the Muslims' desire for Black unity in the form of the Black united front. Nevertheless, throughout Malcolm's tenure and beyond, the NOI remained viable primarily at the level of the individual Black community. It formally shunned involvement in electoral politics at the local or national level and conducted no ongoing foreign relations. The Nation of Islam had no formal links with the religious institutions of the Islamic world.[23]

The theology of the Nation of Islam did not originally view Africa as the ancestral homeland of the Black man. It assigned no special place in its tenets to a revision of the prevailing view of Africa as the "dark continent." Aspects of its theology, in fact, confirmed racist stereotypes of the continent and its people. A reconstructed image of Africa was not then part of the psychological awakening of the Black man which the Nation of Islam sought.[24] The theology of the NOI did not require nor did it necessarily encourage its members to travel to Africa nor to make the *hajj* to Mecca. Dr. Michael Williams, a student of the NOI, noted that Elijah Muhammad rebuked his followers for subscribing financial support to Ghana's independence efforts.[25] He cited a statement of Muhammad which was an excellent example of the Messenger's provincialism on the question of Africa.

> There are some now giving their money to help Ghana's independence...Has Africa ever sent you any help for the past 400 years?...It would be a shame on the part of any independent nation's government to come here begging for help from the so-called Negroes whose status is that of *free slaves*. ...If you have extra money to send abroad, why not use it on SELF and your people here in America...First, help yourself and then if you are able, help others if you want to.[26]

Malcolm X later commented critically on Elijah Muhammad's position on African and Afro-American solidarity. Malcolm said that "he [Elijah Muhammad] was...in a position to unite us with Africa." Malcolm went on to note that the advantage was not exploited by Muhammad:

> But you cannot read anything that Elijah Muhammad has ever written that's pro-African. I defy you to find one word in his direct writings that's pro-African. You can't find it.[27]

Malcolm recognized the need the Nation of Islam to respond positively to the changing realities in Africa and the world. The Nation's changing position on Africa was associated with the emergence of the Afro-Asian bloc and the positive response that Gamal Abdel Nasser gave in the latter 1950s to Mr. Muhammad's desire for recognition in the Arab world. The fact that Nasser extended Muhammad recognition and facilitated his pilgrimage to Mecca in 1959 greatly strengthened the Nation of Islam in its dispute with U.S.-based Sunni Muslims, who denied the authenticity of Mr. Muhammad's movement.[28] Black nationalists in the Harlem community and elsewhere directed scathing criticisms at the Nation of Islam and questioned its Black nationalist credentials specifically for its "softness" on the question of Africa and African redemption.[29] The success of the NOI recruitment efforts depended to a considerable extent on their success in answering these criticisms.

The NOI's sense of racial mission neither required a restoration of African culture nor a cultural rejection of White America. In fact, the cultural orientation of the Nation of Islam was toward a Victorian lifestyle and value system.[30]

Elijah's Model of Organization

The concept of organization embodied in the Nation of Islam was that of an extremely centralized authoritarian theocracy with decision-making concentrated in the hands of Elijah Muhammad. His leadership was legitimized by charisma attendant to his position as the physical link between God and man as "the Messenger" of Allah. At the local level, the Muslim minister had exclusive and authoritarian control of the temples but was strictly circumscribed in his actions by continuous directives from Elijah Muhammad. The ministry itself was personally recruited by Elijah or his national representative Malcolm X and reflected the charismatic characteristics upon which Muhammad's leadership itself was based. Discipline in the Temple was maintained by the para-military Fruit of Islam (FOI). Women had no decisionmaking role in the Nation of Islam at any level.[31]

The Role of Women in the Nation of Islam

The NOI's perception of women was essentially patriarchal. Women's role was in the home or in the institutions specifically tied to the upbringing and education of children. Women were to be respected in their place and protected from the abuse of men outside of their families. They were not to move about unescorted and required strict male supervision because, lacking this, they were prone to promiscuous behavior. The Nation of Islam refused to grant to its female members a decision-making role over men, and strict segregation of the sexes was practiced in the temples and in the agenda of the organization. The Nation of Islam was a sexist, patriarchal, and paternalistic organization. Malcolm X shared this attitude toward women throughout his sojourn in the Nation of Islam and beyond.[32]

Elijah's Constituency

Publicly the Nation of Islam said it desired all members of the Black community to become members of the Nation of Islam. In fact, membership in the Nation of Islam was limited to Black people who had undergone a rigorous ideological training and trial period. Entry into the Nation of Islam was not easy and those who quit after joining were often stigmatized as "hypocrites." Membership was primarily composed of the targeted group, lower-class urban Black people. A disproportionate component of the membership was composed of reformed criminals and other previously anti-social persons.[33]

From the perspective of class, the NOI believed that the deadest of the "dead" were probably the Black middle class. This group would be the last to be awakened, and in recruiting among them the NOI had to be extremely patient. It did not therefore base its movement among better-off Black people but upon the most downtrodden segment of the Black working class whose experience of raw racism predisposed it to a more rapid awakening.[34]

Political Implications of Elijah's Program

Despite its emphasis on the inherent right of self-defense, the Muslim program was politically and economically conservative. Elijah Muhammad discouraged his followers from voting. As reflected in the slogan "do for self," the Muslim ethic was very much that middle-class ethic of accommodation preached by Booker T. Washington, and in that sense it was essentially a program of Black economic nationalism. Here the Muslim advocacy of racial spatial separation reflected a desire in part to acquire a market in which Black producers and consumers were sovereign. Muhammad fashioned his movement to avoid all signs of threat or provocation to the established social power.

In the United States of the 1950s and early 1960s, the pursuit on the part of Black people, Muslim and non-Muslim alike, of constitutionally guaranteed rights of citizenship, including the right of self-defense, was leading to revolutionary situations in the South against legal discrimination and in the North against actual segregation and police brutality. In this context, the NOI's nationalist stance attracted criticism from both the established media and Civil Rights forces, albeit for diametrically opposed reasons.[35] In responding to these attacks, Malcolm X formulated his earliest ideological statements on the nature of the Black Liberation struggle.

Malcolm X: Politicizing Elijah's Theology

Most of Malcolm X's speeches while in the Nation of Islam were more secular and implicitly activist than the official theology of the NOI. Although Malcolm X attributed all of his public statements to the "Honorable Elijah Muhammad," the record suggested that Malcolm X was often significantly more progressive in his thinking than his mentor. Wallace Muhammad reinforced a point made by Michael Williams,who recognized that "Muhammad was in need of someone like Malcolm who would breathe life into his teachings by taking certain ideological liberties with the essential message."[36] Wallace Muhammad noted:

> The thing that distinguished Malcolm X among the ministers was his individuality...He didn't take on the thinking and behavior of the old conservative ministerial body. He just gave Malcolm free reign to preach his doctrine...[Elijah Muhammad] told the old ministerial body "I will never get anywhere with people like you." He said, "All you do is teach the same thing we taught in the thirties...Look at this young man;...he's in modern times, he knows how to help me."[37]

Brotz reinforced this point in a veiled reference to Malcolm X's evangelical style:

> In analyzing the pronouncements of the intellectuals who have become spokesmen for this movement [the NOI], particularly those who travel around the country talking on college campuses, one gets the striking impression that these intellectuals believe no more in this science fiction than do their audiences, because, among other things, they hardly refer to it in serious discussions with educated people.[38]

Up until 1962, Malcolm X faithfully preached the theology of the NOI, but he exploited its political implications through numerous references to the fundamental changes which were occurring in the international and domestic political situation of his time. The theology of the NOI represented the beginnings of a fundamental break with integrationist thinking. It reversed the role of the races in human progress and gave to Black people the superior moral position. Black people were given a new identity which rejected membership in the United States or the Christian faith. According to the NOI, the motive force in the world today stood outside of Western Civilization. It gave a moral justification for the possession and articulation of the intense hatred which most Black people felt for Whites, which Christianity and the morality of its White God would not allow. The NOI's "demonology" was particularly suited to the mood of the alienated, ghettoized Black masses. While this latter group wanted to share in the material advantages of Western Civilization, it might be argued that it had long since given up any respect for the moral superiority of the West's Christianity and its civilization. In a sense, the theology of the NOI represented a challenge to the notion that the primary agent of change in the Black community was its middle class. This challenge was mounted against the middle class for the very reason that its thinking was seen as totally dominated by the integrationist-assimilationist paradigm.

Nevertheless, the NOI program was dominated by a moral code which was Victorian, an economic program based on petty capitalism, and a political program of (Booker T) Washingtonian accommodation. These aspects of the NOI program conformed to the Protestant ethic, and slowed down the radicalization of Malcolm's constituency and dampened his desire to be a social activist.

Constrained by the Ideas of Elijah Muhammad

Malcolm's membership in the NOI represented a constraint on a thoroughly secular statement of his views, and his submission to organizational discipline meant that he could not openly contradict Elijah's theology until his resignation freed him from these restrictions completely.

Suffice it to say that the revelation Malcolm X credited to his 1964 trip to Mecca was probably much longer in its development than he suggested. Malcolm X actually traveled in the Middle East and Africa in 1959 as Malik Shabazz, "so that my brothers in the East would recognize me as one of them."[39] Before the end of the 1950s, he was well-traveled in Third World support circles inside the United States and was even then known as a frequent fixture at Harlem functions concerning Africa. In a similar vein, Malcolm X from the outset of the 60s warned of the impact dispossessed ghetto residents would have on mainstream politics in the Black community. Malcolm X hinted that the NOI could possibly change its position and give electoral leadership to this emerging group. Lincoln reported that Malcolm X put Black politicians on notice that they should not discount the NOI when political decisions were made that affected the Black community.[40]

Minister Malcolm's Growing Problems with Critics

The theology of the NOI placed severe limitations on Malcolm X's ability to respond to critics of the Nation, especially those in the Civil Rights movement, Black nationalists, Sunni Muslims and street people. Black nationalists claimed that the Black nationalism of the NOI was "bogus" because the Muslim program had no role for Africa, and that it was politically conservative.[41] Sunni Muslims in the Black community questioned the authenticity of the Islam of the NOI. They carried their challenge all the way to the Islamic religious authorities in the Middle East.[42] Urban street people grew tired of the NOI's attack against the Civil Rights activists while seeing no direct NOI confrontation with racist and segregationist forces. They wanted the NOI to back up its inflammatory rhetoric with concrete action against the racist and segregationist forces.[43]

A Changing Malcolm Confronts a Changing NOI

By the early 1960s, Malcolm X found himself identifying with many of these critics. He recognized that the NOI would have to move in a much more activist and internationalist direction in order to meet these criticisms and assume the mantle of leadership to which it aspired. It was not only the theology of the NOI but also changes in the organization itself which made such a move unlikely. By the beginning of the 1960s, the character of the NOI as an organization, changed. It was no longer a "sect" with few members dispersed over several cities, but an organization of over 200 temples with at least 50,000 members and many times that number of sympathizers in all of the nation's urban areas. The organization represented a significant power and financial base in the Black community, and it supported an affluent lifestyle for the national leadership in Chicago and many of its ministers. In this context, the media appeal and notoriety of Malcolm X was a potential liability in that it made it more difficult for the NOI to avoid the attention which might attract repression at the hands of the state. With the increasing age and deteriorating health of Elijah Muhammad, the question of succession loomed, and Malcolm's popularity and closeness to the leader attracted envy and jealousy from some members of the inner circle around Muhammad. The NOI by 1962 was confronting its own variation of the dilemma which faced the Civil Rights movement—cooptation or repression. It was prepared to make peace with the White man and await Allah's judgment. It was not prepared to allow its brilliant national spokesperson to mobilize White fears against it.

Michael Williams identified a most important consideration in understanding the dynamics of Malcolm's break with the NOI. Williams claims that conservatives in the leadership of the NOI took issue with Malcolm X injecting the political concept of "Black nationalism" into a movement "which they preferred to keep religious in nature."[44] They used Malcolm and his Black nationalism to transform a sect into a mass-based national movement, but later expelled that nationalism from the NOI to protect its theology from internal criticism and to deflect an activist thrust which would lead to repression. By 1963 the politically progressive role that the Muslim movement played in the Civil Rights mobilization turned into its opposite. It was politically unprepared to move into the next stage emerging in the development of the Black freedom struggle. Malcolm X did not inject Black nationalism into the Black Muslim movement as his NOI critics contend. The NOI blamed Malcolm X for a development over which he had no control. Black nationalism helped mobilize those dispossessed African American ghetto folks who were becoming the most explosive and dynamic feature of urban life. It was they who injected these ideas into all aspects of urban life, including the Nation of Islam. They were unprepared to follow any leadership which did not affirm an allegiance to important nationalist tenets.

Malcolm X and Elijah Muhammad: A Special Relationship

Malcolm X did not immediately recognize the full import of his own evolving thought because of the inhibiting factor of his special relationship with Elijah Muhammad. This special relationship, however, was one of the factors severely compromising Malcolm's ability to move the NOI into a more activist stance.

To some extent, the full power of Malcolm's intellect was held in check due to the magnetism of Elijah Muhammad and the very special and personal role that he played in Malcolm's conversion. Muhammad was a father figure for Malcolm of immense power and prestige, and obviously one that Malcolm X did not subject to his otherwise methodical scrutiny. The break occurred when Malcolm X began to evaluate critically the political essence of all that was closest to him. In looking back over the break, Malcolm said

> When I lost my confidence in Muhammad as a person, I began to reexamine his philosophy, perhaps objectively for the first time, and his doctrines, his entire organization and behavior pattern. He offers something that is unattainable. I believe the Black man needs something more. I try to show my followers how they can get something more.[45]

As Malcolm put it:

> Those of us who split were the real activists of the movement [the NOI] who were intelligent enough to want a new kind of program that would enable us to fight for the rights of all Black people here in the Western Hemisphere.[46]

Malcolm's Political Analysis at the Break

That Malcolm X was committed to resolving the personal crisis of the split through recourse to secular rather than purely spiritual processes was attested to in the following words:

> I was wracking my brain. What was I going to do? My life was inseparably committed to the American Black man's struggle. I was generally regarded as a "leader." For years, I had attacked so many so-called "Black leaders" for their shortcomings. Now, I had to honestly ask myself what I could offer, how I was genuinely qualified to help the Black people win their struggle for human rights. I had enough experience to know that in order to be a good organizer of anything which you expect to succeed—including yourself—you must almost mathematically analyze cold facts.[47]

Malcolm sized up his own suitability for leadership based on his international image and his large following of non-Muslims in New York City. Malcolm attracted non-Muslim followers for three reasons: his historic stand at the 28th Precinct when he led a group of disciplined Muslims into pressuring the police to release the members of his mosque beaten by the police, his ability to draw much larger crowds than the established Black leadership, and his rapport with the Black masses.[48]

Formulating Secular Black Nationalism

Malcolm X formally broke with the Nation of Islam on March 8, 1964. He announced that although he was still a Muslim, "the main emphasis of the new movement will be Black nationalism as a political concept and form of social action against the oppressors."[49] Malcolm X announced the formation of this new organization, Muslim Mosque, Inc., in a press conference in New York on March 12, 1964. In this press conference, Malcolm offered a definition and some discussion of his ideas on Black nationalism. Malcolm's statements at the March 12 press conference were in many ways quite modest. At that event, he identified the aims of the Black Nationalist movement as political, economic, and social, rather than religious. As such, he felt, "it would be better able to work to bring equality for Negroes than the Black Muslims, who never take an active part."

At this press conference, Malcolm X defined Black nationalism in the following terms:

> Our political philosophy will be Black nationalism. Our economic and social philosophy will be Black nationalism. Our cultural emphasis will be Black nationalism...The political philosophy of Black nationalism means: we must control the politics and the politicians of our community. They must no longer take orders from outside forces.[50]

In the economic sphere, Malcolm X followed Elijah Muhammad's Black economic nationalism in encouraging Black people to form their own economic base by owning factories and hiring each other. In addition to taking whatever political action was possible, Malcolm X felt that the Muslim Mosque, Inc. would establish a religious base and a spiritual force necessary to implement the Black nationalist program in the social sphere. He felt it crucial to the advancement of Black people to eradicate alcoholism and drug addiction and all other "vices that destroy the moral fiber of our community."[51]

Malcolm X's most explicit formulations of Black nationalism at this time suggested nothing more than community control of the businesses, institutions, and political representatives of the Black community. The kinship with the earlier nationalism of the NOI was apparent. Nevertheless, a much clearer notion of an international dimension to Black nationalism was now emerging.

Malcolm X was skeptical about whether Blacks in the United States could ever get equality "without outside help." At the March 12 press conference, Malcolm argued that the struggle he and all Black people were involved in was a struggle for human rights, not civil rights. The Negro case should be taken up in the United Nations," Malcolm advised at the end of March 1964."The Negro will never get justice in Uncle Sam's Courts" but will be "forced to take Uncle Sam into the world court."[52]

At the break with the NOI, Malcolm saw the organization he had to build as addressing four problems facing Black people. As Malcolm put it, "It was a big order—the organization I was creating in my mind, one which would help to challenge the American Black man to gain his human rights, and to cure his mental, spiritual, economic and political sickness." For Malcolm X, the Nation of Islam had demonstrated that it could not grow enough and he felt it had "gone as far as it can." He wanted to build an organization differing from the NOI in that it would embrace all faiths of Black men and would practice what the Nation of Islam had only preached.[53] The Muslim Mosque, Inc., was Malcolm's first, if imperfect, approximation of such an organization. Malcolm X was now also thinking seriously about organizational forms beyond the united front which might be required to respond to escalating racist violence.

Absent from Malcolm's March 12, 1964 definition of Black nationalism was his insistence, articulated in the "Message to the Grassroots" speech of November 10, 1963, that nationalism is a revolutionary doctrine and the essence of the nationalist struggle is a violent struggle for land and power. There are, however, no indications that Malcolm X had, at this time or at any time subsequently, abandoned the feeling that the Black Liberation struggle required violent revolutionary methods. His discussion of Black nationalism at this press conference was not as rich and detailed as it had been in many of his speeches in the months before the break, nor would it anticipate the powerful statements which he was to make in the weeks immediately after the break. In order to get the full import of Malcolm's understanding of Black nationalism at the break, we must examine his thinking considerably before and after the formal rupture of relations with the NOI.

The components of Malcolm X's Black nationalist thought were reasonably constant throughout the last period of his sojourn in the NOI through the period of the break and the formation of the Muslim Mosque, Inc. Malcolm's secular Black nationalism was in place before the break with the NOI. In fact, the break with the Nation of Islam came much earlier than Malcolm's formal announcement of departure on March 8, 1964. It even antedated his suspension from public speaking by Elijah Muhammad in December 1963. It dated from the 1962 period when Malcolm's program of major public protest around the police slaying and brutaliza-tion of members of the Los Angeles mosque was vetoed by the Muslim headquarters hierarchy. From this incident through the spring 1964 *hajj* to Mecca, Malcolm X was engaged intellectually in elaborating what he called the ideology of "Black nationalism." This represented an extraction of the secular Black nationalist core of Muslim ideology from its religious form. Malcolm himself stated that "around 1963, if anyone noticed, I spoke less and less of religion. I taught social doctrine to Muslims, and current events and politics."[54]

Malcolm's Criticism of the Civil Rights Leadership"[55]

The beginning of this process of extracting the secular essence from the theology of the NOI occurred near the end of Malcolm X's sojourn in the NOI. It is associated with Malcolm X's response to those in the Civil Rights movement who criticized the NOI. In criticizing the Civil Rights leadership, Malcolm X focused on three crucial aspects of that movement: ideology, leadership, and organization.

Malcolm indicted the Civil Rights movement as suffering from false consciousness, because it defined the goal and objective of the movement as the integration of Black people into the U.S. system. He was concerned that it projected no fundamental critique of U.S. society and erred by restricting its definition of the problem as one of civil rights and its strategy as nonviolent direct action. Malcolm felt that this led African Americans to view them-selves as an isolated minority ultimately dependent on the goodwill of those who oppressed them. He believed that Civil Rights leadership refused to acknowledge the peoplehood of the African American, preferring instead to emphasize those attributes which confirmed its "Americaness." So con-ceived, the movement of African Americans was isolated from the broad sweep of change that convulsed the world, ending White world supremacy and ushering in the era of Afro-Asian hegemony. In addition, the exclusive focus on nonviolence as the guiding philosophy of the movement removed other tactics and strategies from serious consideration, strategies which elsewhere had proved effective in nullifying the overwhelming military-tech-nological might of the imperialists.

This desire to integrate with a fundamentally faulted and wicked system, Malcolm argued, flowed from the nature of Civil Rights leader-ship. This leadership was in the tradition of the "house Negro" of slavery days. Its political frame of reference was defined by the needs and desires of the master, and its cultural values were those of the master's culture. The middle-class Civil Rights leadership, by following in the nonviolent assimilationist tradition of its "house Negro" forebears, embarrassed the race and sold out the masses of Black people.

Organizationally, the Civil Rights movement created no real space within it for the urban working poor and long-term unemployed youth, hustlers, and "street" people, nor did it represent their interests. It created no organizational forms for collective self-defense and made no attempt to forge organizational links with the Pan-Africanist and anti-imperialist forces in the international arena.

Two telling responses greeted Malcolm's critique of the Civil Rights movement: first, a concession to the validity of many of Malcolm's criticisms, swiftly followed by an indictment of Malcolm for having no secular program with which the masses of Black people could achieve first-class citizenship before "Armageddon"; second, the legitimacy of Malcolm's concern was questioned because of the NOI's lack of activist and day-to-day involvement in the mass struggle of Black people for civil rights.

Malcolm X in Search of an Activist Black Nationalism

Malcolm continued to teach a progressively more radical analysis during his last nine months in the NOI. Between November 10, 1963, the date of the "Message to the Grassroots" speech, and the April 22, 1964 departure on the *hajj* to Mecca—a period which encompassed Malcolm's departure from the NOI on March 8, 1964 and the formation of Muslim Mosque, Inc., four days later on March 12,1964—Malcolm X attempted to formulate a more secularized version of Black nationalism than that bequeathed to him from the NOI. This time period constituted a second developmental period in Malcolm X's thinking. There was, however, considerable ambiguity regarding the primary sphere of movement activity. On the one hand, Black nationalism represented an attempt to intensify the self-help efforts toward autonomous Black communities. On the other hand, it was a more activist alternative to policies of the NOI, one which allowed nationalists to participate in the Civil Rights movement. As opposed to the thinking of the NOI, there was a distinct international component in the Black nationalism of Malcolm X and his human rights agenda. In addition, the possibility of Black nationalist revolution in the United States was fully accepted as a serious alternative.

Keeping Up with a Changing Civil Rights Movement

During this period, not only was Malcolm X responding to criticism of the NOI, but he was also attempting to keep pace with developments in the Civil Rights movement. The year 1963 was one of mixed blessings for that movement. There were concrete victories in Birmingham, Alabama and the momentous symbolism of the March on Washington. But there was also the assassination of Medgar Evers and the riots attendant to his funeral. There was the impasse in Danville, Virginia and the defeat of SNCC in the voter registration campaigns in Mississippi. Kennedy was forced to send in troops to stay the hand of Bull Connor in Birmingham, because in the midst of a massive demonstration led by Dr. King, frustrated Black "street" people departed from nonviolence and rioted after racists exploded bombs in the Black community. Finally, in September racist bombers killed four young African American girls in a Birmingham Sunday school.

The movement and its activism came north in 1963 with the Revolutionary Action Movement (RAM) and the NAACP's Cecil Moore confronting building trades' discrimination in Philadelphia. CORE took an activist stance also against building trades' discrimination in Cleveland and New York City. Black nationalism grew in CORE as its membership became predominantly African American for the first time. Retaliatory violence had also appeared in the movement as Robert Williams, the ex-NAACP head in Monroe, North Carolina, had to flee the country to avoid a racist frame-up. The Deacons for Self Defense mobilized in Louisiana to provide armed escorts for nonviolent protesters.

Malcolm's important speeches in this transition period between the summer of 1963 and the spring of 1964 were given in cities like Detroit and Cleveland, which along with New York City had the most militant and nationalistic activists in Black America. These activist cadres pushed Malcolm into a more radical stance as he attempted to clarify his own feelings about what was to be done.

Revolutionary Black Nationalism in Malcolm's Thinking

By this time, Malcolm X defined the African American nationalist tradition as a revolutionary one, a violent struggle for land and self-determination. He saw African American nationalism as an integral part of the worldwide revolution of Afro-Asians against White domination.

75

Even as early as his "Message to the Grassroots" speech, given before his suspension from the NOI, Malcolm X essentially saw Black nationalism in an international perspective. Malcolm saw Black nationalism as a part of a larger revolutionary reaction to White racist oppression which was changing power relationships on a global basis. He said then:

> He [the White man] knows that the Black revolution is worldwide in scope and in nature. The Black revolution is sweeping Asia, is sweeping Africa, is rearing its head in Latin America...All the revolutions that are going on in Asia and Africa today are based on what?—Black nationalism. A revolutionary is a Black nationalist. He wants a nation.[56]

Violence in Malcolm's Revolutionary Black Nationalism

In the "Message to the Grassroots" speech Malcolm attacked the concept of a nonviolent revolution as a phenomenon not confirmed by the facts of contemporary history. After reviewing the various anti-colonial uprisings, Malcolm X said:

> I cite these various revolutions, brothers and sisters, to show you that you don't have a peaceful revolution. You don't have a turn-the-other-cheek revolution. There's no such thing as a nonviolent revolution.[57]

The question of violence was at the center of Malcolm X's conception of the international implications of the Black man's freedom struggle (the struggle against racism and for civil and human rights). Malcolm X generated more controversy around his stance on violence than his analysis of the nature of White people. Malcolm X's position on the role of violence in social change often confused his adherents and his detractors. Liberal Whites such as M.S. Handler of the *New York Times* saw in Malcolm's advocacy of self-defense no more than the mainstream U.S. attitude which drew support from the Declaration of Independence and the United States Constitution.[58] Malcolm X went to great pains to reinforce this interpretation of his many statements on self-defense. He was quoted in the *New York Post* of April 10, 1964 as indicating that he owned a rifle and that he had taught his wife how to use it. Malcolm went on to say that he had instructed his wife to shoot anyone—Black, White, or yellow—who tried to force his/her way into his house. Malcolm X was not a vigilante. He was always careful to preface his statements about the organization of rifle clubs by Black people with the expression "in those areas where the government cannot or will not protect" its Black citizens. Dr. King expressed dismay at Malcolm X's advocacy of armed self-defense and rifle clubs. At the time, he said that such a move would be "a grave error and an inefficient and immoral approach."[59]

Malcolm X disagreed vehemently with Dr. King's rejection of self-defense. On a Philadelphia talk show, Malcolm X defended the former Monroe, North Carolina NAACP head and armed self-defense advocate Robert Williams, and answered the criticisms raised by King and others. For Malcolm, "Robert Williams was just a couple of years ahead of his time; but he laid a good groundwork, and he will be given credit in history for the stand that he took prematurely." Malcolm went on to say that "we don't think that our stand is premature. We think that now things have gotten to the point," where self-defense is necessary.[60]

Malcolm X had something more in mind than a static self-defense responding to individual acts of bigotry and violence. Although couched in the language of self-defense, Malcolm's statement on Black violence in his "Message to the Grassroots" speech mirrored the theory and analysis which later appeared in Frantz Fanon's published works.

> If violence is wrong in America, violence is wrong abroad. If it is wrong to be violent defending Black women and Black children and Black babies and Black men, then it is wrong for America to draft us and make us violent abroad in defense of her. And if it is right for America to draft us, and teach us how to be violent in defense of her then it is right for you and me to do whatever is necessary to defend our own people right here in this country.[61]

The International Perspective

Sizing up the international situation of his time, Malcolm X saw that violence was much more than self-defense narrowly defined. As guerrilla warfare, violence proved effective as a neutralizer of the power of the colonial state. It might be useful in the U.S. context to offset the White backlash and the tremendous military power of the United States government whenever it would be used to buttress the interests of racists. In both his "Message to the Grassroots" speech and at his Cleveland speech, "The Ballot or the Bullet," given at the beginning of April 1964, Malcolm X emphasized the fear guerrilla warfare evoked in white people. Malcolm felt that guerrilla warfare could neutralize the White backlash because "Whites have always been divided. And to get ahead of you, the white man cannot use his big bombs against us; a man does not destroy his own house. We can neutralize his weaponry."[62]

Malcolm X addressed the question of violence as it was addressed by the acknowledged expert on military affairs, Karl von Clausewitz. Violence was a political question, or as Malcolm X put it, a question of the "ballot or the bullet."

> A vote for a Democrat is a vote for a Dixiecrat. That's why in 1964, it's time now for you and me to become more politically mature and realize what the ballot is for; what we are supposed to get when we cast a ballot; and that if we don't cast a ballot, it's going to end up in a situation where we're going to have to cast a bullet. It's either a ballot or a bullet.[63]

Malcolm X did not dismiss the reformist strategies of the Civil Rights movement. He felt that the limits of reform strategies had to be tested and challenged so that African Americans might be encouraged to transcend them. He used the expression "the ballot or the bullet" simply to mean that the only alternative to violence was the real empowerment of Black people through electoral politics—an electoral politics which would allow Black people to break the southern racist stranglehold on the Democratic Party, the gerrymandering of ghettos by northern liberal hypocrites, and the conspiracy of the U.S. government itself to keep Black people powerless. This Black politics had to give Black people control of their own communities. Really to test the effectiveness of electoral politics for Black people, a real unity of identity and purpose and a willingness to punish Black politicians who sold out had to be prerequisites. If this kind of control was not forthcoming or if it did not work, Malcolm foresaw the emergence of urban guerrilla warfare as the natural alternative that would neutralize the superior military might of the racist forces and break the back of racism. As Malcolm put it:

> Modern warfare today won't work. This is the day of the guer-rilla...Nowhere on this earth does the white man win in a guerrilla war. It's not his speed. Just as guerrilla warfare is prevailing in Asia and in parts of Africa and in parts of Latin America, you've got to be mighty naive, or you've got to play the Black man cheap, if you don't think some day he's going to wake up and find that its got to be the ballot or the bullet.[64]

Throughout the early spring of 1964, Malcolm X made reference to the need to "fight for freedom regardless of the odds." His reference to violence here was not just figurative. In Detroit before the Legal Fund

Rally of the Group for Advanced Leadership (GOAL), Malcolm X referred to a Black nationalist convention slated for New York City in the summer of 1964 where delegates would "make up our minds whether we'll form a Black Nationalist party or a Black Nationalist army." Around the same time he told Carlos Russell that the convention was projected for June and that "it will not be unilateral; I mean by this that I will not dictate, but rather it will come from the convention."[65]

Confronting Race, Class, Culture, and Leadership

> If you're afraid of Black nationalism, you're afraid of revolution. And if you love revolution, you love Black nationalism. To understand this you have to go back to...the house Negro and the field Negro back during slavery...The field Negro—those were the masses...The Negro in the field caught hell...He hated his master.[66]

The Black nationalism of Malcolm X was concerned about culture. Malcolm X felt that racial unity required, in part, a reconstructed image of African American culture. To understand Malcolm's reconstruction required an explicit treatment of the impact of class on African American culture and an essentially political conception of the African American's cultural heritage. Through the analysis of the "house Negro" and the "field Negro," Malcolm attempted to reveal the social, historical, and cultural origins of the debate between integrationists and nationalists and the classes involved. For Malcolm X, Black nationalism was the natural political expression of the "field Negro" tradition in African American political culture. This "field Negro" tradition was predicated on a profound hatred of the slave master and all his works. Moreover, it was oriented toward the destruction of slavery by "any means necessary." In no way did it identify with the values of the slave holder, valuing only those things which contributed to the destruction of the slave master and his hated institution. The resurrection of the "field Negro" mentality in the contemporary Negro of Malcolm's day required a psychological acceptance of African roots and identity.

Malcolm X was concerned about the self-image of the race and its impact on Black self-help efforts in every sphere. Independent Black media, he felt, were an indispensable prerequisite to foster such a psychological return to African roots. Malcolm told Carlos Russell in the early spring of 1964, "I mean by Black Nationalism that the Black man must control the radio, the newspapers, and the television for our communities.

I also mean that we must do those things necessary to elevate ourselves socially, culturally, and to restore racial dignity."[67]

The political role that Malcolm assigned to African American culture assumed that the only legitimate Black culture was that of the masses of dispossessed African Americans. For Malcolm, Black culture was significant only to the extent that it contributed to the struggle for Black liberation.[68]

From this identification of African American nationalism as the natural political expression of the masses of dispossessed urban African Americans, Malcolm asserted that the only valid movement leadership was that which was indigenous to and therefore able to establish rapport with the Black urban working classes and the urban street people. Later, as a result of his travels in Africa and the counsel of Pan-Africanists on both sides of the Atlantic, he would recognize that legitimate leadership in the Black community had to have established credentials in international forums and the respect of Third World leadership.

The Muslim Mosque, Inc. concept attempted to attract membership from all classes and groups in the Black community. It was Malcolm X's first serious attempt at building a Black united front. To build this front, Malcolm X wanted to become a member of the Civil Rights movement and to find a principled way of working with the Black middle class.

Malcolm sought the achievement of Black unity at the earliest possible moment. This was reflected in his stand on integration. Appearing with the Black journalist Louis Lomax on a Cleveland television talk show on April 4, 1964, Malcolm said:

> ...my stand is the same as that of twenty-two million so-called Negroes. It is not a stand for integration. The stand is that our people want a complete freedom, justice and equality, or recognition and respect as human beings. That's the objective of every Black man in this country. Some think that integration will bring it about. There are others who think that separation will bring it about. So, integration is not the objective nor is separation the objective. The objective is complete respect as a human being. And the only difference among Negroes in this country isn't in the objective but in the method by which this objective should be reached.[69]

He continued, "I am not out to fight other Negro leaders or organizations. We must find a common approach, a common solution, to a community problem.[70]

Malcolm addressed this theme as it was broached to him by leftist and progressive members of both the Black and White communities. At the March 12, 1964 press conference announcing the Muslim Mosque, Inc., he addressed the question:

> There can be no black-white unity until there is first some black unity. There can be no workers solidarity until there is first some racial solidarity. We cannot think of uniting with others until we have first united among ourselves. We cannot think of being acceptable to others until we have proved acceptable to ourselves.[71]

Around the question of Black unity, Malcolm was prepared to go to any principled lengths to achieve such unity. When he formally announced his departure from the Nation of Islam, he said:

> I am prepared to cooperate in local civil rights actions in the South and elsewhere and shall do so because every campaign for specific objectives can only heighten the political consciousness of the Negroes and intensify their identification against white society...There is no use deceiving ourselves. Good education, housing, and jobs are imperatives for the Negroes, and I shall support them in their fight to win these objectives, but I shall tell the Negroes that while these are necessary, they cannot solve the main Negro problem.[72]

In his "Message to the Grassroots" speech, given on November 10, 1963 before the Northern Negro Grassroots Leadership Conference in Detroit, Malcolm addressed the question of how violence separates the Black community along class lines. He defined the Black middle class as those who aped the thought and attitudes of the White man. Malcolm called this group "house Negroes." The Black middle class he felt was a class with a "house Negro" mentality, most epitomized by their fear of revolutionary violence. This mentality of the Black middle class was at the root of the "Uncle Tom" Civil Rights leadership that was selling out the masses of Black people. Implied here by Malcolm was that in a revolutionary situation the Black middle class had to be written off.[73]

By the early spring of 1964, Malcolm X had moved away from this perception of the Black middle class and its potential for revolution. He told Carlos Russell that "one of the troubles of the Black nationalist is that they have held themselves apart. Since I have gotten involved, I am surprised at how militant some of these 'integrationists' are sounding. Man, sometimes they put me to shame."[74] Malcolm's analysis of the Black middle class by this time was a little more complex. He said again to Russell:

The Black middle class, in its attempt to protect the crumbs the White man gives while trying at the same time to deceive him, is the most acrobatic of Negroes. We have to revolutionize his thinking. He will come around, when he realizes that he is barking up the wrong tree.[75]

Africa in Malcolm's Thinking

Malcolm's perspective on separation and the return to Africa underwent significant modification in the Black nationalist period. At the break, Malcolm said that he still believed, like Muhammad, that "the best solution is complete separation with our people going back home to our own African homeland." But the program Malcolm would now espouse would shed the unrealistic garb of the NOI in order to focus on the practical needs of African Americans *and* Africans. Malcolm now said, "Separation back to Africa is still a long-range program, and while it is yet to materialize, 22 million of our people who are still here in the U.S. need better food, clothing, housing, education and jobs *right now*" (emphasis in the original).[76]

Less than a month later, Malcolm X further clarified his understanding of this notion of separation on a Cleveland radio show:

The white people have clouded the issue by talking this separate state thing. What Mr. Muhammad has always said is give the Negro everything that is his due in this society. And if you can't give it to him in this society, since the Negro today is not going to wait, then there has to be an alternative solution that can be brought about immediately. So what they do is try and make it look like we're asking for some separate states. They hide the fact that it is said give the Negro his due here now. And if you can't do it now take some separate something else somewhere else.[77]

Even at this time, however, Malcolm X recognized, as did all of the nationalist prophets before him, that a blanket return of Blacks to Africa was not only a short-run impossibility but might not even be desirable. In language that paralleled the 19th-century Pan-Africanist, Bishop Henry M. Turner's on this question, Malcolm observed that "the Black Nationalist who will return to Africa will be psychologically ready. He will not go to exploit, but help in the development of the motherland."[78]

Malcolm X's Changing Perception of Whites

Malcolm X retained a suspicion of Whites from his membership in the NOI, but after the break he dropped NOI dogma and focused on the question of leadership and coalitions. Malcolm argued that it was the White man who was the major barrier to unity since White men were brought into leadership positions in Black organizations in order to subvert them. As Malcolm X told Carlos Russell:

> First I believe the Black man must lead his own fight; in fact, the Black Nationalist must become more involved and force the White man out, for he is the most deceitful creature on earth. I intend to prove that you can't get civil rights in this country. Then I intend to elevate the idea of civil rights to the place of human rights; this way we can go to the United Nations and show the world what this country really is.[79]

According to Malcolm, Black unity required the exclusion of White people from Black organizations so that a private airing of differences would be possible. Only in this way could African Americans discover what they agreed on and construct the Black united front. This formulation, while indicating a continued distrust of Whites, should not be construed as the same "White man as devil" analysis common to Nation of Islam demonology. Malcolm feared the hypocrisy of the White liberal, who he felt was not helping Blacks. For him, White liberal hypocrisy paralleled that of the U.S. government in international forums when the question of racism was taken up. It was yet another reason for Malcolm X's desire to expose the United States as a hypocrite in the United Nations.

Nevertheless, Malcolm X's White liberal "hypocrite" was a far cry from the White "devil" of the NOI period. Malcolm was now prepared to accept help from well-meaning Whites exclusive of organizational membership. His position on the role of Whites was by now thoroughly secularized and his distrust of them was couched in pragmatic considerations. As Malcolm frequently articulated it during this period:

> The White groups that want to help can help; but they can't join. The White man who wants to join in with Negroes does nothing but castrate the effort of those Negroes; but when Whites join Negro

groups they aren't joining the Negroes, and they end up by controlling the group that the Negro is supposed to be controlling.[80]

In Search of a Politics of Women's Liberation

The question of women in the struggle is not yet explicitly discussed
by Malcolm in the period immediately after the break with the NOI. The
Moslem Mosque, Inc.,(MMI) did not specifically address the question of
the liberation of women. While it made no formal statements which would
indicate a subordinate role for women, it remained, as an awkward hybrid
of religious and secular organizational forms, essentially tied to the
perception of women inherited from the Nation of Islam. Nevertheless, in
this period Malcolm X began to incorporate a few women into his
planning for a new Pan-African-oriented Black united front. These deliberations would later produce the OAAU.

From Black Nationalism to Pan-African Internationalism

The last period in the evolution of Malcolm's political thought
began on April 22, 1964, when Malcolm embarked upon the first of two
trips to the Middle East and Africa. These trips pushed forward the
development of his thinking. After his return from the first trip in late May
1964, Malcolm X was no longer satisfied with the formulations of Black
nationalism he had articulated in March and April of that year. He no
longer felt that the Muslim Mosque, Inc. could be the proper organizational form for moving toward a politics of African American liberation.
Upon his return from Africa, Malcolm X was committed to Pan-African
internationalism. He founded the Organization of Afro-American Unity
on June 28, 1964.

In this period of Pan-African internationalism, Malcolm X's formulations were not finished theoretical products but a rapidly developing
perspective which he was never allowed to complete. Many questions
which Malcolm addressed, therefore, were incompletely answered or not
answered at all. There were also other important questions he did not take
up before his death. It is clear that Malcolm X felt that the Eurocentric
international system had to be transformed into one which could extend
justice and equality to all of the world's peoples. It is equally clear that
he felt this had to be done in such a way as to preserve the plurality of
cultures and nationalities and not through the forced homogenization of
"integration." He had only begun to formulate the actual contours and

mechanisms which would empower such new social forces, and most often with specific reference not to the entire Third World but only to Afro-America and Africa.

Historically, Black nationalism emerged in response to racism. It had of necessity to be concerned with the status and treatment of the race irrespective of national boundaries. Thus Black nationalism was at one and the same time a legitimate nationalism but also a "pan" movement, an international movement for the redemption of the race (in fact, scholars often refer to 19th-century Black nationalism as "Pan-Negro nationalism"). This might have been obscured in Malcolm X's case because his most explicit formal definition of Black nationalism did not mention an international dimension. Whatever ambiguity existed on this point was clarified by Malcolm in this last period of his development. Late in 1964 at Harvard University, Malcolm X argued that Afro-Americans "are just as much African today as we were in Africa four hundred years ago, only we are a modern counterpart of it."[81]

Malcolm's Critique of Capitalism

As a result of his two trips to Africa in 1964, Malcolm X came to recognize the inconsistency of Black control of Black communities in a monopoly capitalist economy rooted in Western imperialism. Co-existence was impossible. Malcolm X frequently described capitalism as a "blood-sucker." He now felt that it could not be relied upon to eradicate racism and poverty. Shortly before his death Malcolm acknowledged that:

> It is impossible for capitalism to survive, primarily because the system of capitalism needs some blood to suck. Capitalism used to be like an eagle, but now it's more like a vulture...As the nations of the world free themselves, then capitalism has less victims, less to suck, and it becomes weaker and weaker. It is only a matter of time in my opinion before it will collapse completely.[82]

The capitalistic methods associated with the Black economic nationalism which Malcolm carried over from his NOI period now caused him to question his earlier understanding of Black nationalism.[83] By January 1965, Malcolm X felt that the term "Black nationalism" no longer accurately described his thinking.[84] It was not that he had ceased to be a nationalist, but that his nationalism had distanced itself even more from the "reactionary" aspects of Black economic nationalism which he had inherited from the Nation of Islam. Malcolm X was a revolutionary nationalist to the end, but a growing hostility to imperialism rooted his thought in a more anti-imperialist, internationalist, Pan-Africanist direction. This perspective identified the first order of business as establishing an African American liberation movement and giving serious consideration to organizational forms which facilitated collective self-defense, up to and including guerrilla warfare if necessary. In addition, it sensitized Malcolm to the need to explore seriously an alternative to capitalism.

Malcolm X looked closely and favorably on African nationalists' attempts to create an African socialism. He noticed on his travels that most of the newly independent nations "have turned away from the so-called capitalistic system in the direction of socialism."[85] His interaction with heads of state and nationalists in Africa certainly exposed him to the various theories of African socialism that they espoused. Leaders like Nyerere of Tanzania, Nasser of Egypt, Toure of Guinea, and Nkrumah of Ghana, all had some formulation of a "mixed" economy that they were calling "socialist." At his death, however, Malcolm had not established clearly what kind of socialism should supersede capitalism. There is no available information that Malcolm X affirmed a commitment to "scientific" socialism or communism. He was grateful for the support he received from the Socialist Workers Party, while questioning their motivation. The Communist Party of the United States viewed Malcolm X as a dangerous demagogue whose nationalism represented a dead end for African American workers. Those who noted Malcolm's turn toward socialism, like George Breitman and Michael Williams, consistently failed to make a distinction between the Marxist-Leninist tradition of "scientific" socialism and the socialist thought of Malcolm X. There is no information available that demonstrates that Malcolm X seriously studied Marxism-Leninism. In fact, his African mentors in socialism have been scathingly criticized by Marxist-Leninist scholars and activists for their "revisionist" brand of socialism. The various African socialisms and the systems established on that basis in Africa have been criticized by African marxists as veiled apologies for the consolidation of various forms of dependency and dependent capitalism.[86] In some of these countries, the Communist Party was either outlawed or its members harassed by the government as was the case in Egypt under Nasser. The attitude of these African socialists was reflected in Frantz Fanon's rejection of marxism as a thing European and not suitable as the basis for reorganizing post-colonial Africa.

By 1965, however, Malcolm X had shed any previous anti-communism that might have been attributed to him from his NOI period. His intervention in the Civil Rights movement cleared the way for the emergence of the serious study of Marxism-Leninism, which appeared in the latter 60s and early 70s in organizations like the Black Panther Party, The League of Revolutionary Black Workers, and the African Liberation Support Committee.

Emerging Pan-Africanism

It was in Malcolm X's rapidly developing view of the relationship of Africa to the liberation struggle of African American people that we have the most explicit bridge in his thought between the MMI period and his final period of intellectual development as a Pan-African internationalist, the OAAU. In Malcolm X's thinking Africa became less and less the place where African Americans would retreat to create a separate existence while awaiting Armageddon. It became much more a conception essential to the reconstruction of the personality of the oppressed "Negro" in his transformation into an African American. The role of Africa in the thinking of Malcolm was essentially political. The advocacy of a cultural identification with Africa was not advanced as an end in itself. It was a means by which African Americans could reclaim their psyches and their self-respect in order to fight back against racism and exploitation in the Western hemisphere.

Clearly, the African American conception of Africa was a center-piece of the cultural renaissance Malcolm desired. By the time of his return from his summer and fall 1964 trip to Africa, Malcolm X saw that the need for separatism did not require a massive physical return of African Americans to Africa. It did require a strengthened commitment to African redemption. This understanding of separation was closer to the position of the most orthodox 19th- and early 20th-century Black nationalists and Pan-Africanists. On November 29, 1964, he told an OAAU rally, "It is only with a strong Africa, an independent Africa and a respected Africa that wherever those of African origin or African heritage or African likeness go, they will be respected."[87] In this context Malcolm made his final clarification on the question of separatism:

> This doesn't mean that we're getting ready to pack up our bags and take a boat back to Africa. This was not the impression that I was trying to give [in Africa], because this is not true. You don't find any large number of our people packing up their bags going back to Africa. That's not necessary. But what is necessary is that we have to go back mentally, we have to go back culturally, we have to go back spiritually, and philosophically, and psychologically. And when we go back in that sense, then this spiritual bond that is created

makes us inseparable, and they can see that our problem is their problem, and their problem is our problem. Our problem is not solved until theirs is solved, theirs is not solved until ours is solved. And when we can develop that kind of relationship, then it means that we will help them solve their problems and we want them to help us solve our problems. And by both of us working together, we'll get a solution to that problem. We will only get that problem solved by working together.[88]

The OAAU put the image of Africa at the center of African American attention. For Malcolm this was necessary for the emotional and cultural rehabilitation of the African American psyche so necessary for racial unity. The OAAU represented the rooting of Malcolm X's Black nationalism firmly and explicitly within the Pan-Africanist tradition.

Pan-African Internationalism

In the period of Pan-African internationalism, Malcolm X maintained his commitment to revolution as the necessary method of social change. In this last period his perspective on the nature of revolution broadened and deepened. He began to recognize that African Americans could resort to revolution only if international conditions were supportive. It helped that the world was then characterized by many revolutions and revolutionary situations. But what was also required was a high degree of cooperation and coordination across national boundaries between the various oppressed races, peoples, and nationalities. This international setting was characterized by the appearance in the oppressed everywhere of a new self-concept grounded both in their particular histories of oppression and resistance and in a new sense of kinship with all those fighting for a more just world.[89]

Malcolm recognized that defining himself as a Black nationalist complicated his relationship with other valid revolutionaries who were not Black. He credited the Algerian ambassador to Ghana with

show[ing] me where I was alienating people who were true revolutionaries dedicated to overturning the system of exploitation that exists on this earth by any means necessary. ...I had to do a lot of thinking and reappraising of my definition of Black nationalism. Can we sum up the solution to the problems confronting our people as Black nationalism? And if you notice, I haven't been using the expression for several months. But I still would be hard pressed to give a specific definition of the over-all philosophy which I think is necessary for the liberation of the Black people in this country.[90]

Had Malcolm completely jettisoned Black nationalism? He told an OAAU audience:

> I haven't changed. I just see things on a broader scale. We national-ists used to think we were militant. We were just dogmatic. It didn't bring us anything. Now I know it's smarter to say you're going to shoot a man for what he is doing to you than because he is white.

Malcolm X's broadening perspectives never caused him to redefine his primary responsibility as the liberation of the racially oppressed and exploited African American. He told talk show host Les Crane in December 1964 that "this belief in brotherhood doesn't alter the fact that I'm also an Afro-American, or American Negro as you wish, in a society which has very serious and severe race problems which no religion can blind me to."[91]

Legitimizing the Black Revolution

Internationalizing the struggle raised the problem of establishing legitimacy for the African American struggle for human rights in interna-tional law and organization. The quest for legitimacy mandated at a minimum that African Americans speak to international bodies with one voice. On the one hand, Malcolm X asserted that if the alternative of "the bullet" ever had to be resorted to, unity of African American and African people organized in the OAAU and the OAU would have been a necessary prerequisite for successful urban guerrilla warfare. On the other hand, effective participation of Black people in electoral politics in the United States, Malcolm argued, required internationally supervised guarantees of the fundamental human rights of African Americans. International recognition could be achieved only if African Americans could organize as a nationality and present their demands in a "national capacity." This certainly was not the situation within the Civil Rights movement in 1963–64, and for Malcolm X the quickest way to achieve unanimity was not to challenge the established Civil Rights leadership but to form a united front with them within the context of the OAAU. The OAAU was the first major attempt in the 1960s by revolutionary Pan-African nation-alists to form a Black united front.

Malcolm X visualized the OAAU as the organizational vehicle for internationalizing the struggle of the African American. Such an internationalization of the Civil Rights struggle, he felt, was absolutely essential if it were to have any chance of success. As he put it "...I would like to impress upon every African American leader that there is no kind of action in this country that is ever going to bear fruit unless that action is tied in with the overall international struggle."[92] Malcolm X wanted to establish his revolutionary base area in Africa. In this he was steeped in the Pan-African tradition going back to Martin Delany, Bishop Henry M. Turner, and Marcus Garvey. Malcolm argued, as these leaders had before him that

> when you build a power base in this country, you're building it where you aren't in any way related to what you build it on. No, you have to have that base somewhere else. You can work here, but you'd better put your base somewhere else. Don't put it in this man's hand. Any kind of organization that is based here can't be an effective organization. Anything you've got going for you, if the base is here, is not going to be effective. Your and my base must be at home, and this is not at home.[93]

In Malcolm's view, membership within the worldwide majority of Black people would end the perception of African Americans as a minority in White America. Organizationally and politically, Malcolm X saw the United Nations and the search for Bandung-Third World bloc as a counterweight to the domestic political power of the United States. Internationalizing the struggle meant transforming the struggle for civil rights into a struggle for human rights. The advantage of doing this was that the United Nations charter, the Universal Declaration of Human Rights, and the Genocide Convention unequivocally give priority to human rights, but United States law still could not guarantee civil rights to African Americans. Due to U.S. fear of world opinion, internationalizing the struggle of African Americans would give Black people breathing room against the power of racism in the United States. Such breathing room could be used to organize for self-defense, aggressive electoral politics, and Black economic advancement.

Malcolm X repeatedly returned to the theme of self-defense because he truly believed that African Americans would have to fight their oppressors and "that [violence] is the only language they understand," and African Americans needed allies internationally, especially in Africa, to do this.[94]

The OAAU: A New Model for Organization, Leadership, and Women

The OAAU as a united front was patterned upon and reflected the structure of the mass-based nationalist parties which led countries like Ghana, Guinea, Tanzania, and Kenya, among others, to independence. The OAAU concept also reflected the impact that revolutionary organizations in the Portuguese colonies, Southern Africa, and the Algerian Revolutionary experience had on Malcolm. On a more practical level, the OAAU would facilitate the granting of UN observer status to Malcolm X's organizational efforts and make it easier for Malcolm to address this international audience as a legitimate representative of a national liberation movement.[95]

Malcolm X, under the influence of revolutionary thinking in Africa and the Third World, moved away from a messianic conception of leadership toward one more grounded in the collective equality typical of the revolutionary cadre organizations in the liberation movements. From Cairo in July and August 1964, Malcolm wrote home to his associates not to confer upon him any preeminent role in organizational decisionmaking.[96] One of his most important tasks was to establish collective democratic decisionmaking in the OAAU and reverse the legacy of authoritarian leadership carried over from the Nation of Islam.

In the OAAU period, Malcolm continued to build a membership based on the united front orientation that first appeared in his Black nationalist period. The OAAU itself was seen as an improvement over the Muslim Mosque, Inc. because the latter's name had been a significant impediment to attracting the non-Muslim and middle-class Black elements which Malcolm X desired in his organization after he left the NOI. Moreover, the OAAU concept was formulated in terms of the Western hemisphere and not just in terms of the United States. Thus, Malcolm X sought new chapters and potential members from Black communities outside of the United States.

The OAAU concept reflected Malcolm X's growing appreciation of the complexity of the Black middle class, its various strata, and the potential for supporting revolutionary change in several of them. Malcolm X's difficult transition out of the NOI was smoothed by his relationship with Harlem's nationalist-oriented and radical intellectuals. The pilgrimage to Africa was designed primarily by middle-class Pan-Africanists in the Black community in the United States and among expatriate African Americans in Ghana.[97] Upon meeting the nationalist leadership in Africa and the Third World, Malcolm saw that many of these revolutionaries were of middle-class origin but had none of the ideas, self-hatred, and timidity he associated with that same class in the African American community. Lastly, many of Malcolm's middle-class intellectual and activist associates were targeted by J. Edgar Hoover as subversives, and in fact, their association with Malcolm X was used as a pretext for the FBI proscription of the OAAU.[98] Malcolm, no doubt, recognized that this group within the middle class could not at one and the same time be agents of and targets of White power. The united front concept Malcolm attempted to develop in the OAAU was also very much an attempt to find the proper role for the most progressive groups within the Black middle class.

Malcolm X clearly promised a new role for women in the OAAU. On December 27, 1964, he told talk show host Bernice Bass:

> One thing I noticed in both the Middle East and Africa, in every country that was progressive, the women were progressive. In every country that was underdeveloped and backward, it was to the same degree that the women were underdeveloped, or underdeveloped and backward.[99]

Under the influence of the revolutionary examples of the mass-based nationalist parties of Africa and the role of women and women's organizations in them, Malcolm threw his full weight behind the struggle for women's equality. This was arguably his most difficult internal battle. As we shall see in Chapter Five, the success of the OAAU would depend on the acceptance and institutionalization of a new, equal role for women in the very heart of that organization.

The OAAU: What Role for White People?

Malcolm X did not offer OAAU membership to Whites, but his position on their role in social change continued to evolve. Malcolm feared the intentions of White people in the United States, but in the OAAU period, he went to great lengths to establish the material basis for his animosity toward Whites. This he had to do because some of the most nationalistic and radical regimes on the African continent were also the most anti-racist. He would not have been taken seriously by the likes of Nyerere and Nkrumah if he had not repudiated the Muslim devil theory of Whites or any veiled equivalents of it. Upon his return from his final trip to Africa, Malcolm X swore that:

I'm not a racist. I don't judge a man because of his color. I get suspicious of a lot of them [Whites] and cautious around a lot of them—from experience. Not because of their color, but because of what experience has taught me concerning their overall behavior toward us...We are against them because of what they do to us and because of what they do to others. All they have to do to get our good will is to show their good will and stop doing all those dirty things to our people.[100]

Conclusion

In the period between late 1962 and the summer of 1964, Malcolm X articulated a political philosophy which addressed the dilemma which faced the Civil Rights movement in the period 1963–65. This dilemma, the contradiction between reform programs being coopted and revolutionary impulses being repressed by the government, was addressed in Malcolm X's thought through recourse to Pan-African internationalism. Malcolm's ideology addressed cooptation by recognizing that different groups in the Black middle class had different revolutionary potential. It also recognized that the entire middle class vacillated between assimilation and nationalism. Two themes which historically appealed to the more nationalistic segments of the Black middle class as well as to its intellectuals were a sense of racial mission and the placing of the needs of the race over individual desires. Malcolm X made a home in the ideology of revolutionary Black nationalism for these groups in the Black middle class. Moreover, his continued advocacy of community self-sufficiency and development created a space and an outlet for the talents of those Black middle-class entrepreneurs who were not or could not be coopted.

Malcolm's insistence on the centrality of Africa in the Black psyche forced the Civil Rights movement to confront the question of Black identity. The question of Black identity had to be answered if a nationwide Black community—heretofore a numerical expression of people who happened to be Black—was to be molded into a united force for change in the United States. This question of identity made a space for the Black masses to articulate their needs and to compete for leadership positions. This was so because so much of what was African or "Black" about African Americans was tied up with the culture of the Black proletariat. Traditionally, the middle-class assimilationist impulse and its aversion to Africa were most clearly seen in a rejection of the validity of Black working-class culture and its potential for bringing about social change.

From the tradition of African American revolutionary nationalism, Malcolm injected into the Civil Rights movement the notion of facing up to violence and organizing to fight back "by any means necessary." In this tradition, there was always the sense that physical resistance was possible for the African American in the United States because he was part of a larger international community of color which possessed the potential of neutralizing the might of racism in the United States. In its Pan-African formulation, this revolutionary nationalist tradition always emphasized the unity of the struggles of Africans in the continental homeland and in the diaspora. It always pointed directly to the alliance between Pan-Africanists and all other people of color in international forums and institutions. Here the thought of Malcolm X held out hope that the international prestige of the African American struggle might stay the hand of repression if the revolutionary alternative had to be selected.

Malcolm X was finally able to extricate Black nationalism from the cul-de-sac into which the NOI's position on White people had led it. He recognized, as had most of the historical Black nationalist leadership, that the racial sense of mission bound up in the notion of Ethiopianism (the early 19th-century movement of African Americans to redeem the race and execute God's special destiny for Africa) was a mission on behalf of all humankind, a humanist mission. Thus, he was able to redefine separatism into social transformation here in the Western hemisphere and in Europe. By so doing, he defined a role for those Whites seeking a new relationship with the Black revolution.

Chapter Five will examine in detail how successful Malcolm X was in solidifying his most developed insights into the structure, program, and practice of the OAAU. It answers the erroneous charge articulated by Dr. King and most recently by Cornel West that Malcolm was an icon of legitimate Black rage but he lacked a solution to Black oppression. Chapter Five also represents a response to Spike Lee's *X*, which misses the most important developments after Malcolm leaves the NOI, minimizes the impact of his trip to Africa and the creation of the OAAU, and misunderstands Malcolm's growing sophistication as merely a softening on White people. Chapter Four has demonstrated the power of Malcolm X as a thinker and theorist; the next chapter will show the exhaustive lengths to which Malcolm would go to commit his last days to making his ideas a force for creating the Black Liberation movement.

Press Conference at Kennedy Airport, November 24, 1964,
on return from trip abroad.

5

THE OAAU
AND THE
POLITICS
OF THE
BLACK
UNITED FRONT

The Organization of Afro-American Unity, organized and structured by a cross-section of the Afro-American people living in the U.S.A. has been patterned after the letter and spirit of the Organization of African Unity...

Dedicated to the unification of all people of African descent in this hemisphere and the utilization of that unity to bring into being the organizational structure that will project the Black people's contributions to the world;

Persuaded that the Charter of the United Nations, the Universal Declaration of Human Rights, the Constitution of the U.S.A. and the Bill of Rights are the principles in which we believe and these documents if put into practice represent the essence of mankind's hopes and good intentions;

Desirous that all Afro-American people and organizations should henceforth unite so that the welfare and well-being of our people will be assured;

Resolved to reinforce the common bond of purpose between our people by submerging all of our differences and establishing a non-religious and non-sectarian constructive program for human rights...

Statement of the Basic Aims and Objectives
of the OAAU, Preamble[1]

The Formation of the OAAU

The OAAU represented the outcome of numerous discussions that Malcolm X had with militant revolutionary nationalists throughout the country, especially those located in the Cleveland-Detroit area, and with the field secretary of the Revolutionary Action Movement (RAM), Muhammed Ahmed (aka Max Stanford).[2] RAM represented the wing of the Civil Rights movement most committed to revolutionary guerrilla warfare in the United States. It had direct ties to Robert Williams, then exiled in Cuba, and the nationalist wing of the southern student movement and its northern support groups. RAM also had a grounding in Marxist-Leninist ideology which gave to its variant of Black nationalism a particular leftist character. Don Freeman of Cleveland, Ohio, one of the founders of RAM, had been at the press conference when Malcolm X announced the formation of the Muslim Mosque, Inc. (MMI) Muhammed Ahmed had been constantly in touch with Malcolm X from early in 1962. During Malcolm X's break with the Nation of Islam, he spoke frequently in the Cleveland-Detroit axis, and some of his most pointed statements on self-defense and the formation of gun clubs were made in these talks. It is through association with RAM that the formation of the OAAU is linked to Robert Williams and the whole question of revolutionary guerrilla warfare.

In the winter of 1964, Julian Mayfield, a progressive African American expatriate living in Ghana, wrote to Malcolm X about organizing some institutional links between the African American community in the Western hemisphere, the African American expatriate community in Africa, and the developing OAU in Africa.[3] Mayfield suggested that if Malcolm X could get to Ghana, more detailed discussions and planning could be undertaken. Because of this invitation, the idea of an OAAU appeared on the agenda of Malcolm's spring trip to the Middle East and Africa and ultimately consumed the bulk of his time abroad. Malcolm X developed his itinerary and agenda through extensive contacts with friends at the United Nations and received personal tutoring in the fine points of the politics of each country on his itinerary from a close relative of Kwame Nkrumah.[4]

Publicly, Malcolm indicated that his trip abroad was primarily for religious reasons, to fulfill a lifelong obligation as a Muslim to make the religious pilgrimage to Mecca (the *hajj*) and to deepen his knowledge of that religion. Sylvester Leaks argued that Malcolm's prestige and legitimacy as a leader were based, in large part, on his religious credentials.[5] Leeks felt that having discarded the advantages that came with being Elijah Muhammad's spokesperson, it behooved Malcolm to gain the acceptance of orthodox Sunni Islam if he were to retain those who followed him as a religious teacher. While this is certainly true, Malcolm X was just as clear about the political usefulness of his African agenda. He was on a diplomatic mission for the African American people as well as a religious mission to correct the Black Muslim "heresy."

Malcolm X's first 1964 trip abroad commenced on April 13 and ended on May 21. His second trip commenced on July 9, 1964 and ended on November 24, 1964. In these two trips to Africa, Malcolm visited or passed through thirty countries, including Egypt, Sudan, Ethiopia, Kenya, Tanzania, Nigeria, Ghana, and Guinea. He met with several heads of state including Nasser, Nkrumah, Kenyatta, Nyerere, Obote, Toure, and Azikiwe.

The First Trip Abroad

The spring sojourn in Africa and the Middle East was an exercise in "people-to-people diplomacy," with Malcolm X as the ambassador of the Black people in the United States. Speaking to audiences composed mostly of students, radicals, and expatriate Black intellectuals, Malcolm attempted to establish an identity for African Americans, not as popularly conceived in the African continent as U.S. citizens but as subject peoples, colonized by White men and racially oppressed. Malcolm talked to this audience about the condition of African Americans in the United States, speaking the language of human rights, not civil rights. Everywhere Malcolm X went on the continent, he tried to impress "upon them [the Africans] that 22 million of our people here in the United States consider themselves inseparably linked with them, that our origin is the same and our destiny is the same, and that we have been kept apart for too long."[6]

With these audiences he achieved success in establishing Black America as a concern in Third World and human rights discussions. He was the first Black leader of the '60s to take Africa seriously enough to go there and speak directly about conditions in the United States. Mohammad Rahman Babu said at an OAAU rally that Africans recognized this and appreciated Malcolm's gesture. On the first trip to Africa, Malcolm X met with several heads of state and numerous lesser officials, lobbying for a strategic alliance between Africa and Black America and support for his plan to condemn the United States for violating the "human rights of 22 million African Americans."[7]

The reception Malcolm X received in Ghana would not have been possible without the preparatory work of the African American expatriate community. A "Malcolm X Committee" had been formed to plan Malcolm's itinerary while there and it made the necessary media and diplomatic preparations.[8] This expatriate community in Ghana was special in that it was particularly Pan-African in its orientation. Some, like the late Dr. W.E.B. Du Bois, had renounced their U.S. citizenship after years of harassment as radicals and communists at home. They came to Ghana to return to their ancestral homeland and help in its development. Like other expatriate communities, the African American community in Ghana had mixed feelings about leaving the land of its birth. Always sensitive to the accusation of having abandoned the struggle and those left behind, the community constantly sought ways to reaffirm its kinship with those of African descent in the Western hemisphere and the struggle for racial equality being waged there. Malcolm X represented a link with Black America which was politically acceptable to these Pan-Africanists. Their backgrounds caused them to have serious doubts about nonviolence and to be attracted to the grassroots quality of Malcolm's leadership. They thought up the OAAU concept as much as Malcolm did because it resolved the dilemma confronting them.

In May 1963, Pan-Africanists achieved a breakthrough with the creation of the Organization of African Unity (OAU). If the OAAU could work, Africa and its Diaspora would have an organizational link. In that sense the notion of "expatriate" for the Ghanaian African American community would be overshadowed by membership in a transcontinental Pan-African community.

While in Africa and especially in Ghana, Malcolm X solidified ties with representatives of radical Third World nations. He had long discussions with the ambassadors of China, Algeria, and Cuba. He briefed them on the racial situation in the United States and attempted to enlist their support both for his OAAU and the indictment of the U.S. at the United Nations.[9] From them, he received descriptions of their revolutionary programs, accounts of progress made in their countries, and assurances of their support for the struggle of the African American people.

Malcolm X took tea at the home of the Chinese ambassador and later foreign minister, Wang Hua. Hua reminded Malcolm that Mao Tse Tung was the first head of state to declare the open support of his government and its 800 million people for the Afro-American struggle for freedom and human dignity in the United States. Malcolm was impressed with his knowledge of the plight of the African American. Later Malcolm returned to the Chinese embassy for a state dinner given in his honor.[10]

In similar fashion Armando Entralgo, the Cuban ambassador, gave a dinner for Malcolm at his residence, to which he invited the entire diplomatic community. But Malcolm was perhaps most impressed with the Algerian ambassador, Taher Kaid, with whom he had a critical discussion about the relevance of race and revolutionary potential. As we saw in Chapter Four, this discussion caused Malcolm to reconsider his position on Black nationalism. Ambassador Kaid led a delegation of five ambassadors which accompanied Malcolm X to the airport when he was leaving Ghana.[11] Most importantly, Malcolm X was accorded the status of a diplomat and a leader representing a people engaged in a struggle for national liberation. This opened doors on his second trip to Africa and gave him a platform to speak to its leadership and its masses about the human rights struggles of African Americans against the U.S. government.

It is important to recognize that the interest of radical governments like those of Cuba and China in Malcolm X was not simply charity. Malcolm X's popularity in Africa and among Black people everywhere could have benefited Cuba simply by association.[12] Cuba sought to overcome the isolation imposed on it by the United States embargo through greater involvement and a higher profile in the Third World. Castro had identified Africa as a particular arena in which Cuba's involvement in the nation-building process and liberation struggles could pay dividends. The Cubans were familiar with Malcolm X and had made contact with him even prior to the famous two-hour meeting with Fidel Castro at the Theresa Hotel in Harlem in 1960.[13] Malcolm X supported Cuba during the fall 1960 United Nations visit of Fidel Castro. Malcolm's facilitation of accommodations in Harlem for Castro's delegation and the massive and enthusiastic welcome that the Harlem community gave to the Cuban leader represented a major coup for Cuba in the early years of its revolution. Malcolm was fond of comparing the achievements of the Cuban Revolution in race relations with the slow pace of the Eisenhower and Kennedy administrations.[14] Malcolm was a good friend of Cuba, and soon after meeting Castro in September 1960, the Cuban government embarked on a program of cultivating African American activists and intellectuals.[15]

The Chinese also recognized Malcolm X as an asset. From his days in the NOI, Malcolm had spoken in glowing terms of the Chinese Revolution. For Malcolm X, the Chinese Revolution represented the potential of the downtrodden rapidly to reverse their status and assume a major role among the powers of the earth. Malcolm was fond of telling his audiences of the days when a common expression of hopelessness was "not to have a Chinaman's chance." Who in the world today, Malcolm asked, would use that expression in relation to post-revolutionary China. Even more than Cuba, China had experienced an isolation in the world that resulted both from the lack of U.S. recognition and the ideological conflict with the Soviet Union. In 1964, Chairman Mao Tse Tung sent a message to the African American people supporting their struggle against "racism and imperialism."[16] This occurred at a time when China recognized three levels of relations it had to establish in the world. As a sovereign state, there were its state-to-state relations; as a previously colonized nation, it recognized a special bond with the emerging nations of the Third World and established special bonds with independence movements and national liberation fronts; most importantly for the Chinese, they aspired to world leadership of the revolutionary struggle between the classes. Popular uprisings of oppressed races and peoples were seen by the Chinese as integral components of the class struggle, and the Chinese aspired to lead this movement. The African American struggle was so defined by the Chinese, and Malcolm X was seen as its most shining example of working-class leadership.

The human rights, nationalist stance of Malcolm X assisted his discussions and communication with African and revolutionary leadership. Malcolm X now saw the world and spoke of it in the same terms as they did. King and other mainstream Black leaders did not come to Africa and speak the language of revolution. Only when Malcolm arrived in Africa did its militant leadership group receive a briefing on the U.S. racial situation in language immediately recognizable to them.

While in Ghana, Malcolm had long discussions with the representatives of the liberation organizations receiving Prime Minister Kwame Nkrumah's support. Both the African National Congress of South Africa (ANC) and the South African Pan-Africanist Congress of Azania (PAC) representatives in Ghana were much impressed with Malcolm X.[17] He deepened that link with the forces of liberation in Africa on his second trip to Africa, especially at the OAU Summit Conference of Heads of State in Cairo. While there, he was housed with the delegations from the liberation organizations on a boat moored along the Nile. Malcolm X learned as well as taught in these settings. Of his experience on the boat in Cairo Malcolm said:

> I was blessed with the opportunity to live on that boat with the leaders of the liberation movements, because I represented an Afro-American liberation movement—Afro-American freedom fighters...It gave me an opportunity to study, to listen and study the type of people involved in the struggle—their thinking, their objectives, their aims and their methods. It opened my eyes to many things. And I think I was able to steal a few ideas that they used, and tactics and strategy, that will be most effective in your and my freedom struggle in this country.[18]

Founding of the OAAU

The Organization of Afro-American Unity (OAAU) was conceived by Malcolm X in the winter of 1964. It was the product of discussions and planning which took place both in the United States and in Africa. Between Malcolm X's first and second trips to Africa in 1964 he was able formally to establish the OAAU, which occurred on June 28, 1964. Even before Malcolm X formally broke with the Nation of Islam, he recruited Lynn Shifflet, an African American woman and a producer at NBC, to help him pull together a small group of activists and intellectuals to work with him on the creation of a new organization with a Pan-African emphasis.[19] This group began meeting immediately but commenced working in earnest in the middle of May 1964. The group, pulled together in hush-hush fashion, met at least four times at Harlem's only motel at 153rd Street and 8th Avenue. Malcolm X attended at least three of these sessions; and, although Lynn Shifflet chaired these meetings, clearly Malcolm X was in charge. Intellectuals and activists like Dr. John Henrik Clarke, John Oliver Killens, A. Peter Bailey, Muriel Gray, and several of his associates from MMI also attended these sessions. Everyone present participated in the deliberations, but Malcolm X and Lynn Shifflet were clearly in leadership roles. The contributions of Dr. Clarke and the author John O. Killens were important, even crucial, but they were performed in an advisory capacity, which was largely the stance of these people throughout the life of the OAAU.[20]

Peter Bailey noted that the agenda of these organizing meetings dealt exclusively with the projected organization's stance on crucial questions and programs regarding self-defense, education, etc. There was no attempt at this time, he asserted, to deal with the question of the structure of the organization. This had serious consequences, especially when Malcolm X was not in New York City or was out of the country.

At the Riverside Drive apartment of Ms. Shifflet on June 9, the contents of the "Statement of Basic Aims and Objectives of the OAAU" were discussed and preparations initiated for the formal proclamation of the new organization on June 28, 1964. It was John Henrik Clarke who suggested the name "Organization of Afro-American Unity" to Malcolm at this meeting. Malcolm agreed with Clarke that the Organization of African Unity could serve as an excellent model after which the new organization of Afro-Americans could be patterned. Subsequently, Clarke secured from the United Nations' OAU mission the text of the OAU charter and set about to draft the OAAU Aims and Objectives after the letter and spirit of the OAU. In a meeting at Clarke's Harlem apartment, the Aims and Objectives were finalized by Clarke, Malcolm X, and Lynn Shifflet.[21]

Paralleling these discussions, and in as much secrecy, were discussions Malcolm X had with RAM through its field secretary, Muhammed Ahmed. As Ahmed remembered it, in June 1964 he and Malcolm worked out the structure of a revolutionary nationalist alternative to be set up within the Civil Rights movement. They also outlined the role of the OAAU in this alternative.[22]

> The OAAU was to be the broad front organization and RAM the underground Black Liberation Front of the U.S.A. Malcolm in his second trip to Africa was to try to find places for eventual political asylum and political/ military training for cadres. While Malcolm was in Africa the field chairman [Ahmed] was to go to Cuba to report

the level of progress to Robert Williams. As Malcolm prepared
Africa to support our struggle,"Rob" [Robert F. Williams] would
prepare Latin America and Asia. During this period, Malcolm began
to emphasize that Afro-Americans could not achieve freedom under
the capitalist system. He also described guerrilla warfare as a possible tactic to be used in the Black liberation struggle here. His slogan
"Freedom by any means necessary" has remained in the movement
to this day.[23]

These discussions, in fact, reflected the impact of Malcolm's interaction with the representatives of national liberation movements and
guerrilla armies during his trip to Africa. He was very much focused on
establishing an equivalent structure within the African American freedom
struggle. On June 14, 1964, the Sunday edition of the Washington Star
featured an interview with Malcolm X in which he announced the formation of "his new political group," the Afro-American Freedom Fighters.
In this interview Malcolm X emphasized the right of Afro-Americans to
defend themselves and to engage in guerrilla warfare.[24] A change of
direction was rapidly made, however. As Ahmed reported, Malcolm's
premature public posture on armed self-defense and guerrilla warfare
frightened those in the nationalist camp who feared government repression. They feared giving public exposure to organizing efforts for self-defense and guerrilla warfare. Malcolm agreed, and the name of the new
organization became the Organization of Afro-American Unity.[25]

The OAAU was to be the organizational platform for Malcolm X as
the international spokesperson for RAM's revolutionary nationalism, but
the nuts and bolts of creating a guerrilla organization were not to take
place inside the OAAU. The OAAU was to be an above-ground united
front engaged in legitimate activities to gain international recognition for
the African American freedom struggle.[26]

Prior to the founding rally on June 28, the organization was announced to a selected cross-section of Harlem leadership in a letter on
OAAU letterhead, dated June 24, 1964, over Malcolm X's signature. It
read in part:

A cross-section of the Harlem Community has been working for
some time on the formation of an organization that would transcend
all superficial, man-made divisions between the Afro-American
people of this country who are working for Human Rights, and that
would in no way compete with already existing successful organizations. I have been requested, and indeed it is my pleasure, to
announce the existence of the Organization of Afro-American Unity
(OAAU), patterned after the letter and the spirit of the Organization

of African Unity (OAU). Its purpose is to unite Afro-Americans and their organizations around a non-religious and non-sectarian constructive program for Human Rights. The Organization of Afro-American Unity is well aware of your interest, work, and involvement in freedom struggles over the years, and you have proven to be sincere in your area of endeavor.[27]

The recipients of this letter were designated as invited guests at the founding rally, and an informal reception prior to the program was arranged for them. The invited guests included the activist lawyer Conrad Lynn, the Progressive Labor Party leader in Harlem, Bill Epton, the radical journalist William Worthy, and the actor Sidney Poitier.[28] Lynn, Worthy, and Epton did subsequently attend the rally and were introduced to the audience as invited guests along with the following persons: Earl Friedney of the Ghana Press, Ora Mobley of the Central Harlem Mothers Association, William Tatum of the Association of Artists for Freedom, who represented actors Ossie Davis and Ruby Dee, Isaiah Robinson of the Harlem Parents Workshop (who would later become a president of the New York City School Board), Earl Sweeney and his wife from the African American community in Ghana, Mrs. Sidney Poitier, and the author Paule Marshall.[29]

The Basic Aims and Objectives of the OAAU

A close reading of the Basic Aims and Objectives of the OAAU indicated that its first tactical objective was to attack the internalization of oppression on the part of African Americans. In this regard, the OAAU took a vigorous stand on the African American right of self-defense. Second, it projected a "cultural revolution to unbrainwash an entire people." The rationale for this tactic was simply but movingly stated in Point Six of the Aims and Objectives.

After self-defense, education assumed the highest priority as the OAAU's first tactical objective. But this was an expanded definition of education which included the pursuit of quality education through the tactic of the school boycott, and the nationalist goal of establishing alternative schools, cultural centers, and related institutions. Point Six of the Aims and Objectives concluded with a poignant appeal:

> We must work toward the establishment of a cultural center in Harlem, which will include people of all ages, and will conduct workshops in all the arts, such as film, creative writing, painting, theater, music, Afro-American history...This cultural revolution

will be the journey to our rediscovery of ourselves…Armed with the knowledge of the past, we can with confidence chart a course for the future. Culture is an indispensable weapon in the freedom struggle. We must take hold of it and forge the future with the past.[30]

The second tactical objective of the OAAU was to attack the basis of the powerlessness of African Americans. "Basically, there are two kinds of power that count in the United States: economic and political, with social power deriving from the two."[31] Black politics based on greatly expanded voter registration campaigns could bring power in Black localities through bullet voting, which might also allow African Americans to determine the winner in close presidential elections. Economic power would grow as African Americans struggled against the exploitation common to ghetto areas and supported militant actions like rent strikes which attacked such exploitation. We can see here clearly how the OAAU departed from the apolitical stance of the NOI and the go-it-alone orientation of the Black economic nationalism found in both the NOI and the definition of Black nationalism from the MMI period.

The tactics for social uplift advocated by the OAAU were based on the premise that the OAAU's social program had to depend on the internal resources of the Black community. These resources had to be used to rid that community of the "moral and social legacy of oppression." That legacy included police brutality, the impact of organized crime, and drug addiction.[32] The OAAU would lead the way in establishing community acceptance of the responsibility for such socially desirable and necessary services as "a place where unwed mothers can get help and advice; a home for the aged in Harlem and an orphanage in Harlem."[33]"For the youth a guardian system would protect those who got in trouble and would set a good example for all the children of the community," teaching them to be ready to "accept responsibilities…necessary for building good communities and good nations."[34] Such community acceptance of the responsibility for social welfare was not to be construed as a renunciation of rights and entitlement to government services; the OAAU committed itself to facilitating the receipt of all the privileges and entitlement of government social welfare to which Black people as citizens were authorized.[35]

The third tactical objective was to achieve a working relationship between the Civil Rights movement and the emerging human rights movement of the OAAU. The highest priority would be placed on achieving a principled reconciliation with the established Civil Rights leadership. This tactic would be hedged by courting and establishing an immediate working relationship with the radical wings of the Civil Rights movement—its leftist and nationalist wings—with New York City generally and Harlem specifically as its base.

The most important immediate tactical objective of the OAAU was unexplainably missing from the Basic Aims and Objectives. It was the achievement of recognition from the OAU, the United Nations, and the international community as a national liberation organization. With this status the OAAU could indict the United States before these bodies. To this end, Malcolm X lobbied in Africa and Europe for most of the remainder of his life. In his speech at the June 28 rally, however, Malcolm X clearly indicated and talked at length about this latter objective as the first order of business of the OAAU.[36] The remainder of this chapter describes the initial structure of the OAAU and the activities that Malcolm and his supporters undertook in the pursuit of the organization's agenda.

OAAU Structure and Activities

The active membership of the OAAU never exceeded a few dozen souls. It was solidly working class with some students and intellectuals, especially among the OAAU core. The membership was more or less evenly divided between men and women. It was primarily recruited from those who attended the OAAU rallies and participants in the OAAU Liberation School. Every rally and Liberation School session heard a specific pitch for those in attendance to join the OAAU. Hassan Washington estimated that Malcolm X was able to win over approximately 100 Black nationalists from their previous affiliations or their independent stance. In addition, Malcolm X attracted, according to Washington, some old-line Latino Garveyites, especially those of Cuban and Panamanian extraction.[37]

Large numbers of Muslims did not come out of the NOI to join the MMI or the OAAU. This was due to intimidation of NOI members so inclined and a political conservatism among these very same people which oriented them to shun the open advocacy of self-defense and direct challenges to the political hegemony of the U.S. government. Wallace Muhammad, one of Elijah's sons but also his harshest critic, possibly expressed the view of many who had come out of the NOI but had not joined Malcolm when he said that he was a friend and admirer of Malcolm but that he did not wish to be connected with Malcolm because of his "violent image." In fact Wallace himself was competing with Malcolm for disaffected NOI members through a Philadelphia-based organization, African Descendants Uplift Society (ADUS), which he formed in the summer of 1964. He warned his followers there that although Malcolm was his friend, because of Malcolm's association with a violent image, they should avoid joining any organization created by him.[38]

The social base of the OAAU consisted of a large, attentive public of previously unorganizable street people, alienated Black workers, and older, disaffected members of the established Civil Rights organizations. These groups were also courted by Elijah Muhammad. Leftists like Jesse Gray were also attracted to Malcolm X's "new look" but were testing Malcolm to see if he had really changed his position on White people. James Campbell, who came to direct the OAAU's Liberation School, defined himself as one of the group of Black intellectuals and progressives who was listening closely to Malcolm X and found a "complementary mentality in Malcolm." Campbell saw Malcolm X as evolving into the same protest tradition as Frederick Douglass, David Walker, and W.E.B. Du Bois. Between 1962 and 1964, this grouping of intellectuals and progressives watched Malcolm's growing estrangement from the NOI, an estrangement which made it easier for them to reach out to Malcolm X. By the summer of 1964 Campbell joined the OAAU because he "had the notion that Malcolm was moving toward the left: toward a systematic analysis and a systematic scientific organization."[39] It is for this reason that when the Harlem riots erupted less than two months after the establishment of the OAAU, the youth in the streets called for leadership from Malcolm X and the OAAU.

Further Recruitment Activities

Malcolm X organized several chapters of the OAAU among expatriate African Americans in Ghana, Kenya, Egypt, and Paris, France. Chapters gave these groupings some organized way of relating to his mission and at the same time participating in events in the United States. In Ghana, Malcolm's supporters established an OAAU Information Bureau.[40]

Malcolm X had developed an attentive public in Europe based in the expatriate and resident populations of African descent but extending to Third World communities there. Malcolm's impact in England and to a somewhat similar extent in France was to sensitize these communities not only to the African American struggle but to the essential similarities between their conditions in Europe and that of the African American. By doing this, Malcolm X was in part responsible for mobilizing these communities into action against racism in England and France. Malcolm

X struck an anti-imperialist stance in Europe, opposing the Vietnam War and other Euro-American military involvements in the Third World. Consequently, the governments of these countries were notably wary of him, and it did not help that his activities in Africa were of an "anti-imperialist" cast. They saw him as an ally of Nkrumah and Nasser and perhaps an extension of the offensive against the moderate African countries of the Monrovia group. It did not help that Malcolm X was on record with statements like the following:

> His [Nkrumah's] philosophy of Pan-Africanism is the most advanced political doctrine being voiced on the African Continent today, and for this reason President Nkrumah is both feared and hated by the white, Western Powers who are still trying to maintain a neo-colonial foothold on that continent of beauty and wealth.[41]

Abroad, Malcolm X gave the impression that he was trying to organize the resident populations of African descent to oppose the foreign policy and economic interest of European countries in Africa.

Indicative of the extensive international contacts Malcolm X was making in 1964 is the June 14, 1964 meeting Malcolm attended with four Japanese journalists who were part of a delegation in New York for a commemoration of the attack on Hiroshima. This meeting took place in the living room of long-time Harlem activist and Nisei, Yuri Kochiyama. Kochiyama reported that Malcolm X fascinated the writers with his knowledge of the Japanese historical situation and that of the Far East. She remembered that Malcolm claimed that the Japanese resisted the United States and were not intimidated by it due to a lack of a colonial experience at the hands of the West. Malcolm felt Japan had not been colonized because it did not have anything that the West wanted. This, he argued, was not true of other Asian countries like China.[42] Malcolm concluded by saying that "the struggle of the Vietnamese people is the struggle of the Third World."[43]

Membership Meetings and Political Education

Membership meetings could occur at different times but usually were scheduled for Monday evenings at 8:00 p.m., initially at the Marcus Garvey Hall at 2395 Eighth Avenue but later at an office in the Theresa Hotel. Non-members could attend up to five meetings before being required to take out a membership card.[44] Twenty-five to thirty individuals usually met to discuss and act on the pressing but routine work of the organization. The agendas of these meetings focused on the hosts of little things that were the routine work of all organizations. The publication of *The Blacklash* and the drafting and distribution of news releases were often agenda items. When Malcolm was not in town, however, the leading agenda item and the main topic of discussion, Bailey remembered, was how to get people out to the rallies which would not feature Malcolm.

Through the urging of Peter Bailey, James Campbell structured Sunday evening political education sessions for the OAAU leadership. These political education classes were organized around discussions and analysis of the latest speeches and documents Malcolm was sending back from Africa. The Sunday evening sessions took place at Marcus Garvey Hall. Campbell felt that this "Sunday night group" represented the intellectual core of the OAAU "trying to find common ground." Campbell did not recollect that any members of MMI attended these sessions.[45]

Leadership

The leadership remained a handful of middle-class intellectuals and professionals, with the core of MMI providing security. Except for the position of chairperson, which was occupied by Malcolm X, the OAAU had not established officers by Malcolm's death. Its day-to-day operation was run by individuals who assumed certain responsibilities. For a time Lynn Shifflet attempted to provide leadership for the OAAU, and she functioned as a kind of office manager for the organization. Sarah Mitchell, a school teacher, was the OAAU secretary. She was known to the membership as a hard and efficient worker who was dedicated to Malcolm X and enjoyed his confidence.[46]

Malcolm X had a small core of associates upon whom he depended. A few members in the MMI were attuned to what Malcolm was trying to do with the OAAU. Among them, James Shabazz was generally seen as a leader and "in charge." Benjamin Karim described James Shabazz as "an intellectual." Karim added, "His [Shabazz's] father was a Marxist and James was Muslim, but politically he was thinking in terms somewhat mixed with his father. James was an intellectual Muslim, who spoke Chinese and Japanese."[47] Increasingly James Shabazz assumed the leadership position in the OAAU office. He attempted to give direction to the office and make decisions when Malcolm was not around. This happened even though attempts were made to maintain the distinction between MMI and the OAAU.[48] On August 11, 1964 this issue was addressed in an OAAU meeting. An agreement was reached that the MMI and the OAAU should not mix, but "the OAAU would use MMI personnel as public speakers when needed."[49]

It was reported that Lynn Shifflet felt that the administrative and official positions of the OAAU in New York City were kept completely separate from those of MMI on the express direction of Malcolm X. This was to prevent the impression that the OAAU was just another arm of the MMI. Nevertheless, rank-and-file members of the MMI could be members of the OAAU if they so desired.[50]

Decisionmaking

Low attendance at rallies where Malcolm was not speaking continued as a problem and illustrated that the organization's following continued to depend on Malcolm's charisma. Moreover, Malcolm's charisma was affected as he became less of an outlet for the pent-up anger and frustration of the Black masses in the way he had been in the NOI. C. Eric Lincoln felt that the NOI's dilemma was that to expand its constituency, Malcolm had to talk peace and abandon incendiary rhetoric. This undercut the dynamic of hate which was the NOI's vital force.[51] What Malcolm X was trying to accomplish in the OAAU period was to replace the hatred of White people characteristic of the NOI with the more acceptable hatred of oppressive social systems. In addition, he recognized that organizations based on charisma were in jeopardy of falling apart if the leader was removed. He often emphasized the need for the OAAU to develop effective programs which could then replace charisma as the basis for holding its constituency. The evening before his assassination, Malcolm X told Earl Grant, "I did not want an organization that depended on the life of one man. The organization must be able to survive on its own."[52] Only one of the two factions in the OAAU took this admonition to heart.

While Malcolm X encouraged democratic decisionmaking inside of the OAAU and admonished his followers not to build a cult of personality around him, he remained the ratifier of all organizational decisions. Peter Bailey remembered that "the decisionmaking process in the organization saw members discussing issues and problems and then calling Malcolm X for a decision wherever he was."[53] With rather colorful prose Bailey summed up the decisionmaking process and problems as follows:

> Nobody was basically going to basically listen to nobody [sic] else...You had some real serious egos in that organization...The only person that everybody was going to listen to was brother Malcolm.[54]

No one was ever publicly designated by Malcolm as being in charge while he was away, Bailey reported. Malcolm X gave to his most trusted assistants the task of producing a charter for the OAAU. Unfortunately, James Shabazz and Sarah Mitchell could not agree on the wording of the document, and the lack of the promised text was a continued source of embarrassment for Malcolm during the last weeks of his life.[55]

Bailey reported that "on the day he was assassinated, I spoke to brother Malcolm and he said, 'I'm going down to Mississippi at the invitation of SNCC then I am going to come back and spend the next six months working on the building of the OAAU.'"[56] Continuing, Bailey said that Malcolm X realized that the OAAU was not going to get structured if he was not there. Jim Campbell remembered that one week prior to the assassination, Malcolm X chaired an organizing meeting to set up a functioning structure for the organization.[57] At the last business meeting of the OAAU before Malcolm's death, on the evening of February 20, 1965, Malcolm indicated to his associates that he wanted a complete reorganization of the OAAU. He was not satisfied with its operation. He felt that it had not been able to take advantage of the attention drawn to it by his activities. At Malcolm's direction, women were to be given a more clearly defined role in the organization. After this meeting Malcolm X indicated his main concern for the OAAU when he said to a close associate, Earl Grant,"I only want to protect my family and the OAAU. No matter what happens to me personally, it is important that the OAAU continue to exist..."[58]

Committee Structure

Of the projected committees, only two—the Political Committee and the Education Committee—ever held regular meetings and really only for several months.[59] The Education Committee chairperson was Herman Ferguson, a New York City public school principal, who later became a target of FBI repression and a celebrated political prisoner.[60]

Finances

The OAAU financed its activities from several modest sources. Membership fees were $2.00 to join with dues of $1.00 per week. Solicitations were made vigorously at all OAAU public functions—the rallies, the membership meetings, and the sessions of the Liberation School. These solicitations were of the "pass the hat" variety and did not garner very much. At the initial rally of the OAAU, the membership fees netted only $180.00 dollars. The organization lacked funds to cover its basic needs. These needs were the secretary's weekly wages, the monthly rental of the temporary headquarters at the Theresa Hotel ($150.00), and the rental fees for the Audubon Ballroom rallies and the meeting space at Marcus Garvey Hall. James Shabazz reported that on occasion he had to request a second collection at the rallies because the initial call for donations could not pay for the rental of the Audubon Ballroom.[61] In addition, other activities like the publication of the OAAU newsletter, *The Blacklash*, were done in *ad hoc* fashion.[62]

One member described the financial situation as "fighting to keep our heads above water and pay rent."[63] Malcolm X's public position on the question of finances belied the deep concern he had about this question. In an interview in the *Washington Star* of June 14, 1964, Malcolm said of finances, "We are scratching. I do not have any expensive habits. I have never met a true revolutionary who worried about money." Nevertheless, money was a constant concern of Malcolm's whether in his public role as chairman of the OAAU or as the breadwinner for his family. Known universally as being scrupulously honest, Malcolm had to lean on his sister Ella Collins for support on his two trips to Africa, and the income from his speaking engagements did not allow him to accumulate any bank balances.[64] Both the MMI and the OAAU remained afloat on the cash from Malcolm X's advances on the *Autobiography*.[65] The finances of the OAAU mirrored Malcolm's; he died broke and so did his organization.

Interestingly, there is no indication that Malcolm was prepared to resort to the standard fundraising mechanism of the NOI, tithing. This was a question in the minds of the members of the MMI, and they felt that the middle-class membership in the inner core of the OAAU might not have been accustomed to that kind of discipline.[66] As Aldon Morris pointed out, in the Civil Rights movement the initial period of boycotts and the formation of movement centers was largely funded from local sources.[67] Of course as the movement grew, one of its difficulties was its inability to expand its financial base from these sources. Greater dependence on

White contributions had an impact on the policy and independence of the major Civil Rights organizations. Malcolm X was thus caught on the horns of a financial dilemma. On the one hand, if he resorted to the standard method of fundraising proven from the NOI period he might possibly discourage the rapid expansion of OAAU membership. On the other hand, adequate funds would require either an exhaustive speaking and fundraising schedule for him or accepting contributions from White sources which might have compromised the independence of the OAAU. Ironically, one of the major reasons Dr. King avoided any open contact with Malcolm X was the negative impact he thought this might have on major sources of SCLC funding in the New York Jewish community.[68]

Propaganda

The founding rally itself took place at the Audubon Ballroom, adjacent to Harlem in Washington Heights. This locale was to become the site of all subsequent OAAU rallies, and the tone of such rallies was very much reflected in this initial endeavor. In fact, there was no gap between the last MMI rally and the subsequent OAAU founding rally; the usual interval between Malcolm's rallies of two weeks was maintained here.

The OAAU rallies at the Audubon Ballroom represented the complete ideological spectrum in the Black community. When Malcolm was present, the rallies represented a forum in which he presented his ideas on the issues of the transition from reform to revolution. In addition, the rallies were platforms in which Malcolm offered a forum for the Left wing of the Civil Rights movement and revolutionary African nationalists, hoping that these two camps might find common ground. These rallies typically occurred at least bi-weekly and drew between 250 and 800 listeners. From this body the OAAU was able to recruit approximately 200 members.

The OAAU rallies, when looked at collectively, were tending toward a definite pattern and format. Especially after Malcolm X's return from Africa in late November 1964, the OAAU rallies achieved a format which meshed perfectly with the organization's ideology. He opened up his November 29, 1964 homecoming rally by saying:

> ...You and I should realize that the time has come for us to let the world know that we're not only interested in some kind of integrated situation in the United States. but we're interested in taking our place

on the world stage, and we're interested in anything that involves Black people anywhere on this earth.[69]

In all of the rallies, Malcolm X laid out the aims and objectives of the OAAU and in his usual deft fashion highlighted the major themes of unity between African Americans, Africans, and the Third World in an internationalized African American struggle for human rights "by any means necessary." Malcolm's presentation was followed by that of a spokesperson from the militant, somewhat alienated wing of the Civil Rights movement, or a leader of a local movement struggle, which often represented an emerging major front in the next phase of the movement. A spokesperson from Africa or the Third World—either a diplomat, revolutionary, or student—followed and talked about the situation in their area of the world and extended solidarity with the African American struggle. Finally a call was made for new members; for those who wanted to go more deeply into the topics discussed at the rally, an invitation was extended to attend the sessions of the OAAU Liberation School.

There was enough flexibility in this model that it could be adapted to respond to special crisis situations in current events. Some examples were the OAAU's Forum on Police-Community Relations immediately after the Harlem rebellion, or Malcolm's presentation on the underlying causes for the bombing of his house at the February 14, 1965 OAAU rally. The rallies often reached only a small audience, but the rally format described above created an outlook in that audience which survived the demise of the organization itself.[70]

The rallies represented Malcolm's most successful method of political education, not only for his attentive public but also for the inner cadre of the OAAU and MMI. Given his hectic travel schedule, the rallies represented the time when he could make his most extensive presentations to his closest associates. In addition, the rallies offered Malcolm X an opportunity to demonstrate to all that he had established relationships with important leadership figures in the Civil Rights movement, the international revolutionary movements and national liberation fronts, and among the new leadership in independent Africa. The rallies of mainstream Civil Rrights organizations did not present such a spectrum to the Black community. Thus, the OAAU rallies made the concept of Pan-African community and struggle concrete. Their qualitative distinction from other Civil Rights rallies of the period had an impact out of all proportion to the numbers in attendance. For many in the audience, Malcolm's films of Africa represented images free of the traditional stereotypes associated with the continent. The appearances of revolutionary leaders and African diplomats were the first Black people the audiences had ever seen who wielded or aspired to wield state power. The OAAU rallies never approached the massive gatherings of Marcus Garvey's UNIA in its heyday. Nevertheless, the OAAU rallies delivered on the UNIA's promises of future greatness for the Black race.

The OAAU Newsletter, *The Blacklash*

Malcolm X from his days in the NOI placed great weight on the propaganda value of an independent Black press. The journalistic background of Malcolm X was often overlooked, but it was an important part of his whole approach to mobilization and leadership. As far back as his prison years, Malcolm X used the press to project issues and grievances of dispossessed and disadvantaged constituencies. He edited the prison newspaper and used it to advance the grievances of Muslim prisoners. In an attempt to reach a larger audience, he wrote letters to the local press. Later, Malcolm X used his journalistic and editorial skills in numerous contributions to the *Los Angeles Post Dispatch*, a Black paper in that city. Because of Malcolm's articles, this paper was more sympathetic an useful as an outlet for Elijah Muhammad's message than any other Black newspaper in the nation. By 1959 Malcolm X had single-handedly established *Muhammad Speaks*, the official NOI paper, and recruited first-class journalistic talent like Sylvester Leaks to edit the New York edition.

It was in the Black press that Malcolm got his most impartial hearing. In the pages of papers like the *Pittsburgh Courier* and the *Amsterdam News*, Malcolm was more accurately and extensively quoted than in the mass circulation dailies. Malcolm therefore assigned a very important role to the Black press. C. Eric Lincoln quotes Malcolm X as saying that

> the daily [White] press can make even the "Negro" public eat your flesh with its powerful... propaganda...The Negro press may have its shortcomings, but when the die is cast and your 'downtown' friends ready you for the dogs, there must be a Negro Press to present your case to the "Negro" public. The Negro press is our only medium for voicing the true plight of our oppressed people to the world.[71]

Had Malcolm X lived, the OAAU would have placed great importance on and devoted a disproportionate amount of its resources to establishing an organizational publication along the lines of *Muhammad Speaks*. As it turned out, a more modest effort was all that could be mustered.

The OAAU published a small newsletter, *The Blacklash*, which reproduced the full texts of Malcolm's letters and statements from Africa, other information on the developing African American human rights movement, and materials from the OAAU Liberation School's curriculum and discussions. While abroad, Malcolm X either forwarded copy by mail or telephoned copy in from as far away as Africa. These materials were gathered by the office manager of the OAAU, Lynn Shifflet, for possible publication. The newsletter's editor, Peter Bailey, pulled together issues on an *ad hoc* basis and wrote the editorials. Each issue also featured a political cartoon. In all, nine issues of *The Blacklash* appeared.[72]

The Blacklash was limited to four or five pages of dittoed copy which was circulated to the membership, those who attended the OAAU rallies, and those on the organization's mailing list. Average circulation per issue rarely exceeded 200 to 300 copies. The demand for the newsletter far exceeded its circulation since it was the only available source of the full texts of Malcolm X's speeches at home and abroad.[73] The mainstream media was fed a continuous stream of press releases from the OAAU but limited its interest to those aspects of Malcolm X's trips abroad and speeches which could be presented in a sensationalist fashion. As modest as it was then, *The Blacklash* represented the only media source of comprehensive coverage on Malcolm X. Its initial issue appeared within days of the outbreak of the Harlem rebellion.[74]

The Blacklash was financed out of the general funds of the OAAU, and there were no paid positions. A nominal price of 5¢ per copy was charged for those distributed at the OAAU rallies. The paper was not solvent, and it was unable to become the major propaganda vehicle that Malcolm X foresaw. For internal OAAU consumption, he felt it was adequate and was pleased with the paper's content, but Malcolm X recognized that like, *Muhammad Speaks*, *The Blacklash*'s propaganda value would be enhanced only in a printed, full-newspaper format.[75]

Like the rallies, *The Blacklash*'s greatest impact was probably on the core of the OAAU itself. Because of the paper's existence many important speeches of Malcolm X could be studied by the inner membership of the organization. The possibility for such study was not available to the general public until the latter part of the 1960s and the beginning of the 1970s, with the completion of the George Breitman publications of the speeches and other material of Malcolm X.

OAAU Information and Press Bureau

In Ghana, Malcolm's supporters established an OAAU Information Bureau. It was announced at the press club in Accra on August 27, 1964 before a gathering which included African diplomats, Ghanaian government officials, and representatives of the international press. The OAAU Press Bureau was formed to "better acquaint the people of the African continent with the day-to-day struggles of the Afro-American against White supremacy." The Bureau supplied the African American press with information about developments in African states. A spokesperson for the Bureau said that "the biggest difficulty in uniting Africans within and without the continent is that we depend largely for facilities on imperialist organizations. The information bureau of the OAAU is just one small step we are taking to correct this serious problem."[76]

OAAU Liberation School

The most important membership meetings were not the business meetings described above but those held in conjunction with the OAAU Liberation School. The OAAU Liberation School was the brainchild of James Campbell. In the summer of 1964, Lynn Shifflet suggested to Campbell that the OAAU needed an educational component. While she had in mind something more academic, Campbell felt that he should present to Shifflet a process which allowed the students to benefit from the "lessons of history extracted," this being the source of student insights and direction. Campbell saw the Liberation School as a natural outgrowth of the southern "freedom schools," but more far-reaching and in line with the orientation of the OAAU.[77]

Campbell's personal history indicated that he was well placed to bring about a synthesis between the freedom school orientation toward citizenship and the OAAU orientation toward Pan-African internationalism. Campbell was an offspring of what Dr. Du Bois called the "talented tenth." He was from one of the staunchly middle-class Black families of Charleston, South Carolina, a family long associated with higher education for Blacks and personally known and befriended by Dr. Du Bois. Politically, he saw himself in the Pan-Africanist tradition of Du Bois, Robeson, and Alpheous Hunton. A leftist-internationalist orientation was also garnered by Campbell in the late 1950s when he came to New York and studied acting with notables in that field who had been blacklisted and otherwise victimized by the excesses of the McCarthy era. From them

120

he learned world literature. In the early 1960s Campbell was very much a part of the Civil Rights movement. Going South in the summers, he worked with SCLC and with the Student Non-Violent Coordinating Committee (SNCC) in the voter registration and sit-in campaigns. It was here that he got direct experience with the freedom schools which grew up everywhere as a part of the southern Civil Rights movement.[78]

The curriculum of the Liberation School provided weekly school sessions in African and African American history, political education, and consumer information and skills. The Saturday morning sessions focused on African and African American history. First the children and young teenagers (the junior high school ages predominated) came while their parents shopped from 10:00–11:30 a.m. From 11:30 a.m. to 1:00 p.m., the adults held class. Campbell remembered the adult students averaging about thirty-five years of age. For the most part they were family people of solidly working-class background, not *lumpen*. The sessions usually attracted about twenty persons.[79]

As Campbell described the goal of the curriculum , it was to present a "broad worldview which sees us [Afro-Americans] in relation to the broad struggle of peoples around the world who are being victimized by capitalism."[80] Speakers were varied frequently, and the political orientation, language, and terminology of the Liberation School speakers varied also. Campbell attempted to provide a forum for a mix of ideas, but with what he called a "clear scientific analysis." Speakers were usually responsible for a series of two or a maximum of three lectures within which they were to develop a unit of the subject matter under study or a particular theme. Among the presenters at the Liberation School were such ideologically diverse intellectuals and activists as the Garveyites "Pork Chop" Davis and Dr. Joseph Ben Jochanan; the communist Richard B. Moore, who ran the Communist Party Bookstore in Harlem; and James Shabazz, the major intellectual in the MMI and a major actor in the OAAU. Other speakers included the Africanists, Dr. John Henrik Clarke and Dr. Keith Beard. Assisting James Campbell in the operation of the OAAU Liberation School was Herman Ferguson. Campbell remembered the high level of discussion that often graced these presentations. While most often Malcolm X himself was not personally present, he was there to participate in one of the most notable debates at the Liberation School. A doctoral student from Zambia writing a dissertation on Islamic slavery in East Africa engaged Malcolm X in an exchange on the role of this phenomenon in the oppression of Africans. Malcolm X's position was that the impact of Islamic slavery and the Arab slave trade were secondary to the impact the European Atlantic slave trade had on Africa.[81]

The Liberation School also met on Wednesday evenings; these sessions were for couples and focused on a more practical curriculum. Couples were counseled in consumer education, how to shop, buy prescriptions, and care for babies.[82]

Upon completion of the OAAU Liberation School curriculum students were graduated with a certificate over Malcolm X's signature. Twelve people were graduated from the Liberation School with certificates, and a week before Malcolm X's assassination another group was readied for graduation.[83]

Campbell recalled that some members of MMI came to the classes of the Liberation School. Their demeanor there was friendly, pleasant, and they got along with others who attended. He felt that they were supportive of what he was trying to do and very cooperative. On the other hand, there were others in MMI who hung around the office but never came to the Liberation School sessions. James Shabazz, perhaps the major link besides Malcolm X between the MMI and the OAAU was on very good terms with Jim Campbell, and they often debated the merits of Islam.[84]

The Liberation School met for the whole period of the OAAU's life up until the assassination of Malcolm X. Its last session took place one week after the assassination.

The Quest for International and Pan-African Legitimacy for the OAAU

As a result of the groundwork laid on his first trip, Malcolm X returned to Africa, the second week in July 1964 to begin more extensive lobbying for his OAAU and its program of indicting the United States before the United Nations. He returned to Africa as chairperson of the OAAU and in that capacity was accorded diplomatic treatment and observer status at the second meeting of the OAU heads of state in Cairo, which convened on July 17. While not allowed to address the assemblage, Malcolm X was permitted to circulate an eight-page memorandum in which he outlined the condition of 22 million African Americans and exhorted the heads of state to support their brothers in the United States by holding that country accountable for its treatment of African Americans. In part he said:

We pray that our African brothers have not freed themselves of European colonialism only to be overcome and held in check now by American *dollarism*. Don't let American racism be "legalized" by American dollarism.

America is worse than South Africa, because not only is America racist, but she also is deceitful and hypocritical. South Africa preaches segregation and practices segregation. She, at least, practices what she preaches. America preaches integration and practices segregation. She preaches one thing while deceitfully practicing another...

If South Africa is guilty of violating the human rights of Africans here on the mother continent, then America is guilty of worse violations of the 22 million Africans on the American continent. And if South African racism is not a domestic issue, then American racism also is not a *domestic* issue...

We are well aware that our future efforts to defend ourselves by retaliating...could create the type of racial conflict in America that could easily escalate into a violent, worldwide bloody race war.

In the interests of world peace and security, we recommend an immediate investigation into our problem by the United Nations Commission on Human Rights.[85]

It was his hope that the heads of state would publicly endorse the substance of his presentation in their resolutions. This did not happen, but a statement acknowledging with satisfaction the Civil Rights Act of 1964 was tempered with a caution regarding the continued racism existing in the southern United States. In part it said that the OAU Conference "was deeply disturbed, however, by continuing manifestations of racial bigotry and racial oppression against Negro citizens of the United States of America...the existence of discriminatory practices is a matter of deep concern to the member states of the OAU." The resolution concluded by urging the United States government to "intensify its efforts to ensure the total elimination of all forms of discrimination based on race, color, or ethnic origin."[86]

While this resolution was substantially the same concerning the U.S. racial situation as the previous year's, it was not a blanket endorsement of the U.S. government's stance on the issue. Malcolm X accepted this resolution as a very good one and was generally satisfied with the outcome of his activities at the conference.[87] As Malcolm summed up his achievements to Milton Henry, an activist attorney, he concluded that "several of them [African countries] promised officially that come the next session of the UN, any effort on our part to bring our problem before the UN... will get support and help from them. They will assist us in showing us how to help bring it up legally. So I am very, very happy over the whole result of my trip here."[88]

In fact, the most useful aspect of Malcolm X's two sojourns in Africa was that the leadership and masses of that continent were notified that there were other opinions and analyses of the U.S. racial situation than those spread by the United States Information Agency (USIA). Malcolm X was successful in establishing his analysis as that against which subsequent spokespersons and USIA releases were judged in Africa. John Lewis and Donald Harris, in a report of their activities in Africa on behalf of SNCC, stated that "Malcolm's impact on Africa was just fantastic. In every country he was known and served as the main criteria for categorizing other Afro-Americans and their political views."[89]

African and Third World diplomats were not yet prepared openly to indict the United States at the United Nations, but the perspective Malcolm X disseminated in Africa of alleged U.S. hypocrisy in dealing with the domestic civil rights problem was useful in the attempts to embarrass the U.S. and its representative Adlai Stevenson. This was especially true in the debates on the United States-supported Congo "humanitarian" rescue mission of Belgium. At Malcolm X's urging, several African UN ambassadors attacked the hypocrisy of the United States humanitarian concern in the Congo where none was evident in Mississippi or Selma, Alabama.[90] They said the United States was indifferent to the fate of Blacks. M.S. Handler in the *New York Times* of January 2, 1965 took note that Malcolm X had been urging the Africans to employ "the racial situation in the United States as an instrument of attack in discussing international problems...such a strategy would give the African states more leverage in dealing with the United States and would in turn give American Negroes more leverage in American society." He went on to say that the criticism had "profoundly disturbed the American authorities."

The OAAU and the Civil Rights Movement: Building the United Front

One of the cornerstones of Malcolm X's OAAU was the reconciliation he hoped to effect with the major Civil Rights organizations. The first official act of the OAAU was an overture of assistance to the southern Civil Rights forces. On June 30, 1964, Malcolm X as chairman of the OAAU sent the following telegram to Dr. King then engaged in a nonviolent direct action campaign in St. Augustine, Florida:

> We have been witnessing with great concern the vicious attack of the white race against our poor defenseless people in St. Augustine, Florida. If Federal government will not send troops to your aid just say the word and we will immediately dispatch some of our brothers there to organize our people into self-defense units among our people and the Ku Klux Klan will receive a taste of its own medicine. The day of turning the cheek to the inhuman brute beasts is long over.[91]

Later that same day, Malcolm X had his wife Betty send a telegram of the same wording with reference to Philadelphia, Mississippi to the executive director of SNCC, James Forman, then in the midst of the Mississippi Freedom Summer Campaign there. Publicly, the established Civil Rights leadership shunned contact with Malcolm X. Privately, Harlem-based professionals and intellectuals formed a bridge between Malcolm and that leadership which allowed for some dialogue and exploration of the possibilities for further cooperation.[92]

Ossie Davis and other influential Blacks who had links to the established national Civil Rights leadership created off-the-record contacts in the hope of achieving a reconciliation with the established Civil Rights leadership. Among those who became friends of Malcolm in this capacity were Dr. and Mrs. Arthur Logan and the civil rights attorney and legal counsel to Dr. King, Clarence Jones. These channels of communication existed, and they were used. Unfortunately, they had borne little fruit at the time of the assassination of Malcolm X.[93]

There was, however, another group within the general motion of the Civil Rights movement, especially its northern component, which was as attractive and possibly much more accessible to OAAU efforts at joint action. The Aims and Objectives of the OAAU—education, political and economic mobilization, social welfare, and culture—reflected the attempt at a united-front appeal to northern, non-Civil Rights activist leadership. In particular, they reflected the priority issues around which Harlem and Black New York were already organizing. The notables who occupied the OAAU forums in the summer and fall months while Malcolm X was in Africa were associated with the priority issues of the Aims and Objectives. It is not accidental that Malcolm and the OAAU reached out to the likes of Milton Galamison, New York school boycott leader; Percy Sutton and Charles Rangel, Harlem political leaders; Jesse Gray, Harlem housing and rent strike leader; Bill Epton, a leader in the struggle against police brutality; and, in the area of culture, John Henrik Clarke, John Killens and Ossie Davis.

The OAAU and the Radical Wing of the Civil Rights Movement

Outside of Harlem and New York City, Malcolm was also able to reach out to the more militant Civil Rights leadership who were dissatisfied with the pace and programs of their established parent organizations. Though not to the same extent as Malcolm X, these grassroots leaders and organizations were also seen as renegades by their parent organizations. A coalition of this leadership called a meeting and rally in Chester, Pennsylvania on March 14, 1964 to which Malcolm X was invited. Present were Stanley Branch, leader of a militant local NAACP chapter in Chester; Gloria Richardson, head of the Cambridge, Maryland protests; Julius Hobson of Washington, D.C. CORE; Milton Galimison and Lawrence Landry, school boycott leaders from Brooklyn and Chicago, respectively; and Jesse Gray, the Harlem rent strike leader. In many ways this group shared an affinity with Malcolm X, as described by Peter Goldman:

> They shared a common disillusion with the operating style of the national Civil Rights organizations, which seemed to require okays from their front offices and board of directors for anything but the tamest protest actions. The outsiders were further discouraged by the heavy concentration of the energy and money of the movement on the South; they did not question the value of doing away with formal Jim Crow, but the problems that immediately concerned them and their people had to do with rats biting babies and children going hungry and trade unions barring Negroes and men dying of nothing to do. Common interests and the common disapproval of the respectable movement brought the outsiders together...[94]

Although he affirmed his commitment to self-defense, Malcolm supported their struggles and promised to be available for some of their future demonstrations. From the time of these first contacts, Malcolm's speeches and rallies gave explicit attention and endorsement to these struggles. This strategy predated the formation of the OAAU and went back to the period prior to Malcolm X's suspension from the Nation of Islam. In August 1963, Malcolm X was prominent in support of the Brooklyn CORE demonstrations to integrate the building trades workforce at the Brooklyn Downstate Medical Center construction site. He attended the court cases of demonstrators arrested at this construction site in order to support them. Malcolm's presence at the Downstate Medical Center demonstrations was responsible for bringing him new followers who subsequently found their way to the OAAU. Most prominent among them were Hassan Washington and Yuri Kochiyama.[95]

The OAAU and the Developing Student Movement

The ideas of Malcolm X were reaching students. At the time of his death, he was forging organizational links with what was to become an autonomous Black Student movement. As much as it has been suggested that northern urban street people were Malcolm X's natural constituency, a good case could be made that students served that purpose for Malcolm X also. Malcolm was even fond of saying that "SNCC is my favorite Civil Rights organization." While modest, Malcolm X's greatest gains in building a Black united front resulted from his contacts and deliberations with the student wing of the Civil Rights movement. At least a year before his break with the Nation of Islam, Malcolm X had established ties with the more militant and ultimately nationalist wing of SNCC. In 1962 he was invited by the Stokely Carmichael-led Nonviolent Action Group (NAG) to Howard University to address the student body and to debate Bayard Rustin. This was the first activity of NAG's Project Awareness on campus, which was designed to "inform students about social issues."[96] His appearance at that time was controversial, and the Howard University administration attempted to block it. Nevertheless he did speak both publicly and privately with SNCC cadre.

He was to return for deliberations with members of the NAG group and other SNCC cadre who were in Washington, D.C. making preparations for the August 1963 March on Washington. Malcolm X spent considerable time that summer in Washington, D.C. observing the preparations and the march itself. Cleveland Sellers reported that there were meetings between SNCC personnel in Washington and Malcolm X in which Malcolm laid out his position on independent Black politics and its relationship to the empowerment of Black communities.[97] From 1961–63, SNCC had been doing extensive voter registration campaigns in Mississippi and Alabama under extremely repressive conditions. It had been at the center of the formation of the Confederation of Freedom Organizations (COFO), which was in the latter part of 1963 already planning what was to become Mississippi Freedom Summer. In addition, SNCC field workers—along with local Mississippi activists in and out of SNCC like Mrs. Fannie Lou Hamer, Amsie Moore, and Aaron Henry—were planning to challenge the regular Democratic Party in Mississippi. They created the Mississippi Freedom Democratic Party (MFDP). At this time, Malcolm X was arguing for an all-Black political party independent of the two major parties, which through the bullet voting of newly registered Black voters could do away with the "rotten boroughs" of rural southern racism. These "rotten boroughs," in which almost all Black people were disenfranchised, consistently sent White supremacists to the House of Representatives and the Senate and elected their equivalents at the local and state levels.

Malcolm X was able to return to this theme with SNCC workers on several additional occasions. He shared the platform with Mrs. Fannie Lou Hamer in Harlem at Williams Institutional C.M.E. Church in December 1964 and invited her to address an OAAU rally scheduled for that evening.[98] Whenever Mrs. Hamer was in New York she stayed at the house of James Campbell, a close family friend and director of the OAAU Liberation School.[99] Through Mrs. Hamer, Malcolm X was familiarized with the development of the MFDP and the particulars of its unsuccessful challenge to the regular Mississippi delegation to the Democratic National Convention at Atlantic City in August 1964. In his speeches and personal conversations with Mrs. Hamer and other SNCC cadre, Malcolm X constantly raised the theme of independent Black politics because SNCC was experiencing frustration using nonviolent direct action to establish an integrationist alternative within segregationist Dixiecrat state parties.

Malcolm X had rather brief but very effective discussions with the youthful "shock troops" of SNCC's efforts in the South. On December 31, 1964, Malcolm X addressed a group of thirty-seven Mississippi youth sent north on tour by SNCC, who were selected for their outstanding contributions to the Civil Rights struggle in McComb, Mississippi and other communities in that state. He met with them in Harlem and discussed his views on which way the Civil Rights movement had to develop.[100] Later, in early February at the request of SNCC, Malcolm X addressed an audience of local Civil Rights activists at a church in Selma, Alabama. He unequivocally extended his support to their efforts while retaining his commitment to self-defense. His speech was short but impressive, and even Mrs. Coretta Scott King, who shared the podium with him, was impressed by Malcolm X's sincerity. Its greatest impact according to the *New York Herald Tribune* report of the gathering was that "the young crowd cheered [Malcolm] repeatedly, and for hours afterward other speakers tried to simmer off the steam that Malcolm had generated."[101]

Malcolm X was able in these discussions to raise his human rights agenda with SNCC. While Malcolm X was "internationalizing" the Civil Rights struggle on his second trip to Africa, selected SNCC cadre were themselves on a round of African touring organized by James Forman. Malcolm X was able to speak to John Lewis and Donald Harris in Nairobi (when their paths crossed in October 1964). He talked to them about the importance of seeing the Civil Rights struggle in its human rights dimension and the role that Africa could play in supporting the struggle of African Americans for human rights. These two SNCC workers were very much impressed by Malcolm X and what he had to say. Africans had accepted Malcolm's analysis of U.S. race relations. Lewis and Harris like other Civil Rights leaders and dipolomats soon realized that Africans were evaluating what they said against Malcolm's analysis. The impression Malcolm X left on John Lewis was such that he was later to say of Malcolm that "more than any other single personality [he had been] able to articulate the aspirations, bitterness, and frustrations of the Negro people [forming] a living link between Africa and the Civil Rights movement in this country."[102]

The week of Malcolm X's assassination, his itinerary called for him to return to Mississippi to further investigate ways that the OAAU might more effectively join with the popular struggle for freedom in that state.[103]

Black Student Movement and the OAAU

Akbar Muhammed Ahmed (aka Max Stanford) has documented how very close Malcolm X was to a nationalist wing which had developed within the southern student movement. It was composed of students in and out of SNCC who were more oriented to the ideas of Malcolm X and the self-defense philosophy of Robert Williams. Its center was the Afro-American Student Movement (ASM) at Fisk University in Nashville, Tennessee. These students wanted to introduce into the southern Civil Rights movement an explicit self-defense component coupled with a politics of Black empowerment based on nationalist values. At the urging of leaders of the National Liberation Front (the immediate precursor of RAM), student nationalists convened the first Afro-American Student Conference on Black Nationalism at Fisk University from May 1 to 4, 1964. The conference stated that Black radicals were the vanguard of revolution in this country, supported Malcolm X's efforts to take the case of Afro-Americans to the United Nations, called for a Black cultural revolution, and discussed Pan-Africanism. The conference's Thirteen

Points for Implementation included several points that reflected the Basic Aims and Objectives of the OAAU.[104]

Muhammed Ahmed had been in discussions with Malcolm X from January 1964. This was the same period during which Malcolm X recruited Lynn Shifflet to initiate action on the OAAU. The Afro-American Student Conference took place at the beginning of May 1964 while Malcolm X was in the Middle East and Africa. What is interesting is how closely it anticipated many of the positions of the OAAU. The conference was so controversial that the rival Nashville Student Movement brought Dr. Martin Luther King to the campus that same weekend. King's public reaction to the Afro-American Student Conference on Black Nationalism was to attack it as "racism in reverse."[105] The sentiments of the nationalist student conference, however, gained a foothold in the South. Muhammed Ahmed described the aftermath of the conference:

> From the conference BLF-RAM organizers went into the south to work with SNCC. With the permission of SNCC chairman John Lewis, an experimental Black nationalist self-defense project was started in Greenwood, Mississippi.
>
> In discussion with the Mississippi field staff of SNCC, BLF-RAM organizers found the staff was prepared to establish a statewide armed self-defense system. They were also prepared to move in an all-Black nationalist direction. All that was needed was money to finance the project. In the meantime, *Monthly Review* published an article titled "The Colonial War at Home," which included most of [Max] Stanford's *Correspondence* article, "Toward a Revolutionary Action Movement," edited with some of Malcolm's remarks, and excerpts from Robert Williams' "Revolution Without Violence?"
>
> The article was discussed by the majority of the SNCC field staff. SNCC was polarized between Black and White organizers and between left and right wing forces within SNCC...Most of the Black members of the Mississippi SNCC field staff thought that the majority of Black people were beyond the voter registration stage....The integrationist, reformist faction eventually won in the organizational split because they controlled the economic resources of the field staff.[106]

Under the leadership of Bob Moses and James Forman, SNCC attempted to develop an integrationist alternative to the Dixiecrat regular Democratic Party in Mississippi. The Mississippi Freedom Summer, the Mississippi Freedom Democratic Party and its challenge to the regular state delegation at the Democratic National Convention in Atlantic City in August 1964 represented a high point in the integrationist thrust of SNCC. The defeats and frustrations in Mississippi, Atlantic City and later in Selma, Alabama created a renewed sensitivity to the appeals of nation-alist-oriented students in the SNCC ranks. At the end of 1964, SNCC extended invitations to Malcolm X to come to speak and visit their operations in Greenwood, Mississippi and Selma, Alabama. According to Ahmed, this was the beginning of the implementation of the strategy in which Malcolm X was to be the "mass spokesman for armed defense units that would be centered around him and a Black united front."[107] The assassination of Malcolm X disrupted the meshing of Malcolm's own efforts with students and those related efforts of RAM cadre.

Malcolm's student following was not merely Black students nor was it merely in the United States. He was immensely popular with African and Middle Eastern students, as his reception on both trips to that part of the world indicated.

On his first trip in 1964 to the Middle East and Africa, Malcolm was the guest speaker at a lecture arranged by African students in Beirut at the Sudanese Cultural Center. The overflow audience was so enthusiastic in its support of Malcolm X that local newspapers reported a riot there though none had actually occurred. Malcolm later reported that the Suda-nese and Lebanese Muslim students wanted to know how they could help the Afro-American struggle.[108] In Nigeria, Malcolm X spoke to students at the University of Ibadan, where students almost lynched a West Indian professor who tried to defend America against the criticisms of Malcolm X. In that same country, the Muslim Student Society of Nigeria made Malcolm X an honorary member, giving him the name "Omowale," Yoruba for "the child has returned."[109]

He received numerous written testimonials from students he im-pressed on that trip. At the meeting in Harlem mentioned above at which Malcolm was received by Japanese writers on June 14, 1964, Edwardina Brown, an African American teacher who had spent time in Ghana, presented Malcolm X with a three-page letter signed by Ghanaian students expressing the impact Malcolm had on them during his trip to their country.[110]

Malcolm X opened up the podium at OAAU rallies to African students who needed an audience for the struggles they were tied to in their homelands. Similarly the OAAU sought out African intellectuals studying or residing in the United States to enhance the curriculum of the OAAU Liberation School.

Malcolm X saw the tremendous potential of international study for "broadening" the perspectives of African American students. He secured twenty scholarships for African American students at Cairo's Al Azhar

University, and he hoped on the basis of those scholarships to build an organization of African American students in Cairo.[111]

Entree to an Alliance with Whites?

At the time of his death Malcolm X noted that there was emerging a new kind of White student who might relate to the human rights struggle of Black people. Malcolm found that he could talk to these students and that they seemed receptive. He foresaw the possibility that if he were wrong on the question of the potential for change of White people, it would be White youth who would prove him so. To that end, near the end of his life he began to direct a specific message to that audience. This message was based on Malcolm's sense of the role students were actually playing in contemporary history. In one of his last interviews he described this role:

> When I was in the Black Muslim movement I spoke on many white campuses and Black campuses. I knew back in 1961 and '62 that the younger generation was much different from the older, and that many students were more sincere in their analysis of the problem and their desire to see the problem solved. In foreign countries the students have helped bring about revolution...the students didn't think of the odds against them and they could not be bought out. In the United States students have been noted for involving themselves in panty raids, goldfish-swallowing, seeing how many can get in a telephone booth—not for their revolutionary political ideas or their desire to change unjust conditions. But some students are becoming more like their brothers around the world.[112]

Conclusion

The Organization of Afro-American Unity was eight months old when Malcolm X died. It was to continue after his death but in a significantly altered form, with new leadership, goals, and objectives and with greatly decreased membership and effectiveness. Unfortunately the OAAU as conceptualized by Malcolm X did not survive his assassination. In Chapter Six, we will look at some of the difficulties surfacing in the OAAU, and some of the issues it confronted but had not resolved at the time of Malcolm X's death. We will also look at the process by which the OAAU was enmeshed on the horns of the dilemma it was created to avoid.

6

AN
ASSESSMENT
OF THE
OAAU

Introduction

In assessing the Organization of Afro-American Unity (OAAU), we must begin by looking again briefly at the social and movement context within which Malcolm X hoped to intervene. The OAAU was designed to respond to a particular configuration of problems and trends in the Civil Rights movement at a particular and crucial juncture in that movement's development. In the period 1963–65, the Civil Rights movement faced challenges from both processes of cooptation and threats of repression. I will look more closely at the basis for cooptation and how the ideology and practice of the major Civil Rights organizations played into this strategy. As well, I will examine the factors which encouraged those in power seriously to initiate repression toward the more militant wing of the movement and how the ideology and practice of the Civil Rights movement generated demoralization as opposed to resistance in the face of this challenge. Lastly, the OAAU will be assessed both in terms of the appropriateness of its model of struggle and in terms of its achievements or lack thereof.

Cooptation and Repression

In Chapter Three, I explained that the ideological hegemony of the ruling elite is the basis of the false consciousness of those they rule. In the particular case of the African American, that false consciousness had a duality characterized by Dr. Du Bois as double consciousness. Another way of looking at this double consciousness is that in one psyche it combined two ideological orientations, the American Dream and the etiquette of race relations. These orientations often conflicted, causing confusion and indecisiveness or inaction in Black people. On the other hand, these two ideological orientations can be seen as working in tandem to facilitate ruling-class strategies of cooptation or repression.

Cooptation was facilitated by the ideology of the American Dream. The American Dream established not only the material but also the moral superiority of Western Civilization. The United States' "manifest destiny" was to become the epitome of Western Civilization, the only real civilization. It held out the possibility to African Americans that if they could disgard their African roots and assimilate they would be materially and spiritually rewarded. The status quo, through the "invisible hand" in the marketplace, automatically provided for positive social change. It was not to be tampered with by the disgruntled. Any other course of action for a domestic minority was not only irrational but from this vantage point morally bankrupt.

The etiquette of race relations emphasized that the power discrepancies between the races were necessary if Whites were to be able to tutor Black people in the methods of Western Civilization and protect them from their own ignorance, heathenism, and savagery. Force was openly subscribed to as a method to protect the purity of the White race from the pollution of the African strain. Through force, exploitation, and deprivation of social necessities, Black people internalized the notions of minority status, and remained isolated from and ignorant of the larger world. They came to believe that physical resistance was impossible. African Americans were conditioned to believe that the violence which maintained White superiority and Black subordination could be minimized only through conforming with a code of behavior which at every turn symbolized racial power discrepancies and Black acceptance of them.

Double consciousness, embodied in the simultaneous pursuit of the American Dream and conforming with the etiquette of race relations facilitated the success of elite strategies of cooptation and repression. The American Dream caused Black disunity. It raised the needs of the individual above those of the group in an absolute sense. As a condition of success, it required the individual to maximize their cultural and social distance from the mass of Black people. Because the pursuit of the American Dream caused Black disunity, cooptive strategies facilitated repression. Repression, severely punished group cohesion and all strategies which challenged the power inequities between the races. It reinforced the resort to individualistic solutions along lines consistent with the status quo. Repression facilitated cooptation. How were strategies of cooptation and repression implemented during the crucial 1963–65 period?

Cooptation was based on the extension of material incentives, prestige, power and responsibility to Civil Rights leadership. To get these rewards Black leaders either left the Civil Rights organizations themselves or adjusted their programs away from confrontation with the various forms and levels of state power. The organizational characteristics and ideology of the mainstream Civil Rights organizations predisposed them to cooptation.

In the period under consideration the major Civil Rights organizations, especially the Southern Christian Leadership Conference of Dr. King, had limited funds, almost no bureaucracy or chain of command, low salaries, arrears, and a too-heavy dependence on volunteers.[1] They were dominated by clergymen who were authoritarian and male chauvinists.[2] Little or no major decisionmaking was shared with the rank and file of the organization. In fact, much of SCLC was a one-man show built around the leadership and charisma of Dr. King, supported by a few clergymen.[3] Thus, the dangers were high but the individual rewards low. Given the ideological orientation of the Civil Rights mainstream, this situation facilitated cooptation.

The Civil Rights movement defined its tasks as struggling to remove the disabilities of race so Black people could be judged on their individual merits alone. To the extent that the movement was successful, when barriers fell the tendency was for the most meritorious Black people, disproportionately middle class, to be first to take advantage of the new possiblities. These barriers themselves were defined as barriers to individual, not group advancement. Thus, success was often defined in individual terms or as a series of "the first in the race to..." The abandonment of the movement organizations by middle-class leadership was often disguised as taking advantage of the possibilities for making further advances in civil rights "inside the system."

Cooptation was facilitated by false consciousness in Civil Rights leadership. I would argue that the susceptibility to cooptation was an outgrowth of the limitations in the Civil Rights critique of the U.S. system and led naturally to definitions of the problem focused on individual disability and solutions to the problem focused on equal opportunity outlined in Chapter Five. Whatever fruits of victory were achieved deprived the movement of its middle-class leadership resources. In a sense, this process snatched "defeat from the jaws of victory."

Civil Rights ideology appeared to extol the "noblesse oblige" embodied in Du Bois's expression "talented tenth." However, the obligations of the "talented tenth" were often fulfilled symbolically in the pursuit of individual career advancement as opposed to a lifetime orientation of service to the Black community. The NAACP and the Urban League were the first to desert the Civil Rights coalition as a result of their cooptation by 1965, both organizations prematurely felt that African Americans had won unrestricted and routine access to governmental power and by 1965 could work from the "inside" through mainstream political institutions as opposed to the "outsiders'" vehicle of protest.

While the Right wing of the Civil Rights coalition was preparing to jump ship, the government security apparatus had resolved not to depend on processes of cooptation alone to reign in the Civil Rights movement. Kenneth O'Reilly, in his excellent book *Racial Matters*, identified a transition in government thinking regarding the Civil Rights movement as of 1963 which is germane to the thesis of this book. He noted that:

> By the standards of the mid- and late-1960s, FBI surveillance of Black political activists prior to the summer of 1963 was limited and cautious because Hoover [J. Edgar Hoover, director of the FBI] deemed the political risks of more aggressive involvement to be too great. But beginning in the summer of 1963 there was a fundamental change in Hoover's willingness to assume the risks of more aggressive involvement, a change that can be explained by his belief that Blacks had gone too far with their protests and now posed an imminent threat to the established order. Bureau documents immediately before, during, and after the March on Washington are filled with references to an impending "social revolution."[4]

O'Reilly went on to indicate that President John F. Kennedy concurred in this increased surveillance and intervention in the Civil Rights movement. Hoover's position, however, was to destroy the movement as part of his crusade against communism.[5] As a result of the heightened Civil Rights activity and urban rebellions of the summer of 1964, the FBI established in its internal security division a special desk to coordinate its Communist Influence Racial Matters investigation. From that point, detailed files were maintained on the movement under the guise of monitoring "communist infiltration."[6] In the period 1963–65, the combination of the characteristics of the movement and the new demands that emergent urban strata were advancing made repression an attractive alternative for the security apparatus of the United States. The incremental and marginal nature of change fostered by U.S. democratic institutions was unable to respond effectively to the demands for rapid fundamental change coming from the insurgent ghetto dwellers moving rapidly to the movement's center stage. However, the following characteristics of the Black community suggested that there would be relatively low and acceptable costs associated with a policy of repression.

The African American community in the United States, while large, was distinctly in the numerical minority. It was dispersed in urban areas and occupied no significant contiguous part of the country's land mass. The internal organization and solidarity of this race in the United States was low. The African American community at that time was more a loose coalition of organizations and independent institutions which often had to construct consensus around important issues from one crisis period to the next. Racism alienated the community from the domestic White majority, especially in northern urban areas where the new demands of the movement were emerging. The Black community in this country has today—few historic and continuing links to any ancestral power centers in Africa or to sources of support in the international arena.

African Americans were economically and technologically backward. This resulted from their function as a super-abundant pool of unskilled labor. Due to technological change, the Black community was no longer as crucial to the economy as it had been in slavery and later as the rural peasantry of the South.

The characteristics described above, however, were unstable, especially given the activities of the radical wing of the movement as embodied in a leader like Malcolm X. In the 1963–65 period, repression was an option which was viable if promptly initiated but might not have been if its use had been delayed. This fact was not lost on J. Edgar Hoover, who previewed his later COINTELPRO (counterintelligence) program in his treatment and disruption of the OAAU. More will be said of this below. During this period, repression promised significant dividends with few if any costs.

It should be noted here that militant rhetoric was not a major factor triggering repression. Rather, the mobilization of new social forces on a mass scale created the potential for serious disruption of the normal operation of the society and its social institutions. This potential became visible as a result of the early urban rebellions of 1963 and 1964. It was not so much what the leadership was telling its Black following that scared J. Edgar Hoover, but the actual disruptive potential of such a large mobilized mass of Black people, whether as nonviolent activists or as Black nationalists.

Malcolm X recognized that the Civil Rights movement had entered a period of crisis which demanded a new and different direction if it were to make the transition from a reformist, regional movement to a revolutionary international movement. Malcolm X left the NOI and entered the movement in order to make an ideological, organizational, and activist intervention to help the Civil Rights movement turn the corner into the avenue of human rights.

This chapter will evaluate Malcolm X's performance in terms of the transitions he attempted to effect ideologically and organizationally. The ideological transition was that from millenarian-messianism to Black nationalism and then to Pan-Africanism. Another way of approaching this transition is through spiritual and secular concerns, and additionally the change in definition of the problem from a domestic one to one of essentially international dimensions. Organizationally, how successful was Malcolm X in establishing a Black united front? This question can be looked at in terms of his success in uniting organizationally his Muslim and non-Muslim constituency, bringing together African Americans and Africans, and establishing an activist, Pan-Africanist, self-defense-oriented, revolutionary organization as an integral part of the Civil Rights movement.

In facing the crisis of the 1963–65 period, Malcolm X searched for revolutionary options. Such options invited repression in circumstances where a movement was temporarily weakened because it was in transition from its initial goals, objectives, and geographical focus to new ones; where due to changing constituencies and leadership, old allies were lost and new ones had yet to be recruited. This was so because revolutionary goals tended to unite the opposition. As Doug McAdam described this process:

> Truly *revolutionary* goals...are rarely the object of divided elite response. Rather, movements that emphasize such goals usually mobilize a united elite opposition whose minor conflicts of interest are temporarily tabled in deference to the central threat confronting the system as a whole.[7]

In addition, McAdam noted that non-institutionalized tactics pose a distinct threat to elite groups because

> ...[Their use] communicates a fundamental rejection of the established institutional mechanisms for seeking redress of group grievances; substantively, it deprives elite groups of their recourse to institutional power...elite groups are likely to view noninstitutional tactics as a threat to their interests.[8]

It is clear that McAdam was right when he asserted that a weak opponent lessens the costs and risks associated with a strategy of repression and therefore invites such repression.[9] On the other hand, I do not think that McAdam appreciated the difficulty in calculating the relative strength or weakness of a movement once that movement was well under way.

McAdam felt that in the period of movement expansion, which he identified as 1961–66, the movement was characterized by a strong centralized organizational structure, substantial issue consensus, and a certain "geographic concentration" of movement forces. He identified the disappearance of these characteristics in the latter '60s as an element in the decline of the movement. I do not believe it is that simple. McAdam might have agreed, given his arguments about cooptation, that these attributes, when looked at another way, facilitated strategies of cooptation. The strong centralized organizational structure he refers to was clearly beset by oligarchization by 1963. The consensus on issues was narrow and excluded the agenda of new social forces entering the movement, this timidity reflected the extent to which the established leadership of the movement was coopted by its institutional allies who funded the movement and provided it with legislative support. The geographical concentration of movement forces could also be looked at another way. As long as the Civil Rights movement was a southern movement, it was *confined* to areas whose problems became less and less typical of the Black population as a whole. This was one aspect of a danger McAdam discussed, that of dissolution of indigenous support. It results from oligarchization and cooptation but also from tailing behind the development of new constituencies. Despite the clear commitment to reform strategies, the Civil Rights movement had invited repression long before Black Power ideologies became dominant in it. J. Edgar Hoover's COMINFIL program (FBI's way to monitor communist infiltration of the Civil Rights movement) and his conclusion that the urban rebellions of 1963–64 indicated that the movement had gone too far reinforced the fact that there was an important subjective factor determining the resort to repressive strategies. Repression was possible without elite consensus and without an objective commitment to revolutionary strategies on the part of the insurgents. The racist perceptions of those in immediate control of the repressive mechanisms of the state and their relative dependence or independence of control by other segments of the elite had as much to do with repression as did the tactics and strategies of the insurgents. McAdam's model is weakened by its assumption that elite behavior was totally governed by rational calculation. This is as much an error as to assume that insurgent activity was essentially emotional and pathological. Emotions like anger and hatred may have as much to do with elite response as rational calculation, especially when dealing with racism and the legacy of a dual society which resolved racial conflicts with force, not reason.

I would venture to correct McAdam's otherwise insightful analysis by modifying the process of movement growth and decline that he posited. He was right to note that the Civil Rights movement was ensconced on the horns of the dilemma of cooptation or repression. But he was wrong when he saw the transition to the Black Power period as the beginning of movement decline. The nationalism of the Black Power period, I would argue, was a response to the significant erosion of movement dynamism in the 1963–65 period due to cooptation. Its pursuit of a revolutionary option won for the movement a prolongation of life in the period 1965–68. The inability to construct such an option after initial advances facilitated the intensified repression then directed at the movement.

From the NOI to Pan-Africanism

It is clear that at his death, Malcolm X had established himself as a legitimate representative of the African American people in international forums. A reflection of this newly earned status can be seen from the response to Malcolm's assassination.

Thousands of Harlemites came to pay their last respects, and heads of state and revolutionary organizations worldwide acknowledged his passing. President Kwame Nkrumah of Ghana sent the following message read at Malcolm X's funeral: "I have received with profound shock [the news of] the death of Malcolm X at the hands of an assassin. He has left a heritage of dedication so that Afro-Americans everywhere can live in freedom." Among other messages were those of the Jordanian ambassador to the U.S., the African National Congress of South Africa, the London School of Economics, the African Nationalist Liberation Movement, and the Los Angeles branch of the NAACP. On the more militant side of the Civil Rights movement were messages from the Freedom Fighters of Ohio and the Michigan Committee for the Freedom Now Party.[10]

The establishment media, on the other hand, reflected the fear in elite circles of what Malcolm represented in his last period. They steadfastly ignored the transformations which had occurred in his politics and focused on Malcolm as an "apostle of hate." More liberal sentiments portrayed Malcolm as a flawed tragic hero of Shakespearean proportions. Such was the approach of Peter Goldman.[11] The Civil Rights leadership responded with sadness to his assassination but chose to emphasize their disagreement with his advocacy of what they called violence, and did not provide any response to his politics of the united front and his call for Pan-African solidarity. In death, the established Civil Rights leadership refused to accord to Malcolm X the international status he had won in life.

This was a clear indication that this leadership was rapidly losing touch with the sensibilities of its growing new constituency of urban Black people. In addition, the degree of cooptation of this leadership was reflected in its unwillingness to follow up on the great strides Malcolm had made for the movement internationally. SNCC and CORE rapidly parted company with the NAACP and SCLC after Malcolm's death, moving closer to his nationalism and Pan-Africanism than the conservative NAACP and the centrist SCLC. While King and the SCLC kept the churches, nationalist organizations increasingly won over the youth and the urban unemployed. Within the Civil Rights movement, Malcolm's legacy in the most immediate sense was maintained by SNCC and CORE. In Chapter Seven, I will take up a complete discussion of this broader legacy. Now we must ask, What happened to the OAAU?

Despite the outpouring of respect and the belated recognition of Malcolm's international significance, the OAAU was not able to survive the assassination of Malcolm X. The international alliance potential of Malcolm's Pan-Africanism could not quickly be brought to bear on domestic U.S. racial problems. The OAAU could not quickly realize its organizational potential. Malcolm X did not live long enough to surmount practical problems attendant to the formation of the OAAU. Without his charisma, the organization could not survive.

The transition that Malcolm had attempted required considerable time for implementation. This he did not have. His program of Pan-Africanism, human rights, and self-defense consolidated opposition in the U.S. ruling elite much faster than it created solid domestic insurgent organization and firm international alliances. Such a situation invited repression, which fell swiftly and effectively on the OAAU.

Difficulties Forming Effective International Alliances

Malcolm's desire to use international forums to check U.S. repression of the Black Liberation movement was not easily realizable. The majority of African states were in no position to confront the United States in international forums concerning its treatment of African Americans. The OAU was divided ideologically between the radical "Casablanca" and conservative "Monrovia" groups, with the latter being somewhat stronger numerically. This split in part reflected the relative strength of neo-colonial influences in these two blocs, but all African countries at that time suffered from internal problems related to underdevelopment and the colonial legacy, which made the consensus on foreign policy in the OAU problematic.

The United States attempted to influence the policies and the internal political makeup of radical African states through the activities of the CIA and the USIA. Nineteen hundred and sixty-six was the beginning of a decade of coup d'etats in Africa which exposed the weaknesses of state formation in Africa and the relative impotence of these countries in the international arena. Nkrumah's Ghana, the strongest supporter of Malcolm X, was brought down by a right-wing coup a year after the assassination of Malcolm X.

Even if the Afro-Asian bloc had initiated an indictment of the United States on human rights grounds, sanctions above and beyond embarrassing the United States would have been extremely difficult. Human rights law was one of the newest components of international law and organization. At the time of Malcolm's efforts, the Universal Declaration of Human Rights and the Genocide Convention were not universally ratified. The United States had not endorsed the Genocide Convention. Complicating the development of this branch of international law were questions of respect for the territorial integrity and domestic jurisdiction of member states. Violations of human rights law were in the first instance to be corrected by domestic processes wherever possible.

A superpower like the United States had considerable latitude in international forums to block action against it for violations of international law. The "compulsory jurisdiction" of the World Court is a misnomer since it requires the voluntary consent of the parties involved. As the major funder of the United Nations and host to that organization, the United States possessed considerable power to block any embarrassing issues from being raised in that body. Once such issues were raised, the superpower status of the United States made it virtually certain that no effective action could be taken against it. Security Council action could be blocked by veto if necessary, and the General Assembly resolutions carried no effective enforcement mechanisms. To illustrate this latter point, General Assembly condemnations and calls for sanctions had little impact on the consolidation of apartheid in South Africa, the continued illegal occupation of Namibia, or the unilateral declaration of independence in Rhodesia. If the United Nations' actions against these relatively small states was of limited effectiveness and often ignored, what impact could its fiat have against a superpower? The founders of the United Nations recognized that its effectiveness in sanctioning violators of peace and human rights depended on a consensus of the five permanent members of the Security Council. It was recognized that no effective compulsory action could be taken by the organization against a superpower.

New nations in Africa did not always take an unequivocal position regarding support for liberation movements in the Third World, let alone in the United States. The fear of irredentism and secession tempered African advocacy of liberation struggles. The largely artificial nature of the contemporary political boundaries of African states meant that almost without exception the African States were multiethnic in composition. Many of them confronted nationalist-based movements of secession or "pan" movements based on irredentism. They carefully maintained their prerogatives in international law related to both territorial integrity and domestic jurisdiction. The kind of arguments which could be raised to support the petition of Malcolm X might also be used to support movments opposed to many of these African governments. Too precipitous a resort to human rights law might open a Pandora's box on the African continent.

Benjamin Karim reported that Malcolm X recognized that he had not yet gotten anything concrete from African countries regarding his program to indict the United States in international forums. Malcolm told him after he returned from his second trip to Africa that "Wall Street could cause the collapse or overthrow of any African government."[12] Malcolm X recognized that Africa still had problems even in its post-colonial period. But he felt it also had a voice: "In that voice there is strength. And when you and I link our struggle up with his struggle so that his struggle backs our struggle, you'll find that this man over here will pay a little more attention."[13] Malcolm could not have been more correct, as attested to by the activities of the FBI, which will be examined later in this chapter.

As early as 1962, the Cuban missile crisis illustrated the commitment of both the United States and the USSR to recognize each other's spheres of influence and to de-escalate East-West competition. On the other hand, the intensification of the Vietnam War at the beginning of 1965 ushered in a new domestic attitude toward protest rooted in White backlash.

The support of the Islamic Middle East for Malcolm X's human rights mission was probably not unequivocal. His conception of Islam was inconsistent with the social structures of the more conservative Arab monarchies in that part of the world. Certainly his politics were totally unacceptable. There is some indication that Malcolm was made aware of these reservations on his second trip to the area.[14] It should be noted in this regard that Malcolm X never defined for his followers in Muslim Mosque, Inc. what, if any, was the political role of Islam in the Black Liberation struggle. In addition, he was unable to structure any significant organizational developments on the basis of the credentials and influence he procured on his last two trips to the Middle East and Africa. I believe that Malcolm X was confronted with the realization that Islam was *not* the central motive force in any of the revolutions he had studied. Those revolutionaries from Islamic countries who he met were not Islamic revolutionaries but among the most secularized and leftist-progressive nationalists, often trying to diminish further the role of an Islam viewed as a conservative influence in their revolutionary experiments. In Egypt, Algeria, and Guinea, significant opposition to these nationalist movements was located in the most organized segments of Islam and its clergy.

Despite these very real obstacles, in the years subsequent to Malcolm X's death the power of Third World nations did increase in international forums. They demonstrated an increased willingness to embarrass the United States wherever the costs were not excessive, including extending support for human rights causes of domestic U.S. minorities. Both the Puerto Rican independence movement and the Native American movement have been accorded status and given an audience before international tribunals and UN committees and organizations. As we will see in Chapter Seven, African American organizations have continued to develop the notion that the United States is vulnerable to embarrassment in international forums.

Difficulties in Organizing the OAAU

At Malcolm X's death, the OAAU had failed to negotiate several important transformations. The movement from a religious organization to a secular one was never truly completed. Related to this problem was the lack of uniform acceptance and understanding of the new Pan-Africanist orientation. There were also problems with giving effect to the value of building an inter-class united front within the organization. In the area of decisionmaking, OAAU members had difficulty changing from authoritarian heirarchical methods to democratic egalitarian ones. Related to this latter difficulty was the one of accepting a new and equal role for women in the OAAU.

The internal weaknesses of the OAAU were not unexpected. Its model of ideology, organization, leadership, and constituency represented such a departure from those found in the Civil Rights movement at that time that there was little in the experience of the membership to facilitate this transformation and few precedents to guide their action. A charismatic presence like Malcolm X's was necessary to legitimate the new methods and new relationships demanded but not yet validated by practical experience. This was especially true when one considers the trauma associated with the feud between Muslim Mosque, Inc. and the Nation of Islam. Over and above the difficulties just mentioned was the impact of the campaign of disruption and discredit waged by the security apparatus of the state, led by J. Edgar Hoover.

Transition Difficulties

Malcolm's lieutenant in the Mosque, Benjamin Karim, observed that "there were people around Malcolm in the MMI and some of them could not see the value of the OAAU and where he could take it politically. They wanted Malcolm to evangelize for Islam because they felt he could get a whole lot more members this way."[15] Karim expressed his feeling and that of many in the MMI that Islam was automatically an organizing factor because "there are concepts and precepts where Islam was concerned that no matter where Malcolm went there was an organizing factor within it, itself [Islam]. He did not have to say let's organize within the Muslim Mosque; we were already organized. There are certain concepts and precepts and by-laws in the religion of Islam that it organizes you."[16] Whether this was true or not, it could not help but be the source of much confusion in Malcolm X's attempts to build a purely secular political human rights organization. Malcolm X never satisfactorily resolved the question of the relationship of Islam to the social change he desired.[17]

Many disgruntled members of the NOI initially saw Malcolm's resignation from that organization and the formation of Muslim Mosque, Inc. as an attempt to present a reformed version of the NOI. They were encouraged in this belief by many statements Malcolm made in the late winter and early spring of 1964. At that time, he said that he still believed in Elijah Muhammad's program and that he could better implement it outside of the NOI. Thus, many NOI members who respected Malcolm's leadership and were dissatisfied with the leadership of the NOI looked to Muslim Mosque, Inc. as a new home. In Philadelphia and Boston, members of the NOI temples entered into discussions with Malcolm's lieutenants concerning forming chapters of MMI in these cities. Malcolm instructed that they be steered into the OAAU after it was formed. His efforts were unsuccessful in this instance because these groupings where not so much looking for a revolutionary political organization or an activist home within the Civil Rights movement but a way of continuing their religious affiliation away from what they saw was the corruption of the NOI.

Wallace Muhammad, a son of Elijah, who broke with his father's leadership of the NOI, was able to exploit the reformist sentiment in the NOI much better than Malcolm X. In September 1964, in Philadelphia, Wallace formed the African Descendents Uplift Society (ADUS). His initial constituency were members of the Philadelphia mosque. These members had gone to Chicago and were there told by Wallace of the corruption in the NOI and of Elijah Muhammad's fathering of children by various of his female employees. The Philadephia mosque subsequently expelled these members, and they approached both MMI and Wallace about a new organizational home. ADUS was to be an "educational and self-upliftment of the Negroes." It called upon Blacks to obey U.S. laws and to recognize their U.S. citizenship. Members were told to register to vote and encourage their friends to do so. In relation to the then-upcoming presidential election (1964), Wallace expressed the opinion that Lyndon Johnson would be more beneficial to Blacks than Barry Goldwater. ADUS was willing to join with Civil Rights organizations in the fight against bigotry and hatred. Wallace admonished his followers to forget everything his father had taught them, to stop using the X in their names, and to use Arab or African names once their names had been changed legally. Wallace indicated that he had the support of his brother Akbar, then studying Islam in Cairo, in his organizational efforts.[18]

While expressing a personal friendship for Malcolm, Wallace demurred from a closer relationship with Malcolm because of Malcolm's association with violence[19] Malcolm X faced effective competition in attempting to mobilize disgruntled members of the NOI around his new organizational efforts.

While Malcolm X was not successful in pulling large numbers of people out of the NOI and into his new organization, he was successful in creating a space for members of the NOI to criticize their organization and its religious leaders and even to experiment with other forms of religious organization within Islam. Given the very large bloc of African Americans in the NOI, it was important that, through Malcolm X, they realized that its authoritarian orientation and sectarian Islam could be challenged. Most importantly, he was able to guide many people back to the secular tradition of African American nationalism who had first been exposed to that tradition in its more narrow formulation in the NOI. Many people who came to the tradition of Black nationalism while in the NOI were later able to leave that organization and still remain active within the Civil Rights and Black Power movements.

Problems in the Black United Front

The conflict between MMI members and newer members of the OAAU had a class as well as an ideological dimension. These two factors interacted in causing initial difficulties in the new organization.

There was never a major blow-up, but petty bickering and squabbles plagued the OAAU. Its source was the predictable tension between members of MMI and the more bourgeois leadership in the OAAU. Hassan Washington described this contention as based on the division in the organization between the people associated with Malcolm X from the old NOI days and the newer people attracted by the OAAU. These latter were more likely to be intellectuals with verbal skills and formal education. Malcolm X's absence exacerbated these petty squabbles.[20]

It is unclear whether the majority of the membership of the Muslim Mosque, Inc. really understood the need for an OAAU. Peter Bailey felt that some members of MMI saw those males who joined the OAAU as undisciplined "dilettantes." This he felt was true to some extent.[21] The cadre in the MMI felt that they had a monopoly on the question of security procedures in the OAAU. Some of the new membership resented the fact that their input on the question of security was not respected. On the other hand, he noted that these very same OAAU members viewed the members of MMI as hopeless due to their involvement with Islam.[22] "We did not know each other," observed Bailey."It was like two different organizations looking over their shoulders at each other. There were MMI people who never came around the OAAU. There were some people in the MMI who wanted brother Malcolm's new organization to be an exact replica of the NOI," he concluded on this point.[23]

Decisionmaking Problems

No method of decisionmaking was established in the OAAU independent of Malcolm X's personal leadership and charisma. It was never resolved as to who would speak publicly for the organization in Malcolm's absence. In addition, differing organizational and decisionmaking styles, as well as tensions related to the more egalitarian role for women in the OAAU, fed the squabbles.

An FBI informant reported that the OAAU membership meeting of August 17, 1964 was devoted to a heated discussion over the lack of communication between Malcolm X and the OAAU while he was abroad. Members argued over whether Malcolm X should have the final word on all OAAU policies or if the group itself would formulate policies. This latter point echoed the complaint of one of the office staff of the OAAU that Lynn Shifflet "is too cautious and has allowed the OAAU activity to slow down. Consequently, the OAAU is not functioning at full strength and is very disorganized."[24] The informant reporting on the meeting above observed that the "organization almost fell apart at the seams because of the lack of positive leadership."[25] While this was probably exaggerated, it was certainly true that an organization as novel in the Black freedom struggle as the OAAU and held together so much by one man's charisma would need his personal attention and presence during its formative period. He tried to tutor it through its difficulties from abroad. In response to the myriad of petty complaints Malcolm X received in Africa, he responded from Cairo in a letter to his following dated August 29, 1964. In part he said:

> I have been pleased to receive letters from many of you lately,...From the sound of some of the letters there seems to be much dissatisfaction and disunity creeping in among you, and some even seem dissatisfied even with me. This sounds like history repeating itself. I want you to know that this is normal, and therefore it doesn't excite or worry me. I'm not particularly surprised at the ones around whom so much of the controversy and dissatisfaction seems to be raging, because experience has taught me never to take anyone or anything for granted...
> If brothers want to establish another organization, even that is their right. We must learn to wish them well and mean it. Our fight must never be against each other. No matter how much we differ over minor things, our fight must always be directed against the *common enemy* (emphasis in the original).[26]

Malcolm made his most telling point via a disclaimer:

> I know your grievances, much of which is just, but much of which is also based upon inability to look at the problem as a *whole*. It is bigger and more complicated than many of us realize. I've never sought to be anyone's leader. There are some of you there who want leadership. I've stayed away this summer and given all those who want to show what they can do the opportunity to do so. When I return I will work with anyone who thinks he can lead... and I only pray to *Allah* that you will work with me likewise.[27]

What the OAAU needed at this point was more leadership from Malcolm through his direct presence and less experimentation with participatory democracy.

When he returned, this was just what he had planned to provide. On the evening of February 20, 1965, Malcolm met with a dozen of his OAAU stalwarts and indicated that he wanted a complete reorganization of the OAAU. As Earl Grant reported, at this meeting Malcolm X said that the "OAAU had not been operating to his satisfaction. The OAAU had not been able to take advantage of the attention drawn to it by his

[Malcolm's] activities. And, also, he wanted women to be given a more clearly defined role in the OAAU."[28] Late that night Malcolm conveyed what were to be his last hopes to Grant: "I don't care about myself. I only want to protect my family and the OAAU. No matter what happens to me personally, it is important that the OAAU continues to exist..."[29] Unfortunately, for the OAAU to continue to exist and become what he envisioned for it, Malcolm had to be there to guide it. But this was not to be.

New Role for Women in the OAAU

The membership of the OAAU, which was affiliated with the MMI, had difficulty dealing with the leadership roles of women. It was reported, for instance, that Lynn Shifflet would not defer to the chauvinism of some members of MMI.[30] Nevertheless, this tension impeded her activism on behalf of the organization, although she remained an active member while Malcolm was alive. Even within the MMI, Hassan Washington reported that some of the female membership resisted the introduction of classes in the MMI based on the model of the Muslim women's training of the NOI.[31] This resistance caused Malcolm X to abandon this move. Malcolm X's position on the role of women certainly underwent some development. While one of his associates reported that Malcolm did not trust women,[32] by the time of his assassination he was confiding in his associates that "Africa will not be free until it frees its women."[33] Malcolm had moved away from the idea that the woman's role was in the home. Some of his associates reported that he was very disappointed that his wife Betty had not been the type of person who could have taken a more active role in the OAAU.[34] Malcolm X consciously involved women like Lynn Shifflet and Sarah Mitchell in the leadership of the OAAU because he believed that women had a central role to play in the movement for human rights.

In terms of the paid membership, those in attendance at rallies, the students at the Liberation School, and the membership of MMI, the OAAU was overwhelmingly a working-class organization. It was right on target when it attempted to confront the question of how middle-class intellectuals and working-class activists should interact in an essentially working-class organization. Historically, the OAAU experience was important for raising this question in the movement and trying to resolve it. Its experience in this regard illustrated how difficult that question is to resolve.

Interestingly, this question emerged often in a disguised form. The question of the religious or secular orientation of the organization was also a question reflecting the class realities of the organization. The working-class presence in the OAAU was strongest among the members of MMI. Radicalized intelligentsia gravitated to the OAAU's secular Pan-Africanism.

In terms of decisionmaking and leadership, the charismatic and hierarchical models were most firmly established in the orientation and practice of the working-class members of the MMI. The OAAU intellectuals, like their counterparts everywhere, were used to a participatory democracy bordering on anarchism

The question of the role of women in the OAAU had a distinct class component as well. In a patriarchal capitalism, the most oppressed segments of the population would be particularly sensitive to the fact that their males could not play out the same male chauvinist roles associated with those who exercised power over them. In fact, a leading member of the Muslim contingent in the OAAU argued that no people in the process of liberation had a leadership composed of women. He observed that throughout the history of Black oppression in the United States Black women had been disproportionately represented in the community's leadership.[35] In some ways, Black female leadership was being equated with White oppression. Female leadership in the OAAU, then, was seen by some of its working-class members as an essentially petite-bourgeois affectation and a form of Black oppression.

The OAAU was at the beginning of a process of defining crucial questions confronting the Black Liberation movement. Resolving these questions required their proper formulation, stripped of the misstatements and mysticism which had grown up around them over the years. The process of being able to see both a question in all of its forms but at the same time identify its essence is one the African American community is still struggling to master. Malcolm X is to be credited with insisting that absolute honesty be brought to the identification of and pursuit of answers to these questions.

Repression of the OAAU

At Malcolm's death the OAAU was still faced with considerable work in the international arena and at home. It should come as no suprise, then, that the OAAU was the first nationalist organization in the Black freedom struggle that was targeted for destruction by the Federal Bureau of Investigation.

At first Malcolm X was less cautious regarding security concerns and possible provocative behavior. Right after the creation of the OAAU, Malcolm X sent the two provocative telegrams to Dr. King in St. Augustine, Florida and James Forman in Philadelphia, Mississippi. By his second trip to Africa, Malcolm X developed the feeling that the U.S. government was prepared to destroy his movement. While still in Africa, Malcolm noted the actions of the U.S. government to isolate Africans from him and to convince them that the African American was not concerned about Africa. It raised his ire that the USIA (United States Information Agency) was publicizing the 1964 Civil Rights Act in Africa as a refutation of his positions. He was quite angry that as U.S. diplomats and some Black Civil Rights leaders were traveling in Africa to misrepresent the opinions of African Americans regarding Africa.[36] Peter Goldman in his biographical work on this period in Malcolm X's life implied that Malcolm's assertions of a flurry of diplomatic activity in Africa and plans for "dirty tricks" against him were exaggerated and somewhat paranoid.[37] With the record of FBI concern and surveillance available, however, it is clear that his concerns were not without substantial foundation. Certainly, the increased level of government surveillance of Malcolm X and accelerated U.S. State Department activity in Africa to counter his inroads there buttressed his fears, as did his feeling that he had been poisoned by U.S. agents in Cairo.

J. Edgar Hoover initiated the FBI program of destruction of the OAAU in a memo to the New York and Philadelphia field offices dated July 2, 1964. In it he said in part:

> There is indication that Little [Malcolm X] has aligned himself with subversive groups and this matter must be immediately investigated and, if feasible, a counterintelligence program will be initiated to publicly discredit Little.[38]

As an important functionary of the Nation of Islam, Malcolm X had been the subject of FBI surveillance since 1952. With other members of the NOI, Malcolm X's name was added to the FBI's security index. The program instituted by the FBI known as COINTELPRO was not initiated until several years after Malcolm X's assassination. But from its August 1967 description of its program to disrupt and "neutralize" so-called "Black nationalist hate groups," it appears that the FBI program of discrediting Malcolm X was one of its earliest trial runs. In the August 1967 document, the goals of COINTELPRO in relation to Black nationalism are described as

1—Prevent a coalition of militant Black nationalist groups.
2—Prevent the rise of a "Messiah" who could unify, and electrify, the militant Black Nationalist Movement.
3—Prevent *violence* on the part of Black Nationalist groups...Through counterintelligence it should be possible to pinpoint potential trouble makers and neutralize them before they exercise their potential for violence.
4—Prevent militant Black Nationalist groups and leaders from gaining respectability,...
5—A final goal should be to prevent the long-range *growth* of militant Black Nationalist organizations, especially among the youth.[39]

Prior to the COINTELPRO program, the FBI had a major rationalization for investigation and disruption of movements like Malcolm X's. The FBI carried out extensive surveillance of the Civil Rights movement and its offshoots through its Communist Infiltration Program, COMINFIL.

The antagonistic scrutiny of Malcolm X and the OAAU by local and federal security branches of government was an extension of monitoring first directed at the NOI during World War II. It was part of an even earlier trend to ferret out popular Black leadership and movements which had the potential for a mass following based on Black nationalism or more generally the notion of Black equality. A young J. Edgar Hoover moved successfully to destroy the Univeral Negro Improvement Association (UNIA) and discredit the leadership of Marcus Garvey. During World War II, Hoover kept a file on Black organizations which he monitored with reference to communism and German, Italian, and Japanese fifth columnists.[40] The Justice Department in 1942 charged Elijah Muhammad with sedition because of his alleged identification with the "pan-colored" propaganda of the Japanese and his contact with an agent of that government sent to secure allies in the Black community.[41] Elijah Muhammad spent several years in jail as a result of his refusal to be drafted into the wartime armed forces. The FBI opened its surveillance file on Malcolm X because of statements attributed to him in prison in 1952 in which he allegedly stated that he was a communist.

In March 1956, Hoover reported to an Eisenhower cabinet meeting that the Black Muslims was one of the "organizations presently advancing integration(sic)" and "figuring in the rising [racial] tensions."[42] The NOI was described as a group which used "violently anti-white rhetoric" and expressed support for the Mau Mau in Kenya and the Vietminh of North Vietnam.[43] O'Reilly reported that the FBI tried to have the NOI put on the attorney general's list of subversive organizations and to jail its leaders for Smith Act and Selective Service Act violations, but Attorney General Brownell refused. Nevertheless, he approved wiretaps which became the basis of widespread monitoring of Muslims.[44]

Later, during the OAAU period, the FBI investigated Malcolm X because of his association with individuals who had alleged Communist Party or communist front organization links or had previously been put on the FBI's security index. Thus, the OAAU came in for immediate scrutiny because of Malcolm's association on his first trip to Ghana with Julian Mayfield, who was already on the FBI's security index. The initial interest and support of the Socialist Workers Party, Malcolm's appearances at the Militant Labor Forums, the extensive coverage he received in that party's newspaper, *The Militant*, and the frequent reports of Socialist Workers Party leadership's attendance at the OAAU rallies created a certainty within the FBI that Malcolm X was engaged in a subversive enterprise. Other supporters of Malcolm X had significant leftist backgrounds which triggered the paranoia of the FBI. Prominent among the guests at the initial OAAU rally were people like William Epton, former Harlem branch member of the Communist Party and at that time a member of the Progressive Labor Party, Conrad Lynn, a lawyer with a reputation for defending leftist causes and intellectuals like John Oliver Killens who were suspected through a process of guilt-by-association from previous memberships in organizations designated as communist fronts. In fact, not long before his assassination the FBI anticipated that a real possibility existed that they might be able to indict Malcolm X for his "subversive" activities.[45]

Ironically, the FBI also had solid information that the Communist Party was in no way aligned with or encouraging Malcolm X. In a report file relevant to their surveillance of the MMI, an informant reported on the New York district meeting of the CPUSA at the Hotel Woodstock on March 16, 1964. In commenting on Malcolm's break with Elijah Muhammad and his new organizational efforts, several speakers worried about Malcolm X's ideas concerning violence and expressed the opinion that he was hurting the integrationist program.

"Dirty tricks" had been initiated against Malcolm X and the Muslim Mosque, Inc. by the FBI. As indicated in the outline of a plan contained in a memo from the Special Agent in Charge (SAC) in Detroit to Hoover, dated April 10, 1964, a phony letter was drafted over Malcolm's signature and sent to Muhammad's followers in Detroit so as to cause "disruption and deeper disputes between Nation of Islam leader Elijah Muhammad and Malcolm Little of Muslim Mosque, Inc." The FBI's Chicago field office also reported creating a rift between

Malcolm X and Elijah Muhammad.[46] The MMI and the OAAU were well infiltrated by agents and informants of the FBI and other governmental intelligence organizations, including army intelligence, navy intelligence, and the New York Police Department's Bureau of Special Services (BOSS). Gene Roberts, a bodyguard of Malcolm X in the OAAU, later surfaced as a New York City policeman assigned by BOSS to surveillance of the OAAU. Roberts later was at the center of the New York Black Panther 21 trial, turning state's evidence as an undercover agent who had penetrated that organization. Ironically, Roberts reported to his superiors one week before Malcolm's assassination what he and several OAAU members thought was a dry run of the assassination. At the OAAU rally immediately preceding Malcolm X's assassination, a disturbance was created by two men as one cried "Get your hand out of my pocket!" His superiors informed him that they would "get on" this information. In fact, there is no information to suggest that the police did anything positive to follow up on this lead.[47]

McKinley Welch, another BOSS agent, had infiltrated Muslim Mosque No.7 in New York, and when Malcolm X left the NOI, Welch's superiors ordered him to infiltrate the OAAU.[48] The *Big Red* article cited states that the head of BOSS in 1965, Anthony Ulasewisz, later bragged about BOSS's counterintelligence campaign against Malcolm X. Ulasewisz was later convicted as a "bagman" in the Watergate scandal.[49]

Domestic surveillance agencies are not the only ones which have been implicated in governmental measures to remove Malcolm X's influence from the Civil Rights movement. The State Department viewed Malcolm's activities in Africa and his strategy of citing the United States for infractions of African Americans' human rights in international forums as a threat to the national security. Declassified government documents indicated that the State Department asked the CIA division that was later implicated in the overthrow and assassination of several Third World leaders to "take covert action against Malcolm X."[50]

These documents further indicate that on August 11, 1964 Benjamin H. Read, excecutive secretary of the State Department, contacted Richard Helms, CIA deputy director for plans, who, was in charge of both the Domestic Operations Divison and the African Operations Division, urging Helms to use the Clandestine Services Division to investigate Malcolm X. Read identified Malcolm X to Helms as a popular Afro-American revolutionary, who according to information received by Read had been fermenting domestic riots in July 1964 (no doubt a reference to the Harlem riots of that period). Read was also concerned that Malcolm's plan to go to the United Nations might seriously damage the reputation of the United States as a cultural and racial "melting pot." The only other nation besides Nazi Germany to have been so charged was South Africa.[51]

By late 1964, the State Department was disturbed at the progress Malcolm X was making with his petition strategy. He had many friends among Third World diplomats and United Nations representatives, especially among the more radical members of the organization and the radical Casablanca group of African countries. Malcolm's friendship with Nkrumah was about to pay dividends in his petition strategy; as surveillance documents indicated, he had also cultivated a friendship with Alex Quaison-Sackey, Ghana's ambassador to the United Nations, who was about to be elected president of the General Assembly. FBI surveillance also indicated that Malcolm's petition campaign had been supported by such members of the Security Index as author James Baldwin, believed by the FBI at the time to have helped Malcolm draft the petition itself. Revolutionary Algeria was implicated in Malcolm's plans, as the FBI believed that Mahmoud Boutiba, a propagandist for the government of Ahmed Ben Bella, was a personal adviser to Malcolm X of long standing.[52]

CIA documents indicated that the State Department had taken up the matter of Malcolm's UN petition idea with President Lyndon Johnson, who in turn asked J. Edgar Hoover to secure further information. Hoover in turn contacted Burke Marshall of the Justice Department's Civil Rights Section, who initiated inquiries with Malcolm X's biographer, Alex Haley, and other Civil Rights leaders about Malcolm X's foreign ties and financial resources. When Hoover's investigation failed to turn up any legal improprieties on Malcolm's part, Read again approached Helms, asking him to use the Clandestine Services Division to penetrate Malcolm X's foreign connections before the UN petition became a crisis for the Johnson administration. There is no record of the CIA's acting on Read's request.[53] However, FBI documents indicated that the FBI's Newark field office reported to Hoover its attempts to develop new contacts in the Newark NOI temple in the months immediately preceding Malcolm X's assassination. Malcolm's alleged assassins came out of that temple.[54]

The conflict between Malcolm X and the leadership of the Nation of Islam was not, however, merely a creation of FBI "dirty tricks." In the pages of the NOI newspaper, *Muhammad Speaks*, a series of veiled and not-so-veiled threats were made against the "hypocrite," Malcolm X.[55] They came from a variety of NOI ministers and those placed well up in the NOI hierarchy like Minister Louis Farrakhan. Among Farrakhan's veiled threats was the following:

> Only those who wish to be led to hell, or to their doom, will follow Malcolm. The die is set, and Malcolm shall not escape, especially after such evil, foolish talk about his benefactor...Such a man as Malcolm is worthy of death, and would have met with death if it had not been for Muhammad's confidence in Allah for victory over his enemies.[56]

The conflict with the NOI was not merely around personality clashes or ambition but was essentially ideological and organizational. The conditions under which Malcolm X departed from the NOI constituted both an ideological and organizational challenge to the NOI's continued existence—a challenge which the NOI leadership felt it could not ignore.

There was the threat of disruption of OAAU rallies and meetings and numerous clashes between NOI members and MMI followers. OAAU members recruited out of the NOI often could not safely and openly affiliate with Malcolm X. Nevertheless, the FBI, having infiltrated both organizations, was on record as mandating the discredit and disorganization of both. By what it did and did *not* do, it exacerbated this internecine conflict and directed it into channels of self-destruction which ultimately took the life of Malcolm X.

Malcolm X did not handle the conflict with the Muslims well at all. Despite the advice of many friends and associates, he reversed a policy of offical silence regarding allegations of impropriety on Elijah Muhammad's part. He was subsequently entrapped in a running internecine battle over the possession of his residence, the NOI claiming the property as its own. The NOI finally succeeded in getting a court order to evict him from his residence. Reacting to the obvious tactic of embarrassing Malcolm before his family and associates as a man who could not provide for his family, Malcolm fought doggedly and with no holds barred in the verbal tit-for-tat of the several court appearances. In addition, he attempted to get several of the women effected by Elijah Muhammad to file paternity actions against him. Malcolm X even went to the Illinois attorney general on this matter. The intensity of the hostility between the NOI and Malcolm X was not, therefore, all attributable to the NOI. Malcolm X responded to this challenge without considering adequately its impact on the fledgling OAAU or the ability of the security apparatus of the United States to exploit it against the new organization as well as against all he was struggling to establish.

When Malcolm X fully realized the forces committed to his destruction, his response was defeatist and metaphysical. On the one hand, he refused to allow his associates adequately to protect him because he feared for their lives and their families' welfare. On the other hand, he insisted that they carry on and develop the OAAU if something happened to him.[57] What he failed to realize was that the primary resource at that point for making the OAAU a success was Malcolm X himself. The organization's number-one priority should have been to keep Malcolm X alive. While he expressed the desire to build an organization which was not dependent on one man, he should have recognized that the OAAU was not yet such an organization. In addition, Malcolm conceded an omnipotence to the government security apparatus which was unwarranted. The notion that he was a hunted man whose imminent death was inevitable resigned Malcolm to do nothing in his own self-defense. This ultimately resulted in a manner of death which completely terrorized his associates and destroyed their willingness to maintain the organization.

Despite his interaction with revolutionaries abroad, Malcolm had not yet mastered the art of organizing under conditions of repression. He failed to identify the principal conflict confronting the OAAU at this time. Thus, he attributed to his conflict with the NOI an urgency and status which weakened him against a much more potent enemy, the U.S. government.

In the face of threats which ultimately took his life, Malcolm X never flagged in maintaining a regal deportment. His was a lasting example of championing what he believed to be true no matter what the costs. Because of his deportment in the face of death, Malcolm X became an icon of the Black freedom struggle. As Ossie Davis so aptly eulogized him, Malcolm X was the "shining prince" of the Black community.[58] He became a symbol of Black manhood which commanded respect from all segments of the Black community but particularly from urban street youth. Malcolm's own autobiography reflects the transformations that were possible in this stratum of the Black urban community. Better than King, who was a role model of commitment for the Black middle class and the embodiment of the "talented tenth" concept of Du Bois, Malcolm X represented a role model for the new social stratum which entered the movement in the 1963–65 period.

The Demise of Malcolm's OAAU

Peter Bailey described how no one knew what to do with the organization after Malcolm's assassination. Demoralization set in immediately, especially for those members who had come to Malcolm through the auspices of the OAAU.[59] For them, Malcolm had been the organization and much more, and with his death these people had no one to lean on. There was no person in this group who was prepared to give leadership after Malcolm's death and try to pull things back together. The members of MMI were able to hang on a little longer. After the assassination Malcolm X's sister Ella Collins tried to assert leadership in the OAAU.[60] Bailey, who went to only one meeting after the assassination ,said that Ella Collins arrived there and said that Malcolm X had left her in charge. This was the first that Bailey and most others had ever seen of Malcolm's sister; her presence apparently never graced any OAAU membership meeting. According to Bailey, "Everyone went their own way because no one wanted to battle sister Ella for control of the OAAU."[61] Jim Campbell was one of those who left quietly and quickly; he attended only one meeting after Malcolm's assassination.[62]

Hassan Washington also felt that no one came forward to pull the OAAU or any of its committees together to keep the organization going. He saw the members during this period traumatized and running scared.[63] The major attempt at establishing leadership in the OAAU at this time came from two people who had had no real relationship to the organization previously. A rift developed between Ella Collins and Malcolm's widow, Betty Shabazz, over the leadership of the OAAU. Ella Collins emerged victorious and established what amounted to a new organization with the old OAAU name. Washington also noted that after Malcolm's death some of the male members of the OAAU and the MMI drifted away, possibly, he felt, due not only to the shock of events but also to an unwillingness to deal with female leadership.[64]

Conclusion

Malcolm X's OAAU did not successfully negotiate the dilemma between cooptation and repression. Formulated as a united front structure to allow for both middle- and working-class Black people to cooperate organizationally within a newly defined human rights movement without gender discrimination, the OAAU attracted the fear and hostility of the ruling elite. It was subsequently attacked at its weakest links, the physical person of Malcolm X and the young OAAU he had created. The loss of

Malcolm X's charismatic leadership was a blow to the developing human rights movement in the Black community. The loss of the OAAU was salient, because at the time it represented the only significant organizational form with Pan-African links, a working-class constituency, and a united front human rights agenda, explicitly scrutinizing all options including self-defense and revolution. The OAAU was centrally located in Harlem and in the base of operations for the United Nations, New York City. Its demise created a temporary vacuum in a strategic location for the Black Liberation struggle. Repression of Malcolm X and the OAAU, however, did not destroy the movement nor the legacy which Malcolm X bequeathed to it.

Press Conference Announcing break with Nation of Islam.
Park Sheraton Hotel, March 12, 1964

7

Malcolm X's Ideological Legacy

Introduction

I have presented the thoughts, actions, and aspirations of Malcolm so as to get beyond the icon and reveal the dynamic and changing Malcolm who has contemporary relevance in the struggle for Black liberation in the '90s and beyond. Adolph Reid, however, questions the utility of such an enterprise. He argues:

> Attempts to draw on Malcolm for guidance reproduce his inaccurate, simplistic reading of Afro-American history and reinforce inadequate and wrongheaded tendencies in the present...[T]he best way to think of the best of Malcolm is that he was just like the rest of us—a regular person saddled with imperfect knowledge, human frailties, and conflicting imperatives, but none the less trying to make sense of his very specific history, trying unsuccessfully to transcend it, and struggling to push it in a humane direction. We can learn most from his failures and limitations because they speak most clearly both of the character of his time and of the sorts of perils we must guard against in our own.[1]

Reid's comments try to compensate for the excesses of those who would make Malcolm a saint and an icon. By studying Malcolm we do get an entrée into his time, the tumultuous decade of the 1960s, the most recent period of massive social upheaval in U.S. history. The study of Malcolm is important because he was the best critic of an era and a movement which still holds significance for us today. Malcolm asked the right questions, some of which he found answers for. We must know these questions and answers so that we don't "recreate the wheel."

The Black Liberation movement developed in the latter 1960s in marked contrast to the integrationist Civil Rights movement. It was repressed violently by the agents of the state. Even today it represents the only significant alternative to Civil Rights integrationism that African Americans have ever developed. This movement, for a time, energized those groups in the ghetto who are today vilified as "the underclass." Our present oppression as a people is tied to the defeat and destruction of the Black Liberation movement. It is also tied to the sanctification of Black electoral politics within the confines of the Democratic Party, the sainthood of Dr. King, and the canon of nonviolence. This sanctification stood as an alternative to the mobilization of poor and dispossessed African Americans outside of the institutions of electoral, legislative, and executive politics which are institutionally structured to maintain powerlessness. A rejuvenated Black Liberation movement can be constructed only upon an accurate understanding of the strengths and weaknesses, the accuracies and errors of our previous major efforts at rebellion. Critically studying Malcolm X is central to this reconstruction and rebuilding effort.

Malcolm impacted a movement that continued to exist after his death. As he is associated with ideas which in fact preceded him, so these same notions and the insights that Malcolm added to them continued to impact the movement after his death because Malcolm had disciples who attempted to put his model of struggle into practice. Malcolm X bequeathed a legacy to the generation of the '90s. To get at that legacy, however, one must follow the impact of Malcolm in all its mutations through a movement in transition. Malcolm X was a product of social forces which transcended his lifetime. Our task in these concluding chapters is to trace the ideological, organizational, and leadership impact that Malcolm X had after his assassination. By struggling to understand Malcolm and his legacy, many important elements of the present will become much clearer.

Malcolm's Critique of Nonviolence

Malcolm X was an outstanding thinker in the Civil Rights movement. The "collected words" of Malcolm X, appearing in print in 1965 as *Malcolm X Speaks,*[2] represented the domestic equivalent of Frantz Fanon's *Wretched of the Earth.*[3] Malcolm X was like a "John the Baptist" preparing the way for Fanon's book, which became a classic among movement youth and radical intellectuals. It was the multiple impact of Malcolm X and Frantz Fanon which many movement activists feel freed them from the *cul-de-sac* in which the nonviolence strategies of the established Civil Rights organizations had imprisoned them, during a decade of rising violence, White backlash and official repression. Malcolm X's critique of integrationist ideology and Civil Rights leadership was the first effective challenge to the monopoly those forces had over intellectual discourse in the Black community. Malcolm X exposed the hypocrisy behind the philosophy of nonviolence as an aspect of false consciousness. In the "etiquette of race relations," the condition of the oppressed was ameliorated, if at all, through entreaty and supplication and only by the dominant class and at its pace. Because of Malcolm, nonviolence never again exacted the allegiance which it previously had among movement activists. The effectiveness of his critique forced more creative thinking throughout the African American community and prodded the established Civil Rights leadership to rethink its most cherished precepts and acknowledge its responsibility to respond to the agenda of urban street forces.

Malcolm X Identifies a New Social Force

Malcolm's ideological orientation was taken up by new organizations in the Black community after his death. The Black Panther Party of Huey P. Newton and Bobby Seale, which originated in Oakland California's Merritt Junior College in 1966, adopted Malcolm's recognition of street youth as a revolutionary social force. In a similar but more explicitly Marxist-Leninist vein, the African American working-class intellectual James Boggs developed an American communist vanguard party concept based on the leadership of Black street youth.[4] The focus on street youth impacted SNCC in its Black Power period, and the emerging Black Student movement.

Malcolm and the Black Student Movement

Malcolm at the end of his life recognized a potential for change in youth and students that he felt was largely absent from other segments of the population. He certainly felt that if White people were ever going to change, it would first be seen in students. Interestingly, those very campuses where Malcolm X sensed an activist potential in White students experienced shortly after his death a significant increase in the enrollment of Black youth. Many of these new Black college students were ghetto youth, impacted by Malcolm's example and looking to achieve an education relevant to Black liberation. By 1967–68, on previously all-White northern and southern campuses, a Black Student movement was born, consciously identified with the thought of Malcolm X. SNCC and the Black Panthers tried with limited success to organize this new student force, but it was able to maintain an independent existence within the Black Power movement. This Black Student movement was consciously nationalist, anti-Vietnam War and anti-imperialist. It struggled successfully for an organized and institutionalized Black presence on U.S. campuses. The Black Student movement's legacy, achieved through building takeovers and disruptions, is Black student unions and Black Studies programs at many campuses.[5]

In the student campus takeover of 1968, the Students Afro-American Society at Columbia University renamed the college administration building Nat Turner Hall of Malcolm X Liberation University.[6] When students at Duke University and other North Carolina Colleges established an independent, all-Black, Pan-African educational institution in 1970, they named it Malcolm X Liberation University. This same motion created the Student Organization for Black Unity (SOBU), a group which later expanded its conception and metamorphosed into the Youth Organization for Black Unity (YOBO), in order to unite college-educated Black youth and the ghetto-based street youth.[7]

Malcolm X and Black Power

In his "ballot or bullet" analogy, Malcolm suggested that the Civil Rights movement should test the limits of electoral reform as a method for empowering Black people. Malcolm's debates with militants of the Student Non-Violent Coordinating Committee, especially its Non-violent Action Group (NAG) contingent, sharpened their appreciation of the "ballot or bullet" alternative in the quest for Black electoral power.[8] Between 1964 and 1967 SNCC tried to test the "ballot or bullet" approach in their political organizing in Mississippi and Alabama.

Black Power became the orientation of the latter half of the '60s decade because Malcolm X struggled uncompromisingly to restore the African American nationalist tradition. Without Malcolm's ideological intervention the slogan "Black Power" would not have emerged as quickly nor would it have been so rapidly taken up by so many.

Black Power and Pan-Africanism

Although he did not create the ideology of Pan-Africanism, Malcolm X struggled to popularize it in the last months before his murder. He informed his constituency of its rich tradition, one with a considerable literature and adherents in the United States and abroad. During the latter 1960s and early 1970s, activist organizations at the local and national levels could not maintain their legitimacy without addressing a significant portion of their program to Africa-support work. The support of African liberation movements through rallies, pickets, clothing drives, and fundraisers became a standard fixture of militant Black organizations. The pursuit of Pan-Africanism reached its highest level with the creation of the Pan-African Skills Project, the Congress of Afrikan People, Malcolm X Liberation University, and the African Liberation Support Committee. The militants associated with all of these organizations were self-defined disciples of Malcolm X.

After the 1965 Watts riots and the appearance of the Black Power slogan on the 1966 Meredith March Through Mississippi, King was locked in an extensive debate with the ghost of Malcolm X. Author James Cone used the two analogies of life in the United States for Black people that dominate the prose of Dr. King and Malcolm X respectively: the dream and the nightmare.[9] Through Malcolm X, King started to learn much more of the nightmare of the United States for ghettoized Blacks.[10] King's ideological evolution, at the prodding of Malcolm X, can be illustrated by his position on the Vietnam War, his growing engagement with the problems of northern urban ghettos, and his changing perceptions of the role of the federal government. Malcolm's anti-war position was also later taken up by SNCC.

Malcolm's Influence on SNCC

Without the revolutionary nationalism and Pan-African internationalism of Malcolm X, the Student Non-Violent Coordinating Committee's White Paper on Black Power, its White Paper on the Vietnam War, and its subsequent activism in opposition to that war and U.S. imperialism generally would not have occurred when it did. James Forman, former executive secretary of SNCC, explained Malcolm's influence this way:

> I read *Malcolm X Speaks* carefully. His criticism of the term "civil rights," and his advocacy of "human rights" in its place, led me to formulate a resolution that was adopted at the June 1967 staff meeting of SNCC.
> This resolution declared that SNCC considered itself to be a human rights organization working for the liberation not only of Black people in the United States but of all oppressed peoples, especially those in Africa, Asia, and Latin America.[11]

A long debate ensued between SNCC's cadre and Dr. King regarding the movement taking a public anti-war stance. By 1966–67 SNCC's anti-war stance represented a vanguard position both in the Civil Rights movement and in the developing student-led anti-war movement. Given King's perception as an internationally recognized human rights leader, his silence on the war was embarrassing and by the spring of 1967 he unequivocally joined the Anti-War Movement.[12] From that time until his death, Dr. King's nonviolent antiwar activism was dogged by the antiwar "by any means necessary" militancy of SNCC. The militant "by any means necessary" stance of SNCC's members first exploded in their physical disruption of the Atlanta Draft Board and their refusal to report for induction. This miltancy continued at the massive April 12, 1967 antiwar march and rally in New York City when SNCC militants and Stokely Carmichael led a Harlem contingent through Times Square and into physical conflict with pro-war activists. In the winter of 1968, SNCC formed the National Black Anti-War and Anti-Draft Union (NBAWADU). Some SNCC members went to jail rather than serve in the Vietnam War.

Was King Getting Closer to Malcolm?

King's experience with the Chicago Open Housing Campaign in the Winter and Spring of 1966, following his experiences of the devastation in Watts in August of 1965, allowed him for the first time to experience the anger, frustration and alienation of a Black ghetto dweller. Dr. King realized that he had not previously spoken to this alienation as Malcolm X had. He then understood how such alienation could lead to violent explosiveness in this new social force. The future of his nonviolent movement and his "dream" depended on harnessing this urban street force. At his death, King was searching for a militant but nonviolent tactic which could stand as an alternative to violent social disruption. In July 1966, King hinted at that tactic in Chicago; he said:

> We'll use something that avoids violence, but becomes militant and extreme enough to disrupt the flow of the city. I know it will be rough on them when they have to get 200 people off the Dan Ryan [expressway], but the only thing I can tell them is , which do you prefer, this or a riot.[13]

The tactic that Dr. King formulated was the "Poor People's Campaign," a massive nonviolent demonstration in Washington, D.C. If necessary, this campaign would disrupt governmental power so that business as usual could not take place. This tactic was a militant version of the August 1963 March on Washington, a demonstration that Malcolm X scathingly criticized as a sellout. In April 1964, Malcolm X called for a March on Washington to realize the potential he felt was squandered in the 1963 effort. He described his march in the following terms:

> They haven't seen anything like the March we're going to have. Next time we won't take our white friends, we won't take signs already painted and we won't buy round trip tickets.[14]

With the exception of interracial participation, this seems a strikingly similar prescription to Dr. King's "Poor People's Campaign."

The ideological orientations of Dr. King and Malcolm X did not converge. King remained committed to reform as the exclusive tactic of the movement. He sought to force the U.S. government to respond to the needs of his constituency. Malcolm X's presence, in life and in death, encouraged King's nonviolent movement to take a more strident and militant nonviolent stance, openly acknowledging its deficiencies in confronting the need for a cultural "revolution" in the psyche of Black people. King recognized that the government had ceased to be an ally in the struggle against *de facto* racism. King never abandoned his commitment to nonviolence or to the ultimate goal of an interracial society.

Malcolm X and Black Liberation Theology

Beyond the question of tactics and strategy in the Civil Rights movement, Malcolm X's critique of Civil Rights leadership represented a profound indictment of Christianity and the Black church. While King criticized church inaction from within, Malcolm's criticism of Black Christian leadership forced a young generation of ministers and lay people to question what had become of the prophetic role of the Black church.[15] Gayraud Wilmore, in his book *Black Religion and Black Radicalism* reinforces this observation in saying that "since the Muslims, Black churchgoers have measured what their preachers say about the Black condition in the U.S. by what they recognize as the painful truth from the late Malcolm X and other Muslim ministers."[16] This new generation of Black theologians, of whom James Cone was in the vanguard, accepted that the essence of Malcolm's critique was valid. They argued for a new point of departure in the pursuit of the prophetic role of the Black church as a beacon toward liberation in this world as well as the next. Black liberation theology emerged out of their efforts.

Wilmore positioned Malcolm X in the center of the break with the accommodationist variety of Christianity.

> The legacy of Malcolm X belongs to secularists and religionists alike, for during his brief lifetime Malcolm brought Black religion and Black politics together for the spiritual edification and political empowerment of Black people. Although he repudiated Christianity, his prophetic ministry as a Black Muslim contributed to the further development of that indigenous [sic] Black religion which was never exclusively Christian in the historic sense. And what he stood for as an exponent of that ghettoized Black religion—namely justice and liberation—was the continuation of a great tradition of nativistic-messianic religion in the United States, Africa and the Caribbean. Whatever else Black Christianity may be it is also a part of the tradition he shared, and it is precisely for this reason that many Black churchmen are saying today, "The God who spoke by the prophets

and in the fullness of time by his Son, *now in this time, speaks to us through Brother Malcolm*(emphasis in original).[17]

Wilmore's work demonstrated that a source of revolutionary nationalism was the religious radicalism of the Black church. He recognized Malcolm's contribution toward liberating the church from the paradigm of White Christianity and returning it to its founding tradition. In this regard, Malcolm X's impact was truly Pan-African. Rev. Alan Boesak, in both of his major works on the theology of liberation and the role of the church in the struggle against apartheid, identified a role for Malcolm X in the development of a theology of opposition to apartheid in South Africa.[18] Malcolm X had an equivalent impact on the secular Black Consciousness movement among South African students.[19]

Malcolm's impact on religion extended to his own Islamic orientation as well. His critique of Elijah Muhammad and his affirmation of orthodox Sunni Islam were both affected by his commitment to believe only in a religion that would help him to fight back against oppression. He believed Islam to be that religion, not Christianity. From Mecca he wrote:

> The Koran compels all people who accept the Islam religion to take a firm stand on the side of anyone whose human rights are being violated, no matter what the religious persuasion of the victims may be.[20]

However, the relevance of Islam to the Black Liberation struggle was not self-evident, and Malcolm was able only to touch on the question while he was alive. His successors in this country continue to strive to reconcile Islam with the freedom struggle of Black people. In that tradition Yusuf Kly of the Montreal chapter of the OAAU attempted to show the reflection of Malcolm's secular thought in the theology of Sunni Islam.[21] We can find a connection between Malcolm X and the fundamentalism of the Shiite revolution in Iran, which honored the memory of Malcolm X as an Islamic hero with a postage stamp issue.

Putting Revolution on the Agenda

Malcolm X took the concept of an African American revolution beyond rhetorical flourish. After Malcolm X, revolution was a serious topic of discussion and planning within the Black freedom movement. The notion that Black revolution in the United States was impossible was an important part of the ideological hegemony exerted by the Anglo-Saxon-dominated elite in the United States.

Starting with Du Bois, Garvey, and the Harlem Renaissance, the notion that White civilization had entered a period of crisis and decline was introduced to African Americans. Malcolm X, both inside of and later independent of the NOI, projected this analysis to the center stage of the Civil Rights movement. He argued that revolution became a crucial task because African Americans could no longer delude themselves into believing that White people could be persuaded to "save" Black people. With Malcolm X, the movement took up the proposition that there was no solution to the race problem within a Eurocentric civilization. Consequently, the main task for African Americans, Africans, and those in the Third World was to formulate an alternative to the Eurocentric worldview.

Cultural Nationalism

Two related approaches to African American nationalism used Malcolm's "decline of White world supremacy" as a point of departure. These approaches emphasized African American cultural nationalism and are well represented in the works of Maulana Ron Karenga and Imamu Imiri Baraka (LeRoi Jones).[22]

The cultural nationalists identified the essence of Black oppression in the dependence of African Americans on a European or Western paradigm of cultural values. Such dependence produced and reproduced the self-hatred which was a characteristic feature of the Black psyche and one essential to facilitating Black oppression.

By 1970, Karenga's value system, the *Nguzo Saba*, or Seven Principles, had become the frame of reference for the largest formation of cultural nationalists, Imiri Baraka's Congress of Afrikan People.

Using the African language Kiswahili, Karenga set out to establish a value system which constituted the basis for unity among all Black people regardless of their location. The seven principles of his Black value system were: *umoja* (unity), *kujichagulia* (self-determination), *ujima* (collective work and responsibility), *ujamaa* (cooperative economics), *nia* (purpose), *kuumba* (creativity), and *imani* (faith). In several instances, Karenga took great liberties in the English meanings he assigned to these Swahili words. In addition, the major ritual embodying these values, Kwanzaa, was a creation of Karenga which had no explicit equivalent in any African society. What was important, however, was that the adoption of this value system, the cultural nationalists felt, would prevent the kind of psychological contamination which was at the root of Black subservience to White society.

The Land Question and the Class Question

In addition to this notion of a "cultural revolution," Malcolm's disciples developed several different understandings of his legacy on the question of Black revolution in the United States. These different understandings reflected different stages in Malcolm X's own understanding of that concept. Malcolm's concern, as that of later nationalists, was how to establish an independent national existence for African Americans. The NOI and some nationalists believed that physical separation from Whites through emigration represented the best solution to the race problem. Malcolm X initially subscribed to this position, but by the latter part of 1963 and the early part of 1964, he arrived at the position that only a revolutionary struggle would allow for such a solution. As we saw in Chapter Four, Malcolm X argued that nationalists were revolutionaries, and the essence of the revolutionary struggle was the struggle for land. The African American revolution, then, was a struggle to free the national territory of African Americans from White domination. But where was this national territory? Malcolm X himself never specified its location beyond a vague reference to several states and Africa. In the last eleven months of his life, Malcolm was less and less concerned with such a specification.

Malcolm's disciples, especially those in the Detroit area like attorney Milton Henry, seized on Malcolm's statements about the question of land and revolution made in his two speeches "Message to the Grassroots" and "Ballot or the Bullet." Borrowing from the Communist Party (CPUSA) Black Belt Nation thesis but also tapping into indigenous sources that went back to the 19th-century movements of Pap Singleton and McCabe, they had formulated the concept of the Republic of New Africa in 1968 and gave it an organizational existence complete with a shadow government, they described their position in the following terms:

> In the Black Belt, running through the Five States that the Republic claims as the National Territory of the Black Nation (Louisiana, Mississippi, Alabama, Georgia, and South Carolina), we have met all the criteria for land possession required of us by international practice, international law. We have incidentally met these tests too in cities of the North...we give up our claims to these cities as

national territory...in exchange for the five states of the Deep South.[23]

Their arguments followed Malcolm not only in relation to the land but to reparations and human rights under international law. The area of the United States where Black people suffered exploitation under slavery became the focus of the demand for independent land and compensation. This demand for self-determination, land, and reparations was seen as in accord with the human rights and decolonization provisions of international law. Spokespersons for the Republic of New Africa reflected Malcolm in their argument that the provision for the emancipation of African American slaves did not fulfill the dictates of international law. Only when those who were formerly oppressed have the option of choosing through a plebiscite their future political arrangements are those provisions met.[24]

Important aspects of this approach were also taken up by the Black Panther Party in its Ten-Point Program. The tenth point was a demand for "land, bread, housing, education, clothing, justice, and peace." The Party argued:

> This racist government has robbed us [Black people] and now we are demanding the overdue debt of forty acres and two mules...We will accept payment in currency which will be distributed to our many communities.[25]

The Panthers called for an internationally supervised plebescite in the Black community to determine whether Black people wanted to remain part of the United States or separate from it. From Malcolm this branch of nationalism took the notion of self-determination through land, reparations, and internationally supervised justice. The influence of Malcolm X was clearly seen in an alternative formulation on the question of revolution and land. Stokely Carmichael's All African Peoples Revolutionary Party (AAPRP) believed, as did Malcolm X, that the basis for Black revolution could not be located solely within the United States. Carmichael seconded Malcolm's argument when he said that "In the final analysis all revolutions are based on land." He continued, arguing the case for a revolutionary base area in Africa:

> The best place, it seems to me, and the quickest place that we can obtain land is Africa. I am not denying that we might seek land in the United States...but I do not see it clearly in my mind at this time.

We need land and we need land immediately, and we must go to the quickest place for it...[26]

Carmichael and the branch of Pan-Africanism that he represented went much further than Malcolm ever did regarding the relationship of African emancipation to African American freedom. These Pan-Africanists argued that the liberation and unification of Africa under "scientific socialism" would create such a powerful Black political unit in the world that the liberation of the African American would inevitably follow. This position, most strongly articulated by Carmichael as his interpretation of the late Ghanaian prime minister and Pan-Africanist Kwame Nkrumah, implied the almost automatic resolution of racial conflict in the United States as a consequence of the emergence of a united Africa. Consequently, African Americans could best advance their liberation by devoting their energies to facilitating the creation of a base area in Africa from which the unification effort for the continent would be directed. Carmichael did not advance a concrete program of action in the United States for improving Black conditions other than to support the work of continental liberation and general "anti-imperialism."

As opposed to those tendencies which built upon Malcolm's statements on revolution as a struggle for land-based self-determination or focused on Black revolution and African liberation, there appeared in the latter '60s a revolutionary African American nationalism rooted in industrial workers and street people. This new group thought that Black liberation required a fundamental and basic change in U.S. society. Organizationally, this revolutionary nationalism was best represented by the positions of the Revolutionary Action Movement (RAM), the Black Panther Party, and the League of Revolutionary Black Workers.[27] These organizations had direct links to the speeches and organizing efforts of Malcolm X in the spring of 1964, when he said to activists:

> You and I in America are not faced with a segregationist conspiracy, we're faced with a government conspiracy...it is the government itself, the government of America, that is responsible for the oppression and exploitation and degradation of Black people in this country...This government has failed the Negro.[28]

Moreover, Malcolm X, by the end of 1964, saw the U.S. government as part of a Western coalition of powers with a colonial and racist heritage. In Rochester, New York, less than a week before his death, Malcolm X spoke to this perspective:

The three major allies, the United States, Britain, and France have a problem today that is a common problem. But you and I are never given enough information to realize that they have a common problem. And that common problem is the new mood that is reflected in the overall division of the Black people within continental France, within the same sphere of England, and also here in the United States...this mood has been changing to the same degree that the mood of the African continent has been changing...the emergence of African nations into independence...has absolutely affected the mood of the Black people in the Western Hemisphere. So much so that when they migrate to England, they pose a problem for the English. And when they migrate to France, they pose a problem for the French...this same mood is reflected in the Black man in the States...[29]

The Revolutionary Action Movement (RAM)

RAM defined revolutionary nationalism as a rising of the darker races of the world against the racism and colonialism characteristic of modern history. The Black Liberation struggle was an integral part of that world revolutionary process. RAM, the earliest and perhaps foremost advocate of urban guerrilla warfare in the Black Liberation movement, claimed both Malcolm X and Robert Williams as its mentors.[30]

RAM was also the first Black organization of the 1960s to attempt a synthesis of the various strains of Marxism with traditional themes in African American nationalism. [31] RAM took Malcolm X's orientation to the socialism of the Pan-Africanists like Nkrumah and Sekou Toure and attempted to redefine it in relation to both the African American experience and that of more orthodox communism. RAM was the first of many organizations in the Black Liberation movement to attempt to construct a revolutionary nationalism on the basis of a synthesis of the thought of Malcolm X, Marx and Lenin and Mao Tse Tung.

James Boggs and the Black Vanguard Party

RAM's intellectual quest for the proper organizational form to lead Black revolution was taken up in the mid-60s by the late working-class Black intellectual James Boggs. As noted above, Boggs saw the center of revolutionary energy in the United States as located in Black street youth. He felt that this energy had to be captured in a Leninist vanguard party with a core cadre concentrating on "paying special attention to the development of the political consciousness and revolutionary dedication of

Black street youth." Malcolm's successors struggled with the idea of how to harness this social force first identified by Malcolm to a revolutionary organization and program.

The Black Panthers

The Black Panther Party, founded in 1966 in Oakland, California, saw itself as the organizing vehicle for a revolutionary upsurge of the people. It openly avowed its legacy to Malcolm,[32] as can be seen in the text of the following Panther leaflet:

> Huey Newton [Panther Party chairman] is a child of Malcolm X. Malcolm said that we will get our freedom by any means necessary, and 20,000,000 Black people heard his voice and concur in his message. 20,000,000 Black people heard Malcolm's message and that same 20,000,000 felt exactly the same way about it as Huey Newton feels.[33]

The essence of the people, according to the Panthers, were the urban ghetto inhabitants and their most revolutionary offspring, the street youth of the ghetto. The Panthers identified the ghetto as U.S. society's most revolutionary force. They attempted to shape this grouping into a revolutionary force, but the character of their party was marked by a lack of discipline and romanticism characteristic of its *lumpen* members.

The League of Revolutionary Black Workers

By the latter '60s, changes in the workforce found some of the very street people identified by Malcolm X and Boggs at the center of assembly lines in Detroit and other major U.S. cities. On the basis of this structural shift in the workforce, Black activists and intellectuals in the Detroit area joined the debate initiated by RAM and carried on by Boggs. They advanced the argument that Black production workers constituted the vanguard of the U.S. working class and were the revolutionary vanguard in the Black Liberation struggle. In 1968 this ideological orientation emerged in organizational form as the League of Revolutionary Black Workers. The league was centered in the automobile industry and dedicated to "waging a relentless struggle against racism, capitalism, and imperialism." It saw itself not only in a domestic context but as an integral part of a world revolutionary process, playing "a major revolutionary role in the liberation of oppressed people in the world."[34]

180

The ties between Malcolm X and the League were significant. Malcolm X had come from the Detroit area and, after leaving prison in 1952, he worked on the assembly line at the Garwood Truck Factory.[35] He first fished as a neophyte NOI minister among assembly line workers in Detroit. Some of his most important speeches from his Black nationalist period were given in Detroit. The league was the second revolutionary tendency originating in Detroit with definite links to Malcolm X. The other was the Republic of New Africa. Both emerged at about the same time and reflected different aspects of Malcolm's thought.

Malcolm, Marxism, and Black Liberation

The Black Panther Party popularized aspects of marxism among Black students and youth with its advocacy of slogans that appeared in Mao Tse Tung's *Quotations of Chairman Mao Tse-Tung (The Little Red Book)*.[36] Some Black Nationalists adopted Mao because he was not European, and led a non-white people. Mao's works represented an acceptable form of Marxism over and against the "Black and White unite and fight" integrationism of the CPUSA. Mao did not oppose African American nationalism.

Malcolm X was very much impressed by the Chinese Revolution, and the Chinese communists were very much taken with Malcolm X. Malcolm X in his speeches often used the example of the Chinese Revolution as one to be emulated by Afro-Americans.[37] Malcolm prodded the Chinese Communist Party to take a strong position on the African American freedom struggle. During the height of the Black Power period, Mao Tse-Tung issued his second acknowledgement of the African American freedom struggle and said:

> The Afro-American struggle is not only a struggle waged by the exploited and oppressed Black people for freedom and emancipation, it is also a new clarion call to all the exploited and oppressed people of the United States to fight against the barbarous rule of the monopoly capitalist class. It is a tremendous support and inspiration to the struggle of the people throughout the world against U.S. imperialism and to the struggle of the Vietnamese people against U.S. imperialism. On behalf of the Chinese people, I hereby express resolute support for the just struggle of the Black people of the United States.[38]

By 1970, Marxism had become a significant ideological stream in the Black Liberation movement. Several previous streams of left thought—RAM, Boggs and the League of Revolutionary Black Workers, and the Panthers—coalesced with Black student intellectuals to thrust Marxism into the Black Liberation movement. One commentator rightly noted that "Marxists came from the factory or from the campus, but both grew out of the militant Black nationalist revolt of the 1960s."[39]

The Black Workers Congress (BWC) was the first organization of the 1970s to attempt to direct the nationalism of Black workers and street youth in a marxist direction. Formed by former SNCC activists like James Forman (whose intellectual debt to Malcolm has been previously cited) and members of the League of Revolutionary Black Workers, the BWC argued that the Black Liberation movement could emancipate Black people only through a revolutionary union "with the entire U.S. working class...through proletarian revolution." This union was to be part of an international anti-imperialist union of the world's peoples. BWC's impact was largely ideological rather than organizational, as it split into several formations and implemented no significant organizational program. Its adherents, however, were to be found later in all of the important African American progressive organizations of the 1970s.

The OAAU Model after Malcolm

The organizational model represented by the OAAU continued to impact on subsequent movement organizations in the Black Power period and beyond. Malcolm's idea of a Black Nationalist conference was pursued after his death with the convening in 1967 of the National Black Power conference in Newark, New Jersey. A second Black Power Conference was convened in Philadelphia in the following year. The Black united front reached another milestone with the Atlanta convention of 1970, which led directly to the creation of the Congress of Afrikan People (CAP). In this convention the theme "It's Nation Time!" was taken up. Two years before, the same sentiment had created the Republic of New Afrika complete with a government in exile.

In 1972, a structure was actually put in place to validate real grassroots leadership and authorize organizational representatives to the National Black Political Convention. Convened in Gary, Indiana in 1972, the delegates articulated their assessment of the situation in words clearly borrowed from Malcolm's analysis of U.S. society·

> A Black political convention, indeed all truly Black politics, must begin from this truth: The U.S. system does not work for the masses of our people, and it cannot be made to work without radical fundamental change...[The United States is] a society built on the

twin foundations of white racism and white capitalism...the only real choice for us is whether or not we will live by the truth we know, whether we will move to organize independently, move to struggle for fundamental transformation, for the creation of a new direction, towards concern for the life and meaning of Man.[40]

Out of the National Black Political Convention was formed the National Black Political Assembly. Although there was a follow-up convention in Little Rock, Arkansas, the promise of the National Black Political Assembly was not realized.

It is clear that a significant, if not majority, segment of the movement subscribed to ideas associated with Malcolm's leadership. These ideas remained at the center of the programs of the Black Liberation wing of the movement until its repression and remain dear to the remnants of that movement. As we have seen in Chapter One, those remnants were instrumental in bringing Malcolm's words and example to the generation of youth who grew to maturity in the 1980s and the beginning of the 1990s.

What happened when his adherents tried to put his model of Black liberation into practice? What successes did they achieve? What mistakes did they make? What consequences have ensued from these successes and errors? Chapter Eight confronts the practicality of Malcolm's ideas and the radical Pan-Africanist tradition from which they emerged.

8

The
Organizational
Legacy
of the
OAAU

Introduction

Many of the commentators on the significance of Malcolm X stand outside of or even against the struggle of Black people today. There are those who now extol Malcolm who were very much alive and active in the latter '60s and early '70s when his ideas were embodied in the Black Power and Black Liberation movements. Many of these people fought against everything Malcolm stood for. Today some of these same people expropriate the aura of Malcolm to shield from public view their lack of a viable program for Black liberation in the United States. First, because of the repression of the Black Liberation Movement (BLM) in the 1970s and 1980s, these imposters have been able to seize the initiative from Malcolm's true discipline and define the politics of the Black community to suit their own opportunism. This point is made by Adolph Reid.[1] Second, the history of the movement from Civil Rights to the BLM has scarcely been written, let alone told. Unaware of the role that these same political opportunists played in the destruction of the BLM, the younger generation is unable to see the hypocrisy in their posturing as followers of Malcolm X.

A Black ex-political prisoner, Dhoruba Bin Wahad, says that those who now embrace Nelson Mandela and Malcolm X consistently remain silent about the scores of African American political prisoners in jails today. They refuse to see, he argues, that had Malcolm X lived he might very well have become a political prisoner. Those Black political prisoners now behind bars are there either because they faithfully tried to put Malcolm's ideas into action or were victimized by Cointelpro as Malcolm was. Today, Black electoral political leadership, with few exceptions, refuses to make the release of Black political prisoners a part of its agenda. In addition, this same group reduces Pan-Africanism to an unholy conspiracy among the African American bourgeoisie and the most retrograde political leadership and comprador bourgeoisie in Africa, to fleece the continent of its wealth.[2]

Bourgeois Opportunism from Right and Left

Malcolm X today is being exploited by a new type of African American. Amiri Baraka exposed these opportunists in a new essay when he asserted:

> There is even a sector of the newer generation of this backward Negro petty bourgeoisie that has never even lived with Black people,

never lived in the ghetto. Children of Negroes the anti-us apartheid movement of the '50s and '60s allowed to move to the suburbs and be the token. Black people would not move forward, only a small sector of a class as "role models." But now there are more Negroes for whom "Black culture" is abstract or theoretical or a *style*.[3]

Both of these previously cited segments of the Black bourgeoisie, the political opportunists and entrepreneurs and the "buppy voyeurs," have

> ...coopted the people's movement. Baraka argued that they "only 'represent' Black people but are not organically or ideologically connected to the people, they do not *actually* have power. So they become expressions of betrayal, collaboration, cooptation, of the need for actual power, democracy, and self-determination"(emphasis in the original).[4]

Getting the Story Straight

The legacy of Malcolm X exists in the organizational activities of the BLM of the late '60s and early '70s. What happened to Malcolm's legacy can be better understood if we examine the growth and development of the present class of African American bourgeois leadership. We must situate leadership in relation to their position and activities while there was still a major effort to establish the BLM on the radical principles articulated by Malcolm X. Black radicals made serious mistakes which also obscured Malcolm's legacy. The root of these mistakes was in a creeping petty bourgeois approach to political work. In both cases, the problem has very much to do with the growing class differentiation in the Black community. This trend was accelerated in the 1970s due to two deep recessions, which were accompanied by urban fiscal crises and profound economic polarization inside Black America. This polarization was but the sociological reflection of the growing crisis in U.S. capitalism and the impact of permanent structural changes in the U.S. economy. By the 1980s, this crisis was reflected politically in the rise of Reaganism and the political impotence of Black bourgeois political leadership. This impotence was characterized by the emergence of a politics of "deracialization," which in certain forms liquidated the national character and agenda of African Americans.

Leadership among the remnants of the BLM must also come in for its share of responsibility for the deplorable state of affairs. Instead of doing its own independent analysis based on the African American experience, this leadership uncritically attempted to apply to the Black experience the "line" of one or the other socialist state. This "tailing behind" the inappropriate "line" of the Chinese, the Albanians, the Soviets, etc. led to sectarian squabbles, a lack of clear and creative thinking, disunity and demoralization. These errors are typically made by middle-class intellectuals. This is but another fact indicating the growing significance of class in the black community.

SNCC Pursues the "Ballot or the Bullet"

Malcolm's method, the "ballot or bullet" approach, was assumed by SNCC in two important electoral experiments in the period 1964–67. The first of these was the Mississippi Freedom Democratic Party (MFDP). This was a satellite party which, working within the national Democratic Party structure, tried to reform the party's southern Dixiecrat wing. Its strategy was to demonstrate that local integrated MFDP party structures were both more democratically constituted and loyal to the national slate of candidates and the national party platform than the regular Democratic organization. On this basis it launched challenges to the credentials and seating of southern racists in the Democratic Party's national convention and in the Congress.[5]

The MFDP experiment was not only a challenge to the ability of the Democratic Party to reform itself, but also a challenge to the liberal conception of social change and the effectiveness of interracial coalitions of poor Blacks and liberal Whites. The MFDP and other satellite party experiments were not notably successful. The MFDP had not used Malcolm's provisions against cooptation, party independence, and accountability only to the Black masses. It had, however, a direct link to Malcolm X through some of its leaders, including Mrs. Fannie Lou Hamer.

The failure of the MFDP led SNCC to attempt a more perfect approximation of Malcolm X's independent politics. This second experiment was the Lowndes County Freedom Organization (LCFO), whose emblem was the black panther.[6] This political party was independent of the Democratic and Republican parties. It sought to build grassroots Black political power without the need for White cooperation. In a Black Belt county where Blacks were the numerical majority but had been disenfranchised since the end of Reconstruction, the LCFO specifically endorsed self-defense and armed its organizers and militants against racist nightriders and physical intimidation. Through Black electoral power it aspired to take control of governmental and economic power in the county. The LCFO was to be the model for grassroots Black empowerment throughout the Black Belt. In its initial bid, LCFO failed. Nevertheless, the Black Panther Party idea found a lasting position in the movement, and its model of Black empowerment is clearly reflected in several national and local organizations of the Black Power period, most notably the Black Panther Party itself and the Republic of New Afrika. Unfortunately, SNCC, in the Black Power period, made basic mistakes in its treatment of women. During the Lowndes County, Alabama mobilization that led to the creation of the Lowndes County Freedom Organization party, male-chauvinist behavior was very divisive within SNCC. This error became a major factor contributing to the disintegration of this organization.

Cultural Nationalists and Male Chauvinism

The cultural nationalism of United Slaves (US), created by Maulana Karenga and the Congress of Afrikan People (CAP) was also a significant source of male chauvinist attitudes. Cultural nationalists postulated that a major part of the oppression of Black people was rooted in the inappropriate position that Black women enjoyed over Black men in the United States. They argued that the traditional position of women in African society was in the domestic area and in those functions related to the upbringing of children. Women were to be protected by Black men but were not to usurp the decisionmaking and leadership prerogatives of Black men. Extreme forms of this posturing were reflected in the institution in some nationalist organizations of polygamy and forms of public behavior that signified the superiority of Black males over Black women. The stance of the cultural nationalists regarding the role of women had direct links to the position of the NOI on that question.

One of the very important organizational offshoots keyed to the question of women's proper role in the Afro-American struggle was the Third World Women's Alliance (TWWA). TWWA was initiated by SNCC's Fran Beal in 1969 as a SNCC project. It soon outgrew the declining organization. TWWA explored the crucial role that women of color played in the major social movements of the '60s in the United States and in the major liberation movements of the post-World War II period. It examined the relationship between Black liberation, the women's liberation movement, and socialist revolution. As such, it represented a center of critical analysis of the practices of existing Civil Rights and Black Power organizations on the question of male chauvinism. Not limited to questions about male chauvinism, TWWA took positions and engaged in actions on all of the domestic and international issues that were thrown up by the popular struggles of the late 60s and early '70s. More than most organizations of the period, TWWA achieved a decent working relationship between different ethnic groups within the overall rubric of the "Third World."[7]

Spreading the OAAU Model

While SNCC was acting on Malcolm's grassroots empowerment agenda in the Black Belt, grassroots community organizations of nationalist and "Black Power" persuasion were springing up all over the country. There was a tremendous expansion in the number and location of formal movement organizations created in response to a flood of local issues. Even with continued organizational consensus, the "Big Five" Civil Rights organizations were in no position to expand quickly enough to absorb these new organizations. Grassroots organizations succeeded in giving an institutionalized activist role to previously unorganized street forces. Their relatively small size and lack of authoritarian structures and bureaucratic methods were suited to the type and characteristics of their leadership. These grassroots organizations were establishing the kind of leadership and decisionmaking structures that Malcolm X had envisioned for the OAAU and that SNCC had experimented with in the rural South.

Emergence of the "Organic Intellectual"

These new organizational structures based on an OAAU/SNCC model of participatory democracy and grassroots activism were the organizational vehicle, for the emergence of the "organic intellectual" within the street forces. George Lipsitz cited Antonio Gramsci in his study of a grassroots activist of this period, Ivory Perry.[8] Perry was the kind of grassroots leadership the OAAU was trying to energize. Lipsitz says:

> Gramsci had a term for trouble makers like Ivory Perry. He called them "organic intellectuals," and his concept captures the essence of Perry's activism. In Gramsci's view, organic intellectuals direct the ideas and aspirations of their class, even though they hold no formal status or employment as "intellectuals." Social action constitutes the indispensable core of their activity. Organic intellectuals not only analyze and interpret the world; they originate and circulate their ideas through social contestation. As Gramsci explained it: The

mode of being of the new intellectual can no longer consist in eloquence, which is an exterior and momentary mover of feelings and passions, but in active participation in practical life, as constructor, organizer, "permanent persuader" and not just simple orator...[9]

Toward the United Front

This organizational explosion gained its strength and staying power from a combination of a street constituency, small size, direct participatory democracy, political education through the OAAU Liberation School model, and leadership from "organic intellectuals." Malcolm X was its model and legitimizer. Three major organizational attempts were made to create a united front. On balance each attempt represented the dominance of a distinct branch of African American nationalism. All had in common the shared legacy of a particular aspect of Malcolm X's thought.

Malcolm's idea of a Black nationalist conference was not put into effect until 1967 with the convening of the National Black Power conference in Newark, New Jersey. Coming close on the heels of the Newark rebellion, it had the characteristic crisis atmosphere that prompted the periodic gathering of Black activists in national conferences from as far back as the antebellum Black conventions. As with the second Black Power conference in Philadelphia in 1968, all manner of nationalists and even integrationists were present at these gatherings. The dominant theme was networking in pursuit of Black power. The slogan, "Black power," revolutionary in timbre, was more often than not reformist in content. Its militancy was rhetorical, its content reformist, and not always in the progressive sense of reform that Malcolm would have endorsed. It was not necessarily anti-capitalist since it often oriented itself to struggling to give Black people a bigger piece of the pie. The driving force of the Newark conference was an Episcopal priest who secured underwriting for the conference from the Revlon Corporation. SNCC had initiated Black Power to test the limits of reform. By the Black Power conferences, Black Power sounded more and more like conservative Black economic nationalism.

Another major attempt at establishing a Black united front was the Atlanta convention in 1970 that led to the creation of the CAP. This was the high point of action around the slogan "It's Nation Time!" By 1970, the political self-determination of the Republic of New Afrika of two years previous had been displaced in Atlanta by the culturally based notion of a national community whose unity was dependent upon adherence to a "traditional" African value system.

The National Black Political Convention of 1972, which led to the National Black Political Assembly later, moved away from the conception of independent Black politics associated with Malcolm X and gravitated toward Black officials who functioned solely within the context of Democratic Party electoral politics. Although there was a follow-up convention in Little Rock, Arkansas, the promise of the National Black Political Assembly was not realized.[10]

Whose Agenda?

In the pursuit of the Black united front, the movement had to confront the differential impact of its Civil Rights phase on the different classes in the Black community. Therefore, a second salient question that confronted the movement was how to create the common agenda of the united front. Efforts simply to agglomerate all of the constituent agendas either smoothed over essential disagreements or created an agenda which was unwieldy. As the process unfolded, choices had to be made and priorities assigned on the basis of which class or stratum in the Black community represented its center of gravity. The agenda of this class or stratum should enjoy priority status in the agenda of the united front. Unfortunately, a consensus on the question of priorities could not be reached. Today it is an even more complex question than thirty years ago, since the community is more economically skewed today, and polarization has occurred around the diverging life chances of the growing but small Black middle class and the burgeoning so-called Black underclass.

Leading the Black United Front

Those who ascribed to the ethnic-assimilationist model were heirs of the militant-assimilationist posture of the established Civil Rights leadership. They made their peace with Black Power by defining it as no more than the traditional strategy of European ethnic groups applied to the Black problem. Politically, bloc voting within the Democratic Party would increase Black elected representation in the South and in U.S. cities. The resources obtained in this fashion—patronage, influence, and the control of government contracts—would be, as for European immigrants, major sources of African American empowerment. Economically, the construction of civic-minded Black middle-class business persons would be the center of gravity around which Black community development would occur. In this way, the struggle shifted from the arena of protest to the electoral arena, from tactics appropriate to those frozen out of the polity to those who now had access to the polity. This represented an argument for extending leadership credentials to Black politicians and the Black middle class generally. The masses of Black people were to give up the protest option and concentrate on expanding their voting power so as to increase the number of Black insiders who would then seek resources on behalf of the masses. This tendency was responsible for greatly increasing the Black electorate and number of Black elected officials at all levels of government. It was responsible for the establishment of the Congressional Black Caucus, the Joint Center for Political Studies, and TransAfrica, the Washington-based African American lobby on African affairs. Almost all of the largest U.S. cities have experienced the election of a Black mayor, and there is a greatly expanded African American presence in the Democratic Party. The high point of achievement for this tendency was the presidential campaign of Jesse Jackson in 1988 and the election of Ron Brown as Democratic national chairperson.

Nationalist forces generally reflected two alternative responses to this thrust: revolutionary nationalism and cultural nationalism. Both responses were united in viewing the Black predicament as a form of domestic colonialism. Their position was that racism was not an aberration but inherent in the nature of U.S. society.

In the tradition of Malcolm X, revolutionary nationalists focused on the question of the achievement of self-determination for Black people. They saw this task as one of revolutionary dimensions which would involve the destruction of the U.S. system and its imperial manifestations abroad.

Cultural nationalists focused on the psychological damage done by racial oppression. They felt that the major impediment to Black liberation was the effect of cultural imperialism on the Black psyche. They followed Malcolm X in their desire to rehabilitate Black people spiritually by restoring to them a sense of their Africanness and the superiority of traditional African institutions and values.

These tendencies diverged on several important issues: on the question of the role of electoral politics, on the question of whether politics should be put in command of economics, on the question of culture, on the relationship of domestic and international events, and on the question of the role of violence and armed struggle in the liberation of Black people. Those forces which followed an ethnic-assimilation model placed greatest emphasis on electoral politics and eschewed a continuation of the protest tradition. Revolutionary nationalists were committed to an intensification of the protest tradition and its flowering into full-scale rebellion. In their framework, electoral politics was realistic only if independent of the major parties, with Black political representation accountable to the masses. Such an electoral politics was validated only to the extent that it increased the power of Black people in their aspirations to destroy the imperialist system.

Cultural nationalists questioned the effectiveness of electoral politics and tended to put economics in command of politics in their quest for autonomy. In this, they were followed by a segment of the militant integrationists who also felt that more emphasis should be put on the development of economic self-sufficiency than on protest politics.

On the question of culture, the militant integrationists' stance was similar to that taken by European ethnicities. Lip service was paid to the importance of Black culture but its relevance was conceded only to the extent that it produced the kind of group solidarity necessary for accelerating assimilation. For the militant integrationist, Black culture assumed the role that sociologist Herbert Gans calls "symbolic ethnicity," that is, a fawning over particular cultural artifacts as a way of masking the extent to which one's group has in fact assimilated.[11] For cultural nationalists, however, culture is the essence of the struggle and the key to resolving contradictions in the political, economic, and social realms. The re-discovery and re-establishment of classical African culture was to them the centerpiece of Black liberation. Revolutionary nationalists defined the salience of culture in terms of its ability to accelerate and intensify the African American's struggle for revolution in the United States. They recognized that there was a class aspect to African American culture and that not all approaches to Black culture were useful in the struggle against imperialism. To the revolutionary nationalist, the basic cultural unity of African peoples worldwide grew not out of a common cultural heritage but out of a common history of exploitation and oppression at the hands of European racists.

Important divergences existed in the perception of the salience of the international arena in the liberation struggles of Black people. Militant integrationists viewed the struggle of African Americans primarily in domestic terms. They did not look to the international arena as a source of significant alliances and resources. Cultural nationalists recognized an international sphere of African American concern but primarily limited it to the motherland and the African diaspora. The relevance of Third World resources was suspect and not cultivated. Revolutionary nationalists cultivated international contacts and saw in them natural allies. The international arena constituted a necessary counterweight to the numerical and power predominance of Whites in the United States. To revolutionary nationalists, the international context was what made the revolutionary option plausible.

"By Any Means Necessary?"

As one might expect, all three tendencies diverged on the question of the relevance of violence and armed struggle to Black liberation. Militant integrationists dismissed such tactics as foolhardy and counter-productive. Such tactics would isolate Black people from their domestic allies and consolidate an overwhelming White reaction. Cultural nationalists viewed violence and armed struggle as largely irrelevant to the kind of psychological redemption and withdrawal they advocated for Black people. Nevertheless, they endorsed the concept of self-defense. Revolutionary nationalists embraced the necessity of violence and armed struggle since they saw the essence of imperialist oppression as based on institutionalized racist violence. Given the rising tide of revolution in the world and their feeling that urban guerrilla warfare represented a viable tactic, the military option was given considerable examination by revolutionary nationalists.

The question of revolutionary violence, as we have seen, was taken up by RAM, the Black Panther Party, the Republic of New Afrika, and a host of more localized nationalist groupings. Following Malcolm X, these organizations grappled with the question of what options remained to Black people if African American liberation could not be attained within the prevailing political institutions because these institutions were impervious to nonviolent incentives. There was much discussion of urban guerrilla warfare, working-class revolution led by street youth organized into a vanguard party, and land-based revolution in the Black Belt South based on the voluntary relocation and concentration of Black people in that area. The process of instituting such options, however, was little understood within the movement. Serious study of revolutionary theory was not even uniform among those organizations which had opted seriously to consider urban guerrilla warfare. In organizations within which some political education and study were initiated, they were limited to a discussion of the marxist classics and those of Third World revolutionary leaders like Mao Tse-Tung and Che Guevara. Without an extensive and tested analysis of U.S. society and the probable nature of revolutionary change here, rhetoric and slogans from these classics were nevertheless used as mobilizing tools.

Why Was the Black Liberation Movement Defeated?

Some scholars felt that the premature resort to revolutionary rhetoric invited repression and facilitated the isolation of the Black leadership that resorted to violent hyperbole. The Black Panthers and kindred organizations were not prepared, they concluded, to wage the violent struggle that they invited through the self-identification of their organization and program as revolutionary.

While this is an attractive thesis, I find that it is less than persuasive. I argued earlier that the decision to disrupt and discredit the Civil Rights movement occurred prior to any widespread emergence of organizations in the Black community openly committed to self-defense, urban guerrilla warfare, and revolution. Actually, the rhetoric of self-defense and violent retaliation has been a constant feature of urban Black existence for a period far longer than that of the Civil Rights and Black Power insurgencies. What was novel to the situation was the government's decision to disrupt, discredit, and destroy the movement.

Malcolm X was concerned about this kind of strategic response from the government during the period of transition, when the limits of reform would be tested and revolutionary alternatives seriously studied. When the Harlem rebellion erupted, Malcolm X sent instructions from Africa that members of the OAAU were not to provide active leadership to the rioting street forces. He feared the government would use such action as a pretext for repressing the OAAU. Malcolm knew that for some time to come the OAAU could not provide that kind of provocation and survive the subsequent repression.

Given the experience of the OAAU, it is surprising that subsequent nationalist and Pan-African organizations spent so little time actually studying the methods of repression historically used in the United States. Few attempts were made to develop effective responses to such tactics. On the other hand, more recently there has been a concerted effort to get the international community to scrutinize the status of former movement activists who have been convicted and sentenced to long jail terms as common felons. After twenty years, this campaign is starting to bear fruit as the notion of African American political prisoners takes hold in international forums.

As it was, the resort to arms was not so much initiated by movement radicals as it was a response to repression. Police provocations such as those of Police Chief Frank Rizzo in Philadelphia (stripping Panthers naked and inviting them to a shootout) or alleged criminal conspiracies (such as the SNCC dynamite case in Philadelphia) forced members of the Panthers and the Republic of New Afrika, among others, underground for self-preservation.[12] In addition, criminalizing movement activists on trumped-up charges created fugitives who could later be murdered in the process of apprehension or entangled in felony charges associated with their apprehension that would stand even when the original charges were subsequently deemed to have no merit.[13] Repression forced militant activists underground and toward more violent responses and desperate alternatives. The Black Liberation Army, the most explicitly revolutionary organization of this period, was not the product of a detailed analysis of the state of the struggle and the available alternatives. This "army" was, in fact, an *ad hoc* grouping of activists who had escaped the first round of repression, found themselves criminalized and marked persons, and rationalized in revolutionary terms the lifestyle and behavior that had been imposed on them by the severity of the government's Cointelpro program.

SNCC

The international Pan-African aspect of Malcolm X's organizational efforts was the most difficult to maintain, but notable advances were achieved by those who took up this task after Malcolm X. SNCC by 1967 had established an international affairs division to complement its transformation to a human rights organization. This division was to apply to the United Nations for non-governmental organization status on the Economic and Social Council. SNCC actively sought out Third World governments and liberation movements and considered itself part of the "non-aligned world."[14] Unlike Malcolm X, however, SNCC was unable to achieve diplomatic recognition from African governments. At the Kinshasha, Zaire meeting of the OAU in 1967, Foreman arranged for H. Rap Brown to attend the sessions, but at the last minute Brown was denied credentials.[15] Forman went on with other SNCC organizers to take this orientation into movements of working-class orientation in the Black community, most notably the Black Economic Development Conference and the League of Revolutionary Black Workers.

SNCC was unable to achieve the kind of recognition accorded Malcolm X for several reasons. First, the articulation of Black Power in a somewhat chauvinist form after 1966, especially by Stokely Carmichael, was out of tune with the non-racialist positions of many progressive African governments. Carmichael was asked to leave Tanzania because his Black Power rhetoric offended the government. Second, the U.S. government as a result of Malcolm's trips to Africa launched a propaganda counter-offensive which had some impact on SNCC's ability to follow up on its own and Malcolm's initial successes in Africa. Third, as mentioned in Chapter Six, the radical Casablanca powers, who had been the most ardent supporters of Malcolm X in Africa, were in disarray. Nkrumah fell to a coup in Ghana and Nasser had been defeated in the Six Day War. The most important reasons for SNCC's inability to follow up on openings in the international arena, however, were related to internal problems of leadership, constituency, and finances. SNCC never solved the problem of balancing the advantages of participatory democracy with the need for clear lines of authority and well-thought-out positions. It tried to pass over these weaknesses with charismatic leadership, militant rhetoric, and the dogged determination of its cadres. As with the OAAU, it succeeded in attracting the attention of the FBI and was swiftly targeted for disruption and "dirty tricks." SNCC turned toward the revolutionary option but without the prerequisites for avoiding repression.

Pan-African Skills Project

An aspect of SNCC's international orientation which survived the organization was the establishment of the Pan-African Skills Project.[16] This was an idea of Forman's, which reflected Malcolm's desire to provide African American technical-assistance personnel to developing African nations, which came to life in 1969. Foreman's leadership in the Detroit Black Economic Development Conference of 1969 resulted in the development of a practical program for that old nationalist staple, reparations to African Americans. The Black Manifesto presented at New York's Riverside Church on May 4, 1969, resulted in increased funding for programs controlled by Blacks. One of the most effective of these was the Pan-African Skills Project. Headed up by former SNCC chairperson. Irving Davis, the Project sent over 250 Afro-American teachers, technicians, and professionals to Tanzania and a smaller number to Zambia. It was probably one of the two most concrete manifestations of Pan-Africanism to emerge subsequent to Malcolm's initiatives of 1964.

The Pan-African Solidarity Committee

The decade of the 1970s opened with former Pan-African associates of Malcolm X, and nationalist veterans of the Civil Rights and student movements joining with cultural nationalists to form the Pan-African

Solidarity Day Committee. The purpose of the committee was to inject an African American presence into the African Liberation Day celebrations which the OAU and the United Nations had called for and which would take place the third Saturday in May 1970. The committee felt that African Americans had a responsibility to support the liberation movements against colonialism and apartheid in Africa. It also felt that Africans had to recognize that African Americans were an "African people." Thus, the committee established as one of its aims to petition the United Nations to investigate U.S. government violations of the human rights of African Americans.

Here, clearly, was Malcolm X's Pan-Africanist program as he articulated it in his last period. It was also Malcolm's notion of the Black united front in a microcosm. The Pan-African Solidarity Committee was Pan-Africanist in that it included African Americans from nations throughout the Western hemisphere as well as continental Africans. Its membership included Julian Mayfield, one of the formative influences on Malcolm's Pan-Africanism; Malcolm's widow, Dr. Betty Shabazz; Robert Browne, economist and the major theoretician of a separatist solution; Sam Anderson and Bill Sales of the Columbia University student takeovers of 1968 and the CUNY open enrollment struggles of 1969; filmmaker St. Claire Bourne; vocalist Verta Mae Grovesnor; actress Vinnie Burroughs, and Zimbabweian Colistus Ndlovu, later a minister in the Mugabe government. The chairperson of the committee was lawyer Robert Van Lierop, formerly a Civil Rights attorney with the NAACP legal staff. Van Lierop had visited the liberation movements in Africa and had an especially close relationship with those in the Portugese territories like FRELIMO in Mozambique and PAIGC in Guinea Bissau. He would later make two definitive films of the liberation struggle in Mozambique, *A Luta Continua* and *O Povo Organizado*.

The Pan-African Solidarity Committee held a spirited demonstration on African Liberation Day at the United Nations and ancillary cultural commemorations that week in Harlem. The petition campaign was abortive, however, and the committee's activities and orientation were soon to be assumed by a much larger hemispheric Pan-Africanist organization directly in the tradition of Malcolm X, the African Liberation Support Committee (ALSC).

African Liberation Support Committee

The African Liberation Support Committee (ALSC) was established in 1972 after an *ad hoc* grouping of Pan-Africanists and grassroots organizations had successfully engineered a massive African Liberation Day (ALD) march of 50,000 in Washington D.C.[17] This was truly a united front effort, including representation from the newly emergent Black Congressional Caucus. In 1973, the committee was able to commemorate ALD in over twenty cities, on both coasts and in Canada and the Caribbean.[18] In 1974, ALSC again called for and executed a large march in Washington, D.C. It augmented its ALD celebration with several days of conferencing at Howard University devoted to debate and resolution on the question, Which way forward in building the Pan-African united front?[19]

ALSC and the Sixth Pan-African Congresses

Members of ALSC joined with former SNCC cadre, Courtland Cox of Drum and Spear Press in Washington, D.C., and militants in the Caribbean and Europe to design and implement the first Pan-African Congress since the Manchester gathering in 1945 (Six PAC). Hosted by the Tanzanian government in Dar-es-Salaam, Tanzania on June 18-21, 1974, it was by far the largest international gathering of Pan-Africanists ever to take place. The African American delegation dwarfed all others in attendance.[20]

A Critique of ALSC

While the mass character of the Civil Rights and Black Power movements as they were known in the 1960s had disappeared, in the one area of African liberation support work this mass, grassroots character was retained at least through 1974. Significant links were effected between Pan-Africanists in the United States and liberation movements in the Caribbean, like the New Jewel Movement in Grenada, and those in Africa already mentioned. Relationships with progressive governments in Africa were developing, especially in Tanzania, Guinea, and Somalia. A wing of the Pan-Africanists, those closest to the cultural nationalism of the old Congress of Afrikan People (CAP), was courted and "feted" by Idi Amin in Uganda. The African Liberation Support Committee was the most serious organizational advance toward the OAAU model that Malcolm X had envisaged.[21]

In many ways the ALSC developmental process paralleled that of Malcolm X's own personal development. Leading figures in the ALSC accompanied Robert Van Lierop to East Africa in 1972-73. Their sojourn there had many parallels with that of Malcolm in Africa. They went personally to deliver to the OAU Liberation Committee in Dar-es-Salaam the thousands of dollars of support and material aid raised by the ALSC. Some members of the group such as Owusu Sadaukai, headmaster of Malcolm X Liberation University, were at that time strongly influenced by the "nation time" orientation of the cultural nationalist and CAP. They went in order to prepare the way for a general exodus of African American nationalists from the United States. In asking the liberation fighters of FRELIMO what kind of support they could give, they were fully prepared to recruit African Americans to come to fight in Africa with the liberation fighters. Ideologically, their orientation was a cultural Pan-Africanism which at best practiced a petty capitalism while idealizing a traditional African communalism. The African freedom fighters argued with them that kind of Pan-Africanism was not enough. It had reactionary aspects that they were fighting against in their own revolution. Not all tradition was progressive they pointed out. The armed militants indicated that they did not need military aid from their brothers in the United States. They wanted ALSC cadre to recognize that the United States was an imperialist power and an enemy of African people. According to them, African Americans were in a unique position to strike a blow for African liberation because they were inside the "belly of the beast." A U.S. support effort that could prevent the U.S. government from implementing policies against the liberation movements was worth more than fighters or a wholesale emigration back to Africa. The best way to contribute to African liberation, they concluded, was to advance the struggle against imperialism abroad and monopoly capitalism at home.[22]

Toward Marxism-Leninism

These points were far from acceptable to some on the ALSC delegation. The ideological underpinnings of the arguments were Marxist-Leninist, and this ideology was only vaguely familiar to many in the membership of the ALSC. The African revolutionaries admonished their North American guests to take up seriously the study of Marxism-Leninism and see how it might be applied in the United States. Where Malcolm had only a vague notion of socialism as Marxism-Leninism, these cadres in ALSC, starting in 1973, took up the serious study of that body of revolutionary literature and practice.

ALSC was the culmination of a process that started with the OAAU, RAM, the Black Panther Party, the League of Revolutionary

Black Workers, and the Black Workers Congress. It was the major organization which spread marxism among Black youth between 1972 and 1975. Within it was waged the most significant and intense ideological struggle over the relationship of marxism to Black liberation since the 1930s. This debate was positive in that it corrected a tendency in culturally oriented Pan-Africanism toward cynicism about the possibility of achieving success in the struggle against White racism in the United States. This tendency had predisposed the cultural nationalists to stand apart from community-based struggles for reform and to look for the restoration of the "golden age" in Africa. As a result of this debate many cultural nationalists abandoned their elitism, mysticism, and isolation from popular mass struggles. They became seriously engaged in an investigation of the possible relationship between capitalism, racism, socialism, and Black liberation.[23]

Despite this advance, the debate, on balance was poorly handled and quite destructive. Some vociferous members of the leadership of ALSC advocating Marxism-Leninism became dogmatic, anti-democratic, elitist, and sectarian. Rather than preserving the Black united front as an arena for debate and testing the limitations of reform and the possibilities for revolution, the manner in which the debate was conducted destroyed the ALSC Black united front. Too often, the discussions proceeded as if one side or the other was vying to become the "official" U.S. representative of the "line" of one or the other of the major revolutionary powers abroad. There was a lack of critical analysis of these revolutions in terms of strengths and weaknesses and applicability to the situation of African Americans in the United States and the Western hemisphere. Those who participated in the ALSC debate did not emphasize the responsibility of the progressive nations and forces abroad to study seriously the African American experience and to manifest concrete solidarity with it.[24]

The ALSC and National Black Political Assembly also had difficulty with Black elected officials. With a few exceptions like congressman Charles Diggs, a Democrat from Michigan, Black elected officials refused to support these organizations and subordinated their relationship with these grassroots movements to needs of the Democratic Party. The Congressional Black Caucus consistently refused as a body to foster these grassroots organizations because of the fear that their political leadership in the Black community would be jeopardized.

Ten years after the death of Malcolm X, his legacy was alive in a mass-based, grassroots Pan-Africanist organization. But scarcely a year later in 1976, when it was sorely needed as South Africa invaded Angola, the ALSC had been destroyed as a national Black united front, splintering into a host of sectarian chapters while many honest grassroots members left the organization.

The demise of an international option facilitated the repression of the revolutionary wing of the Black Power period, the Black Panther Party, Revolutionary Action Movement, the Republic of New Afrika and the Black Liberation Army. The African American people entered the era of Ronald Reagan with no significant and viable national Pan-Africanist and nationalist formations. Pan-Africanists of the 1970s were not totally prepared to provide organizational resources and leadership to the support effort that emerged among students when the South African situation exploded again in 1984 and thereafter.

With a few notable exceptions in the tradition of Malcolm X, like the National Black Independent Political Party and the National Black United Front from the period 1979–81, the dominant strategic motion in the Black community has come from those in the tradition not of Malcolm X but of Martin Luther King, Jr. Their bankruptcy and that of Black electoral politics, from the perspective of resolving the pressing needs of the masses of ghettoized Black people, has engendered a renewed interest in Malcolm X and the Pan-African nationalist and internationalist tradition of which he was the most elegant spokesman in the latter part of the 20th-century.

My purpose in this chapter was not to recapitulate the history of defunct organizations but rather to situate various forces in the Black community today with reference to their origins and their relationship to all that Malcolm X held dear. While many years have passed, the questions which the Black Liberation Movement addressed are still with us. The groupings in the Black community are even more distinct and opposed than in Malcolm's time. And we should not forget that, as Malcolm X said, if you want to know a thing you must know its origins.

9

Malcolm X's Legacy of Leadership and Charisma

Introduction

In this concluding chapter we will sum up the historical and contemporary relevance of Malcolm X—the man, the Pan-African internationalist, and the ideas and movement he represented. It has been our aim throughout this book to demonstrate that Malcolm X is more than an icon. He was a multi-faceted thinker and organizer who is worthy of serious study by scholars, activists, and anyone else looking to understand our world today. His method of confronting the world in his maturity is worthy of study and emulation.

Malcolm X: Grassroots Leader

Malcolm X established in the Civil Rights movement the principle that street elements could rise to leadership in the struggle for Black liberation. He did not establish this principle by romantically "tailing after" the *lumpen* element. Rather, through his own life's witness, Malcolm X demonstrated that this social stratum was capable of self-emancipation. As Dr. King represented the living example of W.E.B. Du Bois's "talented tenth," so Malcolm X represented the manifest leadership potential of the newest stratum to join the Civil Rights struggle. He demonstrated that the experience of exploitation and degradation at the hands of a racist system could be turned to a source of insight and emancipation through study, knowledge, morality, and self-discipline.

The Source of Malcolm's Charisma

The source of Malcolm X's charisma was his ability to help others break with the paradigm of ruling-class thought. He was above all a great teacher, and his closest associates remember him in that way above all else. Moreover, his lack of a formal education allowed his street constituency to see clearly the essence of the intellectual endeavor without the mediation of formal academic institutions and processes. The model of Malcolm X, the intellectual, challenged every ghetto youth to be a serious intellectual, that is, knowledgeable about her/himself and the society in which she or he lived. Malcolm's example mandated that the essence of the intellectual endeavor was the unity of self-knowledge and social practice, since all acquired knowledge, he argued, established its validity only through the process of its application to making the world a better place in which to live.

One commentator observed that:

More than any other person Malcolm X was responsible for the new militancy that entered the Movement in 1965. Malcolm X said aloud those things which Negroes had been saying among themselves. He even said those things Negroes had been afraid to say to each other. His clear uncomplicated words cut through the chains on black minds like a giant blowtorch…He spoke directly and eloquently to black men, analyzing their situation, their predicament, events as they happened, explaining what it all meant for a black man in America.[1]

Malcolm X had a profound respect for the power of the word. He strove to master the English language in all of its connotative meanings and nuances. Even before religion, it was the word which ushered in Malcolm's first major personal transformation. At Charlestown Prison, Malcolm embarked on the ambitious project of memorizing the dictionary. Later at the Norfolk Prison Colony, he wrote for the prison newspaper and was an important member of the debating team. Malcolm applied this skill immediately in negotiating with the prison authorities concessions for Muslims to practice their religion behind prison walls.[2] Peter Bailey, a journalist and associate of Malcolm X in the OAAU, related an incident reflecting Malcolm X's deft editorial skills. He instructed Bailey to substitute the word,"killing" for "murder" in the organization's report of an incident which had triggered the Harlem riots. In this way, Malcolm X anticipated that many potential lawsuits could be avoided.[3]

Malcolm's speech was shocking, vivid, graphic, visceral but always precise and never wordy. Although articulated in a language whose formal conventions were determined by bourgeois intellectuals, Malcolm's speech reflected the nobility inherent in the modes of articulation of the African American masses.

Malcolm X's public speeches, however, were not brilliant merely as exercises in rhetoric. As we saw in Chapter Four, Malcolm sought facts through history as a basis for establishing the truth of the Black experience. But he sought historical verification for the truth from a new perspective, that of the person at the bottom of the ghetto heap. The reawakened interest in Black history characteristic of the Black Studies aspect of the Black Power movement owed a great debt to Malcolm X's example, approaching the Black experience from the vantage point of the most oppressed segment of the Black community.

John Henrik Clarke described the differences between the oratorical impact of Dr. King and Malcolm X:

When inquiring of someone the next day who had heard Dr. King, they would typically respond as to how moved they were by his oratory. When asked, however, what did King say, they usually could not remember the specifics of his discourse. On the other hand, those who had heard Malcolm X speak, when asked the next day about that experience would typically respond "Malcolm said" and then recall the specifics of Malcolm's line of argument and his factual verifications.[4]

Malcolm X led by activating the intellect as well as the emotions. He was honest. His associates almost universally spoke of Malcolm X as the most honest person they ever knew. He taught his constituency that an honest appraisal of their own degradation and self-destruction was the beginning of their self-emancipation. Malcolm's honesty, however, also set a new standard of responsibility for middle-class Black self-awareness. He taught this class that their existence transpired within a gilded cage whose essence was no different from the cell that had incarcerated Malcolm. Malcolm called for honesty, not opportunism, from the Black middle class.

Malcolm taught the means of self-emancipation to the lowest stratum of the ghetto. He taught them how to impose reason on a previously incoherent existence. Discipline was at the center of Malcolm X's intellectual and activist methodology. He identified and executed his task on time. Malcolm was punctual to a fault. He once chastised activist Muhammad Ahmed for being a few minutes late by leaving the meeting place and forcing Ahmed to wait hours for his return. Once returned, Malcolm informed Ahmed: "Brother, don't you realize that a revolution is run on time."[5] Malcolm's X's self-discipline made it almost a fetish for him to keep his word. His associates remembered that whatever he promised, he went to extraordinary lengths to deliver.

Malcolm X's honesty was not only personal but intellectual as well. For Malcolm honesty was facing up to facts, to the truth as the only basis for change. He did this no matter what the costs. It was Malcolm's honesty which was the basis of his openness to people and ideas with which he differed. He listened and learned from the opposition and saw debate as a way of winning over the uncommitted and shaking the confidence of the opposition. Malcolm's honesty commanded respect from friend and foe alike.

In the OAAU, Malcolm's honesty was manifested in two important ways: his changing position on decisionmaking and his role within the organization, and his abandonment of the NOI's position on the organizational role to be played by women. The NOI's position reflected Victorian notions of femininity and the perception that women were weak, subject to moral compromise and seduction, and needed, therefore, to be watched and protected. Malcolm X had held the same position. His experiences in Africa caused him to see that the rate of progress of a country could be measured by the progress made by its women. He observed that those countries whose women were most advanced were also themselves the most rapidly developing, and vice versa. Malcolm X had firsthand knowledge of the crucial role of Black women in the major Civil Rights organizations. Malcolm X's closeness to SNCC, probably the most progressive in regard to the question of the role of women, reinforced his position on this question. The intervention of female Black leadership in the person of Ella Baker led to the creation of SNCC. The late Ruby Doris Robinson was an essential worker in SNCC's inner circle; and the grassroots activist and co-founder of the SNCC-inspired Mississippi Freedom Democratic Party, Mrs. Fannie Lou Hamer, was Malcolm X's personal friend. Consequently, he repudiated his earlier position on women and called for their participation and leadership in all aspects of the work of the OAAU. He recruited Lynn Shifflet and gave her a leadership position in the OAAU to emphasize the importance of a new role for and perception of women. When her leadership was challenged, Malcolm wrote from Africa reminding his following back home of the tremendous strides women were making in the African revolution. Malcolm's position on these issues created a space in subsequent organizational efforts to challenge the authoritarian charismatic model of leadership inherited from the Black church and the male chauvinism deeply embedded in Civil Rights organizations. Malcolm X's prestige was added to that of the great Black women leaders of the African American freedom struggle, legitimizing a freedom agenda that recognized the question of the liberation of women. Malcolm's ability to change when confronted with good new ideas and facts was given no better verification than in his changing position on women. He spoke explicitly about this question and gave leadership to the African American liberation struggle on this issue.

One can now make a few observations about the basis of Malcolm's leadership, especially among his close associates. Malcolm's closest followers were most impressed with Malcolm's intellect and discipline. They remembered most his ability to teach and "make it plain." For them, Malcolm was unique in his ability to help people learn with their intellect and their emotions. He was a straightforward and open person who put himself totally at the disposal of his friends and associates. Muhammad Ahmed observed that "Malcolm was a very shocking person, the most flexible person I've ever met in life. You meet people who have less stature and are very rigid...Malcolm actually blew me away. He said, "Brother what do you want me to do?"[6] Malcolm's words best describe the essence of his intellectual methodology. At an OAAU rally in Harlem he promised that:

> I'm not going to be in anybody's straitjacket. I don't care what a person looks like or where they come from. My mind is wide open to anybody who will help get the ape off our backs.[7]

Malcolm's Contribution to the Movement

This book has highlighted the problem confronting the Civil Rights movement at a crucial stage in its transition, that in which it attempted to institutionalize itself as a national movement representing and including all groups of the African American community. This transition required important tactical and strategic choices between programs of reform and revolution. A dilemma of this transition was that reform strategies might dissipate support from the most deprived segment of the Black community while revolutionary strategies might present those in power with unacceptable risks. Cooptation or repression represented the horns of this dilemma.

African American nationalism emerged as a major ideological force in the Civil Rights movement because it offered a plan of action to transcend the dilemma of cooptation or repression associated with the tactical and strategic choices between programs of reform or revolution. The intervention in the movement of Malcolm X was important because he clearly saw this dilemma and developed a multi-faceted response to it. This response consisted of an attempt to find an alternative model to the American Dream in the rich tradition of African American nationalism, especially in its Pan-Africanist variant. In the realm of politics, Malcolm X confronted the dilemma associated with reform or revolution by advocating that the limits of reform be tested and the revolutionary option be given serious consideration. In the face of cooptation or repression, on the one hand, he advanced the need for a cultural revolution in the psyche of African Americans while on the other hand arguing for the necessity of self-defense options and international protection for Black human rights. In the area of methodology, Malcolm X asserted that "by any means necessary" would transcend the dilemmas of this transition period while the philosophy of nonviolence would not. Lastly, he saw the motive force for change in the U.S. not as King's *agape* (love) but as the organized anger of a new social force, the ghettoized street people. Malcolm X attempted in the OAAU to implement the beginnings of a revolutionary option within the Civil Rights movement. Through internationalization of the Civil Rights movement into a human rights movement and the serious consideration of all options including self-defense and urban guerrilla warfare, Malcolm hoped to negotiate successfully the dilemma of cooptation or repression. We have seen that Malcolm's strategy precipitated a united elite stance committed to repressing his leadership and the OAAU. This coalescence of elite opposition occurred before the OAAU had consolidated any advantages which might have accrued from the new approach. As a result, the OAAU was destroyed as an effective organization and Malcolm X was physically removed from the African American freedom movement.

Nevertheless, Malcolm X's intervention in the movement and the concept of the united front as embodied in the OAAU have had a lasting impact on the Black freedom struggle. If anything, that impact has grown significantly over the intervening years. Among African American youth today, the image of Malcolm X rivals and perhaps outshines that of Dr. Martin Luther King, Jr. as a Black icon and commitment to Black people. Malcolm X's legacy has been of unquestioned symbolic significance, but it has also left a more mundane but lasting impact on the organizations which forged the transition from Civil Rights to Black Power and those nationalist organizations that came thereafter.

Malcolm X sought to discover and implement the organizational form proper to the period of the Civil Rights movement's break with ruling-class ideas and the transition from reform to revolution. To do this, Malcolm X called upon the well-recognized and historical longing of African Americans for viable racially based united fronts. This tradition had its genesis in the Negro Convention movement and continued into the Civil Rights decade in the Black Power conventions. The OAAU grappled with the questions of the united front of organizations and classes in the Black community, democratic leadership and decisionmaking, and the proper structure to articulate international networking between Africa and its diaspora. The Civil Rights forces assumed Malcolm's organizational agenda in the Black Power period and continued to pursue answers to questions he first raised.

African American nationalism was not an aberration or a residue of the spent energies of the Civil Rights mobilization. The nationalism and Pan-Africanism of Malcolm X, the OAAU organizational model, are rooted in historically derived institutions and trends indigenous to the African American community. I have attempted to demonstrate, as

Charles Tilly[8] has demonstrated for revolutions generally, that the strength and staying power of the African American nationalism of Malcolm X and the OAAU resulted from its close correlation with the mood and orientation of ghettoized Black people. It accorded with their prevailing standards of right and justice, and its method of political education followed their daily routines: street-corner debates, open-air rallies, and national conventions with deep roots in the style and oratorical tradition of the Black church. African American nationalism reflects the internal organization of the Black community. It mirrors the creative tension characteristic of the conflict between two strong African American traditions, charismatic leadership and participatory democracy. The self-defense posture of Malcolm X and the OAAU, as opposed to Dr. King's nonviolence, was much more grounded in the actual accumulated experience of African Americans with collective action and the society's patterns of social control and repression. While grounded in African American intellectual and scholarly protest traditions, Malcolm X reworked this historical material in search of a new paradigm of Pan-African liberation. African American nationalism represented a historically grounded and indigenous alternative available to the African American community when the limitations of Dr. King's approach became clear. In order to understand the social mobilization of African Americans in the 1960s, both the integrationism of Dr. King and the nationalism/Pan-Africanism of Malcolm X must be understood. In fact, African American nationalism, especially as represented in the thought and legacy of Malcolm X, is a continuing and rich tradition that African Americans call upon as they continue to confront the questions broached between 1963 and 1965 even as they approach the 21st century.

Conclusion

Where are we today? Today the international influence of African countries is negligible. The United Nations has been coopted by the United States and the North Atlantic Treaty Organization (NATO). These two important factors influencing Malcolm X's political ideology are not as they were while he lived. Black electoral politics without an independent base and a viable protest option have proven impotent in the face of the conservative White backlash and racist reaction. There has been plenty of ballot, but no bullet. Black electoral politics continue to be coopted by Black middle-class political entrepreneurs and opportunists unaccountable to the masses of African Americans. Malcolm X's hemispheric conception of African Americans is threatened by more narrow and ethnically sectarian notions of who is an indigenous African American. Our political perceptions must continue to embrace immigrants from the Caribbean and other parts of the African diaspora as allies. We must uphold Malcolm's perception of the basic solidarity of all dispossessed Third World peoples.

The "field Negro" tradition so important to Malcolm's analysis of the politics of Black liberation still lives in our youth and in their street culture. Its potential for disruption was displayed again in open rebellion in South Central, Los Angeles; Atlanta, Georgia; and other locales. Events in Eastern Europe, the former Soviet Union, Lebanon, and Somalia clearly indicate that urban guerrilla warfare allows well-entrenched and committed minorities to immobilize a society and destroy its way of life. Malcolm X was right to argue that no oppressed people can ever give up this option and retain any hope of liberation. It would appear that Africa is not now able to serve as a base area for African American resistance. Important changes are now underway in southern Africa. These changes will have important consequences for the future of Black liberation for decades to come. If South Africa is finally liberated and the industrial base comes into the unrestricted control of Africans, then there will be a renaissance throughout the whole southern African region, and African Americans will again have a viable base area in the continent.

What does the OAAU idea of Malcolm X tell us about confronting the New World Order? It is essential that our politics not be constricted to the electoral arena alone. In that arena Black politics must work to be organizationally and programmatically independent of both parties of the ruling class. Malcolm X taught that only under particular and exceptional conditions can lasting gains be made by Black people in the electoral arena. Our politics must be a "field Negro" politics that will not hesitate to disrupt the normal operation of society whenever that becomes necessary. It must seek organizational forms that are democratic, provide for collective leadership, and energize as equal participants men, women, and youths. This politics must be internationalist and Pan-Africanist. Our politics must continue to affirm the belief that Black liberation is possible and that it is right to rebel. The recent events in Eastern Europe and the former Soviet Union must not weaken our understanding that Black liberation cannot occur within the context of capitalism. These are the kinds of insights that flow from Malcolm's legacy.

We want freedom by any means necessary. We want justice by any means necessary. We want equality by any means necessary...we want it now or we don't think anybody should have it.

If something is yours by right, then fight for it or shut up. If you can't fight for it, then forget it.

NOTES

1. The Year They Re-discovered Malcolm

1. May 19-25, 1990.
2. Dennis O'Neill, "Malcolm's Message in Rap," *Forward Motion*, vol. 9, no. 1 (March 1990), p. 22.
3. Especially after 1965, Dr. King also developed a much better appreciation of the nightmare of urban ghetto life. While his coopted image is rooted in the "I Have A Dream Speech" of 1963, King by his death in April 1968 had made several major attempts to adapt nonviolent direct action methods to the struggles which he felt had to be waged for economic, social, and political justice in ghettoes like those in Chicago and Memphis, and all over the United States. In his monumental April 4, 1967 anti-Vietnam War speech at Riverside Church in New York City, King echoed sentiments spoken by Malcolm X in 1963 and 1964. Dr. King and Malcolm X were in no sense ever completely in accord or for the most part struggling for exactly the same thing. Nevertheless, the conditions that produced Malcolm X also impacted on the thinking and behavior of King. It is ironic that Black youth in their search for a more militant icon than King have not only resurrected Malcolm X but forced scholars to pursue a more serious presentation of King's thinking and activities.
4. John E. Jacobs, "Black America 1991: An Overview," *The State of Black America 1992* (New York: National Urban League, 1992), p. 1.
5. Ibid., p. 2.
6. David H. Swinton, "The Economic Status of African Americans: Limited Ownership and Persistent," in *The State of Black America 1992* (New York: National Urban League, 1992), p. 90.
7. Ibid., pp. 90-91.
8. Jacobs, p. 3.
9. Swinton, p. 100.
10. Ibid., Table 20, p. 101.
11. Ibid.
12. See David H. Swinton, Melvin L. Oliver, and Thomas M. Shapiro, "Race and Wealth," *Review of Black Political Economy* (Spring 1989), pp. 5-25.
13. Michael Specter, "Tuberculosis: A Killer Returns," *New York Times* (five-part series) October 11-15, 1992.
14 See Margery A. Turner et al., *Opportunities Denied, Opportunities Diminished: Discrimination in Hiring*, (Washington, D.C.: The Urban Istitute, 1991).
15. Margaret Burnham, "The Great Society Didn't Fail," *The Nation*, July 24/31, 1989, p. 123.
16. Ibid.
17. Michael Katz, *The Undeserving Poor: From the War on Poverty to the War on Welfare* (New York: Pantheon, 1989) p. 204.

18. Ibid., p. 196.

19. Ibid.

20. Ibid., p. 204.

21. Burnham, "The Great Society Didn't Fail," p. 123.

22. See William W. Sales, Jr., "Comments on the Controversy Surrounding the Nomination and Confirmation of Judge Clarence Thomas to the Supreme Court," *The Black Scholar*, vol. 22, nos. 1 & 2 (Winter 1991/Spring 1992), pp. 85-90.

23. See Joseph McCormick II and Charles E. Jones, "The Conceptualization of Deracialization: Thinking Through the Dilemma," *Dilemmas of Black Politics: Issues of Leadership and Strategy*, ed. Georgia A. Persons (New York: Harper Collins, 1993), pp. 66-84.

24. Claire Cohen, "The Legacy of Malcolm X and The Black Liberation Movement Today," *Bulletin in Defense of Marxism* (February 1991), p. 18.

25. Katz, *The Undeserving Poor*, p. 195.

26. See James Ridgeway, *Blood in the Face: The KKK, Aryan Nations, Nazi Skin Heads, and the Rise of a New White Culture* (New York: Thunders Mouth Press, 1991).

27. Malcolm X, "Prospects for Freedom in 1965," *Malcolm X Speaks: Selected Speeches and Statements*, ed. George Breitman (New York: Grove Press, 1965), p. 151.

28. Cornel West, "Nihilism in Black America: A Danger That Corrodes From Within," *Dissent* (Spring 1991), pp. 221-2

29. O'Neill, "Malcolm's Message in Rap," pp. 22-23.

30. Ibid.

31. Cornel West, "On Black Rage," *The Village Voice*, September 7, 1991.

32. Ibid.

33. Frantz Fanon, *The Wretched of the Earth* (New York: Grove Press, 1965). p. 206.

34. See Sidney Verba and Gary Orren, *Equality in America: The View From the Top* (Cambridge, MA: Harvard University Press, 1985).

35. W.E.B. Du Bois, "The Propaganda of History," Chapter XVII of *Black Reconstruction in America: 1860-1880* (Cleveland: Myridian Books, 1964).

2. The Gestation of a Revolutionary

1. Throughout this work, I use variations of the phrase "street people" to describe the core of Malcolm X's constituency. These strata are most usually so described in the popular "movement" literature of the Civil Rights and Black Power period. In fact, this phrase is a very imprecise description of an amalgam of the most dispossessed economic strata in the Black ghetto. It includes the most unstable segments of Black blue-collar and service workers in marginal industries and on assembly lines, the long-term unemployed and discouraged workers, and the anti-social elements described by Karl Marx as *lumpen*. The notion of "street people" includes unemployed youth and high school dropouts, pregnant teenagers and impoverished single parents. C.E. Wilson, "Leadership: Triumph in Leadership Tragedy," *Malcolm X: The Man and His Times*, ed. John Henrik Clarke (New York: MacMillan, 1969), pp. 29, 37.

2. Malcolm X, *The Autobiography of Malcolm X* with the assistance of Alex Haley (New York: Grove Press, 1966).

3. *Black Liberation Month News*, February 1965, p. 2.

4. Ibid.

5. See Alain Locke, *The New Negro: An Interpretation* (New York, 1925).

6. Robert A. Goldberg, *Grassroots Resistance: Social Movements in Twentieth Century America* (Belmont, CA: Wadsworth, 1991), p. 70.

7. Theodore Vincent, "The Garveyite Parents of Malcolm X," *The Black Scholar*, vol. 20, no. 2, pp. 10-13.

8. Ibid.

9. Interview with Ella Collins, April 29, 1988.

10. Ibid.

11. Ferruccio Gambino, "Malcolm X, Laborer: From the Wilderness of the American Empire to Cultural Self-Identification," *Studies on Malcolm X: Newsletter of the Maclolm X Work Group*, vol. 1, no. 1 (Fall 1987), p. 10.

12. Bennett Harrison, "Institutions of the Periphery," *Problems in Political Economy: An Urban Perspective*, 2nd. ed. (Lexington, MA: Heath, 1977), pp. 102-7.

13. Ibid., p. 106.

14. *BLM News*, February 1965, p. 2.

15. Ibid., p. 4.

16. Ibid., pp. 12-13.

17. Ibid., p. 11.

18. Ibid., p. 16.

19. Ibid., p. 5.

20. Ibid., p. 6.

21. See Paul Baran and Paul Sweezy, *Monopoly Capital: An Essay on the American Economic and Social Order* (New York: Monthly Review, 1966).

22. See Charles S. Johnson, Edwin Embree, and Will Alexander, *The Collapse of Cotton Tenancy* (Chapel Hill, NC: Univ. of North Carolina, 1935).

23. Jack M. Bloom, *Class, Race and the Civil Rights Movement* (Bloomington: Univ. of Indiana Press, 1987), p. 5.

24. Doug McAdam, *Political Process and the Development of Black Insurgency: 1930 to 1970* (Chicago: Univ. of Chicago Press, 1985)

25. Aldon Morris, *The Origins of the Civil Rights Movement: Black Communities Organizing for Change* (New York: Free Press, 1984).

26. "The Hate That Hate Produced," CBS Documentary, aired in July 1959.

27. "Memo From Director, FBI, to SAC New York, Philadelphia, Organization of Afro. American Unity," *OAAU Surveillance File* (Internal Security-Miscellaneous. 100-442235, July 2, 1964), p. 2.

3. A New Model in the Civil Rights Movement

1. Representative of the mainstream 1960s scholarly reaction to Black nationalism are Theodore Draper, "The Fantasy of Black Nationalism," *Commentary* 48, September 1969, pp. 27-54: Kenneth B. Clark, "Some Personal Observations on Black Separatism," *Black Separatism: a Bibliography*, ed. Betty Jenkins (New York: MARC, 1976), pp. xiii-xv. Kenneth B. Clark, "The Booby Trap of Black Separatism," Speech Delivered at the University of Chicago (May 1971): Kenneth B. Clark,"Thoughts on Black Power," *Dissent* 15, March-April 1968, pp. 178-92.

The emotion-laden content and diffuseness of the "Black Power" slogan influenced scholarly perceptions of the newly emergent African American nationalism. With the exception of Carmichael and Hamilton's book there was a dearth of scholarly effort on the "Black Power" concept. While their book was a good first effort, there was no systematic follow-up. It is ironic that one of the intellectual underpinnings of Afro-American nationalism and Black Power, the colonial analogy, was first popularized in intellectual circles in the 1960s by Dr. Kenneth Clark. In his excellent book *Dark Ghetto*, Clark defined the Black ghetto as a social, political, and above all, an economic colony. This theme became the organizing concept for Carmichael and Hamilton's work and the definitive article of Robert Blauner on internal colonialism. Kenneth Clark, *Dark Ghetto:Dilemmas of Social Power* (New York: Harper and Row, 1965); Stokely Carmichael and Charles V. Hamilton, *Black Power: The Politics of Liberation in America* (New York: Vintage, 1967); Robert Blauner, "Internal Colonialism and Ghetto Revolt," *Social Forces*, vol. 16, no. 4, Spring 1969, pp. 393-408.

2. Doug McAdam, *Political Process and the Development of Black Insurgency: 1930 to 1970* (Chicago: Univ. of Chicago Press, 1985).

3. Ibid., pp. 26-27.

4. Frances Fox Piven and Richard A. Cloward, "Introduction to the Paperback Edition," *Poor People's Movements* (New York: Vintage Books, 1979), p. xv.

5. Building on the work of Tilly and others, Doug McAdam and Aldon Morris fashioned their major theoretical work on the Civil Rights movement. McAdam used a modified form of Tilly's political process model in his theoretical and empirical work on the social insurgency of Afro-Americans in the period 1930-1970. He identified the broader social forces rooted in the urbanization process as they impacted the South, which facilitated the ethnic mobilization of Afro-Americans. Morris effectively answered Cloward and Piven's thesis that the Civil Rights movement, as a "Poor People's movement," was largely the creation of spontaneity. His work clarified the process by which the forces identified by McAdam coalesced a new elite of young, highly educated and itinerant political entrepreneurs, working within a traditional but transformed Afro-American institution, the church, to create and institutionalize the central mobilizing vehicle of the southern Afro-American community, the "movement center." In so doing, Morris gave an account of the growth, development, and impact of the Southern Christian Leadership Conference (SCLC), with important subsidiary analyses of the Congress of Racial Equality (CORE), the Student Non-Violent Coordinating Committee (SNCC), and the southern wing of the

National Association for the Advancement of Colored People (NAACP). The more descriptive accounts of August Meier and Claybourne Carson of CORE and SNCC, respectively, completed the organizational history of the Civil Rights phase of the 1960s mobilization. These latter two works devoted more space to the emergence of nationalism in both organizations but offered little in the way of the rigorous analysis.

6. McAdam saw the nationalist phase of the Civil Rights movement as the phase of movement dissolution. By so doing, he missed the many significant developments which characterized this period, often mistaking newly emergent strengths as weaknesses. Aldon Morris ended his study with the 1963 SCLC campaign in Birmingham, an event he viewed as the high point of the movement. He provided no postscript or epilogue which would give any indication of the process of transformation from the "movement center" led struggle to what emerged thereafter. Neither work did very much in the way of explaining the rapid emergence of Afro-American nationalism. McAdam identified the rising level of frustration of movement activists in the 1963-64 period as the major source of Black Power policies. This harkened back to the Durkheimian approaches that his work consciously repudiated. One of the indigenous resources which McAdam completely overlooked, but Tilly acknowledged, was the intellectual and protest traditions of the insurgents. Charles Tilly, *From Mobilization to Revolution* (Reading, MA: Addison-Wesley, 1979), p. 162.

7. McAdam's terminology is "insurgency."

8. See Antonino Gramsci, *Selections From the Prison Notebooks of Antonino Gramsci*, eds. trans. Quintin Hoare and Geoffrey Nowell Smith (New York: International Publishers, 1971).

9. This notion of power rooted in the manipulation of symbols is discussed. Peter Bachrach and Morton Baratz, *Power and Poverty: Theory and Practise* (New York: Oxford University Press, 1970).

10. The notion of the "mobilization of bias" is associated with the work of Schattschneider and is discussed in Bachrach and Morton, *Power and Poverty*, 1970.

11. Michael Mann, "The Social Cohesion of Liberal Democracy," *American Sociological Review* 35, June 1970, p. 437.

12. Tilly, *From Mobilization to Revolution*, p. 162.

13. "Has Discrimination Declined?," *Problems in Political Economy: An Urban Perspective*, ed. David Gordon (New York: Heath, 1978), Table, p. 161.

14. Firdaus Jhabvala, "The Economic Situation of Black People,": Ibid.

15. See Kenneth O'Reilly, *Racial Matters: The FBI's Secret File on Black America*, 1960-1972 (New York: The Free Press, 1989).

16. B. Ringer and E. Lawless, *Race, Ethnicity and Society* (New York: Routledge, 1989), p. 83.

17. Sidney Verba and Gary Orren, *Equality in America: The View From the Top* (Cambridge, MA: Harvard University Press, 1985). This work sees as lying " at the heart of the policymaking and political struggle" in the United States. It describes and analyzes "American values about particularly the values of American leaders, in order to give a better understanding of American politics." As such, it was very useful in clarifying the central ideological contention between the ruling class and the rising nationalist leadership in the Civil Rights movement like Malcolm X.

18. See E.U. Essien-Udom, *Black Nationalism: The Search for Identity in America* (Chicago: Univ. of Chicago Press, 1962).

19. H. Brotz, *The Black Jews of Harlem: Negro Nationalism and the Dilemmas of Negro Leadership* (Glencoe, N.Y.: Free Press, 1962), pp. 97-98.

20. James Cone,"I Have a Dream," *Martin & Malcolm & America: A Dream or a Nightmare* (Maryknoll, NY: Orbis, 1991), Chap. 4.

21. Ibid.

22. David Garrow, *Bearing the Cross: Martin Luther King and the Southern Christian Leadership Conference* (New York: William Morrow, 1986), p. 484.

23. See David Garrow, "The Intellectual Development of Martin Luther King, Jr.: Influences and Commentaries" (Xerox).

24. Aldon Morris, *The Origins of the Civil Rights Movement: Black Communities Organizing for Change* (New York: Free Press, 1984), p. 247.

25. Claybourne Carson, *In Struggle: SNCC and the Black Awakening* (Cambridge, MA: Harvard University Press, 1985), pp. 103-4.

26. See Robert Williams, *Negroes With Guns* (Chicago: Third World Press, 1973).

27. Julius Barker and Jesse McCrory, Jr., "The Nature of the System," *Black Americans and the Political System* (Boston: Little Brown, 1980), pp. 68-78.

28. Tilly, *From Mobilization to Revolution*, p. 177.

29. Garrow, *Bearing the Cross*, p. 420.

30. Linda Wagley and Marion Harris, Minorities in the New World (New York: Columbia Univ. Press, 1958) p. 280 ff.

31. See J.B. McConahy and J.C. Hayh, Jr., "Symbolic Racism," *Journal of Social Issues*, vol. 32, no. 2, pp. 23-46.

4. The Political Thought of Malcolm X in Transition

1. As quoted in *Malcolm X in Context: A Study Guide*, eds. Don Murphy and Jennifer Radtke (New York: School Voices Press, 1992), p. 25.

2. Malcolm X, "Twenty Million Black People in Prison," *Malcolm X: The Last Speeches*, ed. Bruce Perry (New York: Pathfinder, 1989), p. 35.

3. *Malcolm X on Afro-American History*, ed. George Breitman (New York: Merit Publishers, 1967), pp. 4-5.

4. Malcolm X, "Interview With Les Crane, December 2, 1964," *Malcolm X: The Last Speeches*, p. 87.

5. Malcolm X, *The Autobiography of Malcolm X* with the assistance of Alex Haley (New York: Grove Press, 1966), pp. 153-5.

6. Ibid., p. 177.

7. Malcolm and Surveillance File (Scholarly Resources, Wilmington, Del, 1978, March 16, 1954).

8. Interview with Benjamin Karim, April 29, 1988.

9. Ibid.

10. Martin R. Delany, *The Condition, Elevation and Destiny of the Colored People of the United States* (New York: Arno, 1969), pp. 38-39.

11. Ibid., p. 39.

Notes

12. See *Malcolm X on Afro-American History*, George Breitman, ed., (New York: Pathfinder Press, 1970)

13. Milton D. Morris, *The Politics of Black America* (New York: Harper and Row, 1975), p. 120; Gabriel Almond and Sidney Verba, *The Civic Culture* (Boston: Little, Brown, 1963), pp. 13-14.

14. Alphonso Pickney, *Black Americans*, 4th ed. (Englewood Cliffs, CA: Prentice Hall, 1993), p. 215.

15. Ibid.

16. E.U. Essien-Udom, *Black Nationalism,* p.14.

17. Interview with Hassan Washington, New York, N.Y., May 11, 1987.

18. Elombe Brath, Speech at the Annual Symposium of the Malcolm X Work Group (New York, N.Y., May 20, 1989).

19. Interview with James Smalls, New York, N.Y., February 19, 1988.

20. Interview with Sylvester Leaks, New York, N.Y., February 3, 1988.

21. The following description of Nation of Islam theology is taken from C. Eric Lincoln, "The Faith and the Future," *The Black Muslims in America,*

22. H. Brotz, *The Black Jews of Harlem,* p. 106.

23. Lincoln, *The Black Muslims in America*, pp. 17-20.

24. Unpublished speech by Elombe Brath at the Fannie Lou Hamer Institute, New York, N.Y., February 11, 1987.

25. Michael Williams, "The Split: Some Ideological and Organizational Implications of Malcolm X's Break With the Nation of Islam," (Department of Afro-American and African Studies, *University of North Carolina-Charlotte, 1990),* p. 7 (Xerox).

26. Essien-Udom, *Black Nationalism*, p. 321.

27. Malcolm X, *Malcolm X Speaks*, p. 139.

28. Lincoln, *The Black Muslims in America*, p. 222.

29. Brath interview

30. Lincoln, *The Black Muslims in America*, p. 82.

31. Ibid., p. 83.

32. Karim interview and interview with James Shabazz, Brooklyn N.Y., October 20, 1988.

33. Lincoln, *The Black Muslims in America*, p. 24.

34. Ibid., pp. 111-2.

35. "The Hate That Hate Produced," *Newsbeat* (New York: WNTA-TV, July 10-17, 1959).

36. Williams, p.7.

37. Ibid.

38. Brotz, *The Black Jews of Harlem,* p. 108.

39. Lincoln, *The Black Muslims in America*, p. 110.

40. Ibid., p. 39.

41. Ibid., p. 222.

42. Ibid., pp. 169-72.

43. Brath interview

44. M.S. Handler, "Malcolm's Plans Irk Muslims," *New York Times*, November 8, 1964.

45. African Opinion 2 as quoted in "Memo to FBI Director from SAC Philadelphia, October 27, 1964," *OAAU Surveillance File*.

46. Malcolm X, *Malcolm X: The Last Speeches*, p. 134.

47. Malcolm X, *Autobiography*, p. 309.

48. Ibid., pp. 309-10.

49.]*New York Times*, March 9, 1964.

50. Malcolm X, *Malcolm X Speaks*, p. 21.

51. Ibid.

52. Ibid., p. 34.

53. Malcolm X, *Autobiography*, p. 315.

54. Ibid., p. 294.

55. The following critique is extracted from several speeches of the period. "Message to the Grassroots," *Malcolm X Speaks*, "Twenty Million Black People in a Political, Economic and Mental Prison," "America's Gravest Crisis Since the Civil War," *Malcolm X: The Last Speeches*, pp. 25-58, 59-80.

56. Malcolm X, "Message to the Grassroots," *Malcolm X Speaks*, p. 9.

57. Ibid.

58. Malcolm X, *Autobiography*, "Preface."

59. *New York Herald Tribune*, March 15, 1964.

60. FBI, "Transcript of the Joe Rainey Show, WDAS Radio Philadelphia, PA., March 20, 1964." *Muslim Mosque, Inc. Surveillance File*, March 26, 1964, pp. 13-4.

61. Malcolm X, "Message to the Grassroots," *Malcolm X Speaks*, p. 6.

62. Malcolm X, "The Ballot or the Bullet," *Malcolm X Speaks*, p. 37.

63. Ibid., p. 30.

64. Ibid., pp. 37-38.

65. Carlos Russell, "Exclusive Interview With Brother Malcolm X," *Liberator*, vol. 4, no. 5 (May 1964), p. 13.

66. Malcolm X, "Message to the Grassroots, pp.10-11.

67. Russell, "Exclusive Interview With Brother Malcolm X," p. 12.

68. Malcolm X, "Speech at the OAAU Founding Rally," *By Any Means Necessary: The Speeches, Interviews and a Letter by Malcolm X*, ed. George Breitman (New York: Pathfinder, 1970), p. 54.

69. FBI, "Transcript of Bud Dancy Show, KYW TV, April 4, 1964," *Muslim Mosque, Inc. Surveillance File (Memo From SAC Cleveland to Director FBI, April 14, 1964)*, p. 1a.

70. Ibid.

71. Malcolm X, *Malcolm X Speaks*, p. 11.

72. Ibid. p. 18.

73. Ibid. p. 11.

74. Russell, "Exclusive Interview With Brother Malcolm X," p. 13.

75. Ibid., p. 16.

76. Malcolm X, *Malcolm X Speaks*, p. 20.

77. FBI, "Memo to FBI Director from SAC Cleveland," *Muslim Mosque, Inc. Surveillance File*, April 10, 1964, p. 9.

78. Russell, "Exclusive Interview With Brother Malcolm X," p. 13.

79. Ibid.

80. FBI, "Transcript of Joe Rainey Show", p. 15.

81. Malcolm X, *The Speeches of Malcolm X at Harvard*, ed. Archie Epps, (New York: William Morrow, 1968), p. 182.

82. From Interview with *Young Socialist*, March-April 1965, *Malcolm X Speaks*, p. 199.

83. Williams, p. 16; Malcolm X, *Malcolm X Speaks*, pp. 66, 121-2: Malcolm X, *By Any Means Necessary*, p. 49.

84. George Breitman, *The Last Year of Malcolm X: The Evolution of a Revolutionary* (New York: Merit, 1967), p. 65.

85. Malcolm X, *Malcolm X Speaks*, p. 65.

86. Representative of African critical thinking on " African Socialism" is Issa G. Shivji,*Class Struggles in Tanzania* (New York: Monthly Review, 1976).

87. Malcolm X, "Speech at the OAAU Homecoming Rally," *By Any Means Necessary*, p. 136.

88. Ibid., p. 146.

89. Malcolm X, "Not Just an American Problem, But A World Problem," *Malcolm X: The Last Speeches*, pp. 152-53.

90. Malcolm X, *The Last Year of Malcolm X.*

91. Malcolm X, *Malcolm X: The Last Speeches*, p. 86.

92. Malcolm X, *By Any Means Necessary*, p. 153.

93. Malcolm X, *Malcolm X Speaks*, pp. 129-30.

94. Malcolm X, *By Any Means Necessary*, p. 154.

95. Karim interview.

96. Malcolm X, "Letter From Cairo: August 29, 1964," *By Any Means Necessary*, pp. 111-12.

97. Peter Goldman, *The Death and Life of Malcolm X,* 2nd ed. (Urbana: Univ. of Illinois, 1979), p. 181.

98. FBI, "Memo From Director FBI to SAC New York, Philadelphia, July 2, 1964" *OAAU Surveillance File*, p.2.

99. Malcolm X, "Bernice Bass Interview, December 27, 1964," *Malcolm X: The Last Speeches*, p. 98.

100. Malcolm X, *By Any Means Necessary*, p. 152.

5. The OAAU and the Politics of the Black United Front

1. George Breitman, *The Last Year of Malcolm X: The Evolution of a Revolutionary* (New York: Merit, 1967), p. 105-6.

2. Interview with Muhammed Ahmed (Max Stanford), New York, NY, December 28, 1987.

3. Peter Goldman, *The Death and Life of Malcolm X,* 2nd ed. (Urbana: Univ. of Illinois, 1979), p. 174.

4. Ibid. p. 172

5. Interview with Slyvester Leaks, New York, NY, Feb.3, 1988.

6. Malcolm X, "Speech at OAAU Homecoming Rally, November 29, 1964," *By Any Means Necessary*, George Breitman, ed., (New York: Pathfinder, 1970) p. 145.

7. Malcolm X, "We Are All Blood Brothers," *Liberator*, vol 4, no. 7 (July 1964), p. 5.

8. Interview with Victoria Garvin, New York, NY, June 15, 1988.

9. Ibid.

10. Malcolm X, "We All All Blood Brothers," p. 6.

11. Ibid.

12. See Carlos Moore, *Castro. The Blacks and Africa* (Los Angeles: UCLA-CAAS, 1989).

13. Reinaldo Penalver, Presentation at Symposium, "Malcolm X Speaks to the 1990's," Havana, Cuba, May 23, 1990.

14. Cited in FBI, *Malcolm X Surveillance File*, November 20, 1960.

15. Harold Cruse, *The Crisis of the Negro Intellectual: From Its Origins to the Present* (New York: Morrow, 1967), pp. 356-7.

16. Abdul Alkalimat, *Introduction to Afro-American Studies* (Chicago: 21st Century Books, 1985), p. 334.

17. Garvin interview.

18. Malcolm X, *By Any Means Necessary*, p. 141.

19. Interview with Peter Bailey, Richmond, Virginia, February 16, 1988: Interview with John Henrik Clarke, New York, NY, September, 8, 1988: Interview with James Shabazz, New York, NY, October 20, 1988.

20. Bailey interview.

21. Clarke interview.

22. Ahmed interview.

23. Maxwell C. Stanford (Muhammed Ahmed), *Revolutionary Action Movement (RAM): A Case Study of An Urban Revolutionary Movement in Western Capitalist Society* (Dept. of Political Science, Atlanta University, May 1986), p. 104.

24. *Washington Star*, June 14, 1964, p. 1.

25. Ahmed interview.

26. Stanford, *Revolutionary Action Movement (RAM)*, p. 105.

27. FBI, *OAAU Surveillance File* Letterhead Memo, July 15, 1964.

28. Ibid.

29. Ibid.

30. Malcolm X, *By Any Means Necessary*, p. 111.

31. Ibid., p. 109.

32. Ibid.

33. Ibid., p. 110.

34. Ibid.

35. Ibid.

36. Malcolm X, "Speech at OAAU Founding Rally, June 28, 1964," *By Any Means Necessary,* p. 37.

37. Washington interview.

38. FBI, "Letterhead Memo to Director from SAC New York," *OAAU Surveillance File*, October 19, 1964.

39. Interview with James Campbell, New York, N.Y., December 2, 1987.

40. Malcolm X, "We Are Blood Brothers", p. 6.

41. "OAAU Information Bureau" *Liberator*, October 1964, p. 16.

42. Interview with Yuri Kochiyama, New York, NY, November 5, 1987.

43. Ibid.

44. FBI, "Summary Report," *OAAU Surveillance File*, September 23, 1964, p. 32.

45. Campbell interview.

46. Bailey interview.

47. Interview with Benjamin Karim, Richmond, VA, February 15-16, 1988.

48. Shabazz interview.

49. FBI, p. 32.

50. Ibid.

51. Lincoln, *The Black Muslims in America*, pp. 207-8.

52. Earl Grant, "The Last Days of Malcolm X," *Malcolm X: The Man and His Times*, ed. John Henrik Clarke (New York: Collier Books, 1969), p. 91.

53. Bailey interview.

54. Ibid.

55. Ibid.

56. Ibid.

57. Campbell interview.

58. Grant, pp. 90-91.

59. FBI, p. 32.

60. Ibid., p. 22.

61. Shabazz interview.

62. Bailey interview.

63. Washington interview.

64. Interview with Ella Collins, Boston, MA, April 29, 1988.

65. Shabazz interview.

66. Ibid.

67. Morris, *The Origins of the Civil Rights Movement: Community Organizing for Change* (New York: Free Press, 1984), pp. 57-58.

68. Interview with Clarence Jones, New York, NY, February 9, 1989.

69. Macolm X, *By Any Means Necessary*, p. 134.

70. For a detailed description of each OAAU rally see William W. Sales, Jr.,"Malcolm X and the Organization of Afro-American Unity: A Case Study in Afro-American Nationalism," PhD. Dissertation, Dept. of Political Science, Columbia University, 1991, pp. 276-89.

71. Lincoln, *The Black Muslims in America*, p. 142.

72. Bailey interview.

73. Ibid.

74. Ibid.

75. Shabazz interview.

76. Liberator, October 1964, p. 16.

77. Campbell interview.

78. Ibid.

79. Ibid. FBI, "Summary Report," p. 32.

80. Campbell interview.

81. Ibid.

82. Ibid.

83. Ibid.

84. Ibid.

85. Malcolm X, "Memorandum to Meeting of OAU Heads of State, Cairo, Egypt, July 17, 1964," Breitman, *Malcolm X Speaks* ed., pp. 75-77.

86. Milton Henry, "Interview With Malcolm X in Cairo Egypt,"

87.Malcolm X, "Memorandum to Meeting of OAU Heads of State, Cairo, Egypt, July 17, 1964," Breitman, *Malcolm X Speaks* ed., p. 79.

88. Ibid., p. 84.

89. Ibid., p. 85; Claybourne Carson, *In Struggle: SNCC and the Black Awakening* (Cambridge, MA: Harvard University Press, 1985), p. 135.

90. Shabazz interview.

91. FBI, "LHM New York to Director," *OAAU Surveillance File* (June 30, 1964).

92. Leaks interview.

93. Ibid.

94. Goldman, *The Death and Life of Malcolm X*, p. 143.

95. Kochiyama; Washington interview.

96. Carson, *In Struggle*, p. 103.

97. Cleveland Sellars, Unpublished Speech at the "Hands on the Prize School," (Boston, MA, April 28, 1987).

98. Breitman, ed., p. 105.

99. Campbell interview.

100. Breitman, ed., *By Any Means Necessary*, pp. 137-46.

101. Ibid., p. 225.

102. Carson, *In Struggle*, p. 136.

103. Ahmed, Campbell, Bailey interviews.

104. Ibid., pp. 92-93.

105. Ibid.

106. Stanford, pp. 94-95.

107. Ibid., p. 103.

108. Malcolm X, "We Are All Blood Brothers," p. 4.

109. Ibid., p. 5.

110. Kochiyama interview.

111. FBI, "Summary Report," September 23, 1984.

112. Breitman, ed., *Malcolm X Speaks*, p. 221.

6. An Assessment of the OAAU

1. Aldon Morris, *The Origins of the Civil Rights Movement: Black Communities Organizing for Change* (New York: Free Press, 1984), pp. 103-4.

2. Ibid.

3. Ibid.

4. Kenneth O'Reilly, *Racial Matters: The FBI's Secret File on Black America, 1960-1972* (New York: Free Press, 1989), p. 132.

5. Ibid., p. 133.

6. Ibid., p. 140.

7. Doug McAdam, *Political Process and the Development of Black Insurgency: 1930 to 1970* (Chicago: Univ. of Chicago Press, 1985), p. 58.

8. Ibid., p. 57.

9. Ibid., p. 56.

10. O. Sykes, "The Week That Malcolm X Died", *Liberator*, vol. 5 no. 4 (April 1965), p. 6.

11. Peter Goldman, *The Death and Life of Malcolm X*, 2nd ed. (Urbana: University of Illinois Press, 1979).

12. Interview with Benjamin Karim, Richmond, VA, February 15-16, 1988.

13. Malcolm X, *By Any Means Necessary*, ed. George Breitman (New York: Pathfinder, 1970), p. 137.

14. Interview with James Smalls, New York, NY, February 19, 1988.

15. Karim interview.

16. Ibid.

17. Ibid.

18. FBI, "Memo From SAC Philadelphia Office to Director," *Muslim Mosque, Inc. Surveillance File*, October 8, 1964.

19. Ibid.

20. Interview with Hassan Washington, New York, NY, May 11, 1987.

21. Interview with Peter Bailey, Richmond, VA, February 16, 1988.

22. Ibid.

23. Ibid.

24. FBI, "Summary Report," *OAAU Surveillance File* (September 9, 1964), p. 29.

25. Ibid

26. Malcolm X, *By Any Means Necessary,* p. 110-11.

27. Ibid., pp. 111-12.

28. Earl Grant, "The Last Days of Malcolm X," *Malcolm X: The Man and His Times*, ed. John Henrik Clarke (New York: Collier Books, 1969), p. 90.

29. Ibid.

30. Bailey interview.

31. Washington interview.

32. Interview with James Shabazz, New York, NY, October 20, 1988.

33. Karim interview.

34. Washington interview.

35. Shabazz interview

36. Malcolm X, *By Any Means Necessary,* p. 139.

37. Goldman, *The Death and Life of Malcolm X*, p. 212.

38. FBI, "Memo from Director, FBI to SAC New York, Philadelphia "Organization of Afro-American Unity,." *OAAU Surveillance File* (Internal Security. Miscellaneous. 100-442235-July 2, 1964), p. 2. Earlier "dirty tricks" had been initiated

against Malcolm X and the Muslim Mosque, Inc. by the FBI as indicated in the outline of a plan contained in a memo from the SAC to Hoover dated April 10,1964 Detroit in which a phony letter was drafted over Malcolm's signature and sent to Muhammad's followers in Detroit so as to cause "disruption and deeper disputes between Nation of Islam leader Elijah Muhammad and Malcolm Little of Muslim Mosque, Inc."

39. Maxwell C. Stanford (Muhammed Ahmed), *Revolutionary Action Movement (RAM): A Case Study of An Urban Revolutionary Movement in Western Capitalist Society* (Dept. of Political Science, Atlanta University, May 1986), p. 182.

40. Kenneth O'Reilly, *Racial Matters,* p. 18.

41. Ibid.

42. Ibid., p. 42.

43. Ibid.

44. Ibid.

45. FBI, *OAU Surveillance File,* July 2, 1964.

46. *Big Red News,* July 28, 1990, p. 2.

47. Elaine Rivera, "The Man Who Spied on Malcolm X," *New York Newsday,* July 23-24, 1989.

48. Interview with Muhammed Ahmed (Max Stanford), New York, NY, December 28, 1987.

49. *Big Red News,* July 28, 1990, p. 2.

50. Ibid.

51. Ibid.

52. Ibid.

53. Ibid.

54. FBI, "Memo From SAC, Chicago to Director," *Muslim Mosque, Inc. Surveillance File* (April 10, 1964).

55. Louis Farrakhan, "Minister Who Knew Him Best Rips Malcolm's Treachery, part 1," *Muhammad Speaks,* May 8, 1964, p. 13.; Louis Farrakhan, "Fall of a Minister, part 2," *Muhammad Speaks,* June 5, 1964, p. 8.; Louis Farrakhan, "Truth and Trials of a Righteous Prophet," *Muhammad Speaks,* July 31, 1964, p. 11. Louis Farrakhan, "Malcolm–Muhammad's Biggest Hypocrite," *Muhammad Speaks,* December 4, 1964, p. 11.

56. Ibid.

57. Earl Grant, "The Last Days of Malcolm X," in *Malcolm X: The Man and His Times,* ed. John Henrik Clarke (New York: Collier Books, 1969), p. 90.

58. Ossie Davis, "Why I Eulogized Malcolm X," *Malcolm X: The Man and His Times,* pp. 128-31.

59. Bailey interview.

60. Interview with Ella Collins, Boston, MA, April 29, 1988.

61. Bailey interview.

62. Interview with James Campbell, New York, NY, December 2, 1987.

63. Washington interview.

64. Ibid.

7. Malcolm X's Ideological Legacy

1. Adolph Reed, Jr., "The Allure of Malcolm X and the Changing Character of Black Politics." *Malcolm X: In Our Own Image,* (New York: St. Martin's Press, 1992) p. 226, 232.

2. Malcolm X, *Malcolm X Speaks: Selected Speeches and Statements,* ed. George Breitman (New York: Grove Press, 1965).

3. Frantz Fanon, *The Wretched of the Earth* (New York: Grove Press, 1965).

4. James Boggs, *Manifesto for a Black Revolutionary Party* (Philadelphia: Pacesetters Publishing House, 1969).

5. William W. Sales, Jr. "Response to a 'Negro Negative,'" Immanuel Wallerstein and William Starr, eds. *University in Crisis: a Reader,* vol. 1 (New York: Vintage Books, 1971) p.371.

6. See *Mojo, Newsletter of the Black Student Congress,* vol. 1, no. 2 (May 1968), p. 1.

7. *Afro-Americans and the African Revolution: A Documentary History of the Two Line Struggle in ALSC* (Chicago: 21st Century Books, 1987), hereafter referred to as ALSC.

8. Claybourne Carson, *In Struggle: SNCC and the Black Awakening* (Cambridge: Harvard University Press, 1985), pp. 103-4.

9. See James H. Cone, *Martin, Malcolm and America: A Dream or a Nightmare* (Maryknoll, NY: Orbis, 1991).

10. Ibid.

11. James Forman, *The Making of Black Revolutionaries* (New York: MacMillan, 1972), p. 480.

12. See Dr. King's April 4, 1967 Speech at Riverside Church in opposition to the Vietnam War.

13. David Garrow, *Bearing the Cross: Martin Luther King and the Southern Christian Leadership Conference* (New York: William Morrow, 1986), p. 491.

14. FBI, "Letterhead Memo, SAC Cleveland to Director," *Muslim Mosque Surveillance File* (April 17, 1964).

15. James Cone,"I Have a Dream," *Martin & Malcolm & America: A Dream or a Nightmare* (Maryknoll: Orbis, 1991), Chap. 4., p. 296.

16. Gayraud S. Wilmore, *Black Religion and Black Radicalism* (Garden City, NY: Doubleday, 1972), p. 238.

17. Ibid., p. 256.

18. See Allan Boesak, *Coming Out of the Wilderness: A Comparative Interpretation of the Ethic of Martin Luther King, Jr. and Malcolm X* (Kampen, Holland: J.H. Kok, 1976).

19. See Bill Sales, *Southern Africa/Black America, Same Struggle, Same Fight* (New York: Black Liberation Press, 1977).

20. As quoted in James Booker, "Is Mecca Changing Malcolm X?," *Amsterdam News,* May 23, 1964, p. 14.

21. See Yusuf N. Kly, ed., *The Black Book: The True Political Philosophy of Malcolm X (El Hajj Malik El Shabazz)* (Atlanta: Clarity Press, 1986).

22. Representative of their work is Ron Karenga, *Kawaida Theory: An Introductory Outline* (Inglewood, CA: Kawaida Publications, 1980) and Imamu A. Baraka, "Black Nationalism: 1972," *The Black Scholar*, vol. 4, no. 3 (September 1964), pp. 23-29.

23. Abdul Alkalimat, *Introduction to Afro-American Studies* (Chicago: 21st Century Books, 1985), p. 308.

24. Imari Obadele, "Comments," Symposium: Malcolm X Work Group, New York City, May 19, 1989 (Audio Tape).

25. Black Panther Party, "Ten Point Program," *The Black Experience in American Politics*, ed. Charles V. Hamilton (New York: Capricorn Books, 1973), pp. 213-14.

26. Alkalimat, *Introduction to Afro-American Studies*, p. 309.

27. RAM emerged at predominantly Black Central State College in Ohio in the Spring of 1962. It was an outgrowth of the campus Students for a Democratic Society chapter. Its members entered various Civil Rights organizations and also became strong supporters of Robert Williams, the controversial NAACP leader in Monroe, North Carolina. The Black Panther Party was formed in 1966 at Oakland, California's Merritt Junior College by Huey P. Newton and Bobby Seale. It initially reflected the northern support effort for the Loundes County Freedom Organization of SNCC and in 1967-68 enjoyed a short merger with SNCC. Its armed confrontations with police and its rhetorical style became characteristic features of the organization, especially when Eldridge Cleaver became one of its leading figures. Both RAM and the Panthers were targets of the FBI Cointelpro operation. The League of Revolutionary Black Workers was formed in 1969 as a merger of various Black caucuses that had emerged on the shop floor in the automobile industry. In 1968 the Dodge Revolutionary Union Movement (DRUM) at Crysler's Hamtramch Assembly Plant in Detroit was the first of several of these caucuses to disrupt the assembly line to advance an agenda against the management and the UAW for its alleged racial discrimination.

28. Malcolm X, "The Ballot or the Bullet," *Malcolm X Speaks*, pp. 28-31.

29. Malcolm X, *Malcolm X: The Last Speeches*. ed. Bruce Perry (New York: Pathfinder, 1990), p. 154.

30. Akbar M. Ahmed, "A Brief History of the Black Liberation Movement in the 1960s: Focus on RAM," Unpublished Speech (Chicago: Northeastern University, 1978).

31. Ibid.

32. The profound impact of Malcolm X on a Black Panther leader is represented in Eldridge Cleaver,"Initial Reactions on the Assassination of Malcolm X," *Soul on Ice* (New York: Delta Books, 1968), pp. 50-64.

33. "Huey Must Be Set Free," *The Black Panther,* November 23, 1967 *The Black Experience in American Politics*, p. 219.

34. Alkalimat, *Introduction to Afro-American Studies*, p. 305.

35. Ferruccio Gambino, "Malcolm X, Laborer: From the Wilderness of the American Empire to Cultural Self Identification." *Studies on Malcolm X, Newsletter of the Malcolm X Work Group* vol. 1, p. 13.

36. Mao Tse Tung, *Quotations From Chairman Mao Tse Tung* (Peking: Foreign Language Press, 1972).

37. FBI, "New China News Agency Interview With Malcolm X," *Malcolm X Surveillance File* (January 14, 1965).

38. Alkalimat, *Introduction to Afro-American Studies*, p. 334.

39. Ibid.

40. Ibid., p. 258.

8. The Organizational Legacy of the OAAU

1. Adolph Reed, Jr., "The Allure of Malcolm X and the Changing Character of Black Politics." *Malcolm X: In Our Own Image,* (New York: St. Martin's Press, 1992) p. 226, 232.

2. Interview at Patrice Lumumba Forum on Political Prisoners, Harriet Tubman School, New York, N.Y., July 1993.

3. Amiri Baraka, "Malcolm as Ideology," *Malcolm X: In Our Own Image*, p. 23-24

4. Ibid.

5. See Hanes Walton, *Black Political Parties: An Historical and Political Analysis* (New York: Free Press, 1972), Chap. 3.

6. Ibid., pp. 131-57.

7. Frances Beal, "Slave of a Slave No More: Black Women in Struggle," *The Black Scholar*, vol. 4 (March 1975), pp. 2-10.

8. George Lipsitz, "Grass Roots Activists and Social Change: The Story of Ivory Perry," UCLA, *Center for African and Afro American Studies Newsletter*, vol. 9, no. 2 (1986), p. 8.

9. Ibid.

10. Walton, *Black Political Parties*, pp. 56-59.

11. Herbert J. Gans, "Symbolic Ethnicity: The Future of Ethnic Groups and Cultures in America," *Majority and Minority : The Dynamics of Race and Ethnicity in American Life,* 4th ed., Norman Yetman, ed. (Boston: Allyn and Bacon, 1985), pp. 429-41.

12. James Forman, *The Making of Black Revolutionaries* (New York: MacMillan, 1972), p. 467.

13. Assata Shakur, *Assata: An Autobiography* (Westport, CT: Lawrence Hill, 1987), p. 252.

14. Claybourne Carson, *In Struggle: SNCC and the Black Awakening* (Cambridge, MA: Harvard University Press, 1985), p. 263.

15. Forman, *The Making of Black Revolutionaries,* p. 507.

16. Ibid., 481-92.

17. *Afro-Americans and the African Revolution: A Documentary History of the Two Line Struggle in ALSC* (Chicago: 21st Century Books, 1987), hereafter referred to as ALSC.

18. Ibid.

19. Ibid.

20. See the special issue "Focus on the Sixth Pan-African Congress," *Black World*, March 1974, pp. 5-70.

21. ALSC.

22. Ibid.

23. Abdul Alkalimat and Bill Sales, "Lessons of ALSC," *The City Sun*, May 20, 1987.

24. Ibid.

9. Malcolm X's Legacy of Leadership and Charisma

1. Julius Lester, "The Angry Children of Malcolm X," eds. August Meier, Elliot Rudwick, and Francis Broderick, Black Protest Thought in the 20th Century (Indianapolis: Bobbs-Merrill, 1965) p. 479.

2. Ferruccio Gambino, "Malcolm X, Laborer: From the Wilderness of the American Empire to Cultural Self Identification" *Studies on Malcolm X Newsletter of the Malcolm X Work Group*. vol. 1, pp. 4-9.

3. Interview with Peter Bailey, Richmond, VA, February 16, 1988.

4. Interview with John Henrik Clarke, New York, NY, September 8, 1988.

5. Interview with Muhammed Ahmed (Max Stanford), New York, NY, December 28, 1987.

6. Ibid.

7. George Breitman, *The Last Year of Malcolm X: The Evolution of a Revolutionary* (New York: Merit, 1967).

8. Charles Tilly, *From Mobilization to Revolution* (Reading, MA: Addison-Wesley, 1978), p. 156.

SELECTED BIBLIOGRAPHY

Ahmed, Akbar M. "A Brief History of the Black Liberation Movement in the 1960s: Focus on RAM." Unpublished Speech, Chicago, Northeastern University, 1978.

Alkalimat, Abdul. *Malcolm X for Beginners*. New York: Writers and Readers Press, 1990.

_____.Studies on Malcolm X: A Review Essay and Reseach Design. *Sage Race Relations Abstracts*. Vol. 17, no. 11 November, 1992.

_____. Why Remenber Malcolm. *Forward Motion*, vol 9, no.1 (March 1990). p.3-7.

Black, Pearl. "Malcolm X Returns," *Liberator*, vol. 5, no. 1 (January 1965), pp. 5-6.

Blake, J. Herman. "Black Nationalism," *The Annals of the American Academy of Political and Social Science*, vol. 382 (March 1969), p. 15-25.

Boesak, Allan. *Coming Out of the Wilderness: A Comparative Interpretation of the Ethic of Martin Luther King, Jr. and Malcolm X*. Kampen, Holland: J.H. Kok, 1976.

Bracey, John, August Meier, and Elliot Rudwick, eds., *Black Nationalism in America*. Indianapolis: Bobbs-Merrill, 1970.

Brath, Elombe. Unpublished Speech at the Fannie Lou Hamer Institute, New York, N.Y., February 11, 1987.

_____. Speech at the Annual Symposium of the Malcolm X Work Group, New York, N.Y., May 20, 1989.

Brotz, Howard. *The Black Jews of Harlem: Negro Nationalism and the Dilemmas of Negro Leadership*. Glencoe, N.Y.: Free Press, 1964.

Breitman, George. *Malcolm X: The Man and His Ideas*. New York: Pathfinder, 1965.

_____. *The Last Year of Malcolm X: The Evolution of a Revolutionary*. New York: Merit, 1967.

_____(ed.). *The Assassination of Malcolm X*. New York: Pathfinder Press, 1970.

Carson, Claybourne. *Malcoln X: The FBI Files*. New York: Carrol and Graf, 1991.

Cone, James H. *Martin and Malcolm and America: A Dream or a Nightmare*. Maryknoll, NY: Orbis, 1991.

Davis, Linwood. *Malcolm X: A Selected Bibliography*. Westport, CT: Greenwood Press, 1984.

Essien-Udom E.U. *Black Nationalism: A Search for Identity in America*. Chicago: University of Chicago Press, 1962.

Evanzz, Karl. *The Judas Factor: The Plot to Kill Malcolm X*. New York: Thunder Mouth Press, 1992.

Gambino, Ferruccio. "Malcolm X, Laborer: From the Wilderness of the American Empire to Cultural Self Identification," *Studies on Malcolm X: Newsletter of the Malcolm X Work Group*, vol 1, no. 1 (Fall 1987).

Goldman, Peter. *The Death and Life of Malcolm X*. 2nd ed. Urbana, Illinois: University of Illinois Press, 1979.

Johnson, Timothy. *Malcolm X: A Comprehensive Annotated Bibliography*. New York: Garland, 1986.

Karim, Benjamin. *Remembering Malcolm: The Story of Malcolm X from Inside the Muslim Mosque by his Assistant Minister Benjamin Karim*. New York: Carrol and Graf, 1992.

Kly, Yusuf N. ed. *The Black Book: The True Political Philosophy of Malcolm X (El Hajj Malik El Shabazz)* Atlanta: Clarity Press, 1986.

Lincoln, C. Eric. *The Black Muslims in America*. Boston: Beacon Press, 1961.

Lomax, Louis. *When the Word is Given: A Report on Elijah Muhammed, Malcolm X and the Black Muslim World*. Cleveland: World Publishing, 1993.

Malcolm X. *The Autobiography of Malcolm X,* with the assistance of Alex Haley. New York: Grove Press, 1965.

_____. *By Any Means Necessary*. George Breitman. ed. New York: Pathfinder Press, 1970.

_____. *The End of White World Supremacy: Four Speeches of Malcolm X.* Benjamin Goodman. ed.New York: Merlin House,1971.

_____. *Malcolm X on Afro-American History*. edited by George Breitman (expanded) New York: Pathfinder, 1972.

_____. *Malcolm X Speaks*. George Breitman. ed. New York: Pathfinder, 1976.

_____. *Malcolm X Talks to Young People*. New York: Pathfinder (no date).

_____. *The Speeches of Malcolm X at Harvard*. Edited with an introductory essay by Archie Epps. New York: Morrow, 1968.

_____. *Two Speeches of Malcolm X*. New York: Pathfinder (no date).

_____. "We Are All Blood Brothers," *Liberator*, vol. 4, no. 7 (July 1964).

Obadele, Imari. "Comments", Symposium: Malcolm X Work Group, New York City: May 19, 1989 (Audio Tape).

Perry, Bruce F. "Malcolm X in Brief: A Psychological Perspective," *Journal of Psychohistory*, vol. 11 (Spring 1984).

Sales, William W., Jr. *Malcolm X and the Organization of Afro-American Unity: A Case Study in Afro-American Nationalism.* Ann Arbor: Dissertation Services, 1991.

Stanford (Muhammed Ahmed), Maxwell C. "Revolutionary Action Movement (RAM): A Case Study of An Urban Revolutionary Movement in Western Capitalist Society." unpublished Master's essay, Dept. of Political Science, Atlanta University, May 1986.

Sykes, O. "The Week That Malcolm X Died," *Liberator*, vol. 5, no .4 (April 1965).

T'Shaka, Oba. *The Political Legacy of Malcolm X.* Chicago: Third World Press, 1983.

Vincent, Theodore, "The Garveyite Parents of Malcolm X," *Black Scholar*, vol. 20, no. 2, (1989), pp. 10-13.

Williams, Michael. "The Split: Some Ideological and Organizational Implications of Malcolm X's Break With the Nation of Islam," Unpublished paper, Department of Afro-American and African Studies, University of North Carolina at Charlotte, 1990, p. 7 (Xerox).

Wilmore, Gayraud. *Black Religion and Black Radicalism* (Garden City, N.Y.: Doubleday, 1972).

Wolfenstein, *The Victims of Democracy: Malcolm X and the Black Revolution.* New York: Columbia University Press, 1990.

Wood, Joe. *Malcolm X: In Our Image.* New York: St. Martin Press, 1992.

Selected Interviews

Hassan Washington-interviewed in New York City, May 11, 1987.

Yuri Kochiyama-interviewed in New York City, November 5, 1987.

James Campbell-interviewed in New York City, December 2, 1987.

Akbar Muhammad Ahmed-interviewed in New York City, December 28, 1987.

Sylvester Leaks-interviewed in Brooklyn, New York, February 3, 1988.

Benjamin Karim-interviewed in Richmond VA, February 15-16, 1988.

A. Peter Bailey-interviewed in Richmond VA, February 16, 1988.

James Smalls-interviewed in New York City, February 19, 1988.

Ella Collins-interviewed in Boston, Massachusetts, April 29, 1988.

Victoria Garvin-interviewed in Jamaica, New York, June 15, 1988.

John Henrik Clarke-interviewed in New York City, September 8, 1988.

James Shabazz-interviewed in Brooklyn, New York, October 20, 1988

Clarence Jones-interviewed in New York City, February 9, 1989.

Government Documents

Federal Bureau of Investigation (FBI). Malcolm X FBI Surveillance File (2 Reels Microfilm). Wilmington, Delaware: Scholarly Resources, 1978.

Federal Bureau of Investigation (FBI). Muslim Mosque, Inc. FBI Surveillance File (100-441765), unpublished.

_____. Organization of Afro-American Unity (OAAU) FBI Surveillance File (100 442235), unpublished.

_____. FBI Malcolm X Little Elsur Logs [Phone Tap Logs] June 3, 1964 to October 3, 1964 (105-8999-Sub 1), unpublished.

Abbreviations

AAPRP	All African Peoples Revolutionary Party
ADUS	African Descendants Uplift Society
ALSC	African Liberation Support Committee
BPP	Black Panther Party
CORE	Congress of Racial Equality
BWC	Black Workers Congress
CAP	Congress of Afrikan People
COFO	Confederation of Freedom Organization
FOI	Fruit of Islam
GOAL	Group for Advanced Leadership
LCFO	Lowndes County Freedom Organization
LRBW	League of Revolutionary Black Workers
MMI	Muslim Mosque, Inc.
NAG	Non-violent Action Group
NBIPP	National Black Independent Political Party
NOI	Nation of Islam
OAU	Organization of African Unity
OAAU	Organization of Afro-American Unity
PAC	Pan-African Congress
RNA	Republic of New Africa
SCLC	Southern Christian Leadership Conference
SNCC	Student Non-Violent Coordinating Committee
UNIA	Universal Negro Improvement Association

Index

A

African American Expatriate Community in Ghana, 101-102
African American Nationalism, 15, 19, 21-22, 23, 27, 41, 42, 48, 59-60, 71
   cultural nationalism in, 175-176, 190
   definition, 59
   and Pan Africanism, 85
   revolutionary nationalism in, 27, 73, 75-76, 79, 106, 129, 176-181
   and violence, 196, 197
African Americans,
   economic conditions, 6-7, 13, 28-29, 32, 34-35, 44
   political culture, 57
   social conditions, 9, 11, 13, 29, 34, 35, 42-43
   urban rebellions, 12, 17, 44
African Descendants Uplift Society (ADUS), 109
African Liberation Day 1972, 16, 201
African Liberation Support Committee, 16, 23, 170, 201-204
African National Congress, 18, 104, 142
African Nationalist Liberation Movement, 143
African Nationalist Pioneer Movement, 60
Afro-American Freedom Fighters, 106
Afro-American Student Conference on Black Nationalism, 129-130
Afro-American Student Movement, 129
Ahmed, Muhammed Akbar (Max Stanford), 58, 99, 105, 129-130
Alkalimat, Abdul, 3, 28
All Afrikan Peoples Revolutionary Party, 16, 177

American Creed, 45, 47
American Dream, 45, 46, 135-136
Anderson, S.E., 200
Anti-apartheid movement, 16-18
Apartheid, 144
Atlanta Convention, 192
Audubon Ballroom, 116
The Autobiography of Malcolm X, 27-28
Azikiwe, Nnamdi, 100

B

Babu, Mohammad Rahman, 101
Bailey, A. Peter, 106, 112, 113, 114, 119, 149, 160, 208
Baird, Keith, 22, 121
Baker, Ella, 210
Baldwin, James, 157
Baraka, Amiri, 175, 187-188
Basheer, Ahmed, 60
Bass, Bernice, 92
Beal, Fran, 190
Beard, Keith, 22
Ben, Bella Ahmed, 157
Ben, Jochanan Joseph, 60, 121
Ben, Wahad Dhoruba, 187
Biko, Stephen, 16, 17
Bimbi, 33, 54
Bishop, Maurice, 18
Black Arts Movement, 22
Black Belt Nation Thesis, 176
Black Convention Movement, 192, 212
Black Economic Development Conference, 199
Black Liberation Army, 198
Black Liberation Movement, 8, 17-18, 20-21, 167-168, 182, 188-189
   critique of, 197-198
Black Liberation Press, 16

241

Black Manifesto, 199
Black New York Action Committee, 23
Black Panther Party, 169, 177, 180,
  181, 190, 202
  Ten-Point Program, 177
Black Power, 21, 170-171
Black Power Conferences, 182-183
Black Power Movement, 170, 208
Black United Front, 192-196
Black Workers Congress, 182, 203
Blacklash The, 113, 116, 118
Blacks in Solidarity With Southern Af-
  rican Liberation (BISSAL), 16
Boesak, Alan, 174
Boggs, James, 179-180
Bourne, St. Claire, 200
Boutiba, Mahmoud, 157
Brath, Elombe, 23, 60
Brotz, Howard, 45, 66
Brown, Edwardina, 131
Brown, H. Rap, 198
Browne, Robert, 200
Burnham, Margaret, 9
Burroughs, Vinnie, 200
Bush, George, 10, 11, 12

C

Campbell, James, 22, 112, 114, 120,
  121-122, 128, 160
Carmichael, Stokely (Kwame Ture),
  16, 127, 178, 199
Castro, Fidel, 103
Central Intelligence Agency (CIA),
  143, 156
Chicago Open Housing Campaign, 172
China, Peoples Republic of,
  position on Malcolm X, 103
Civil Rights, 35, 42-43
Civil Rights Act of 1964, 123, 153
Civil Rights Movement, 21-22, 27, 44-
  46, 48, 75, 136-137, 141-142
  role of ideology in, 45-46
Clarke, John Henrik, 22, 60, 105, 121,
  212
Clinton, Bill, 11, 12
Cole, Johnnetta, 11

Collins, Ella, 30, 31, 60, 115, 160
Columbia University student uprising
  of 1968, 22-23
Communist Party (CPUSA), 155, 176,
  181
Cone, James, 3, 46, 173
Confederation of Freedom Organiza-
  tions (COFO), 127
Congo Crisis, 124, 143
Congress of Afrikan People (CAP),
  170, 175, 182, 199, 202
Congress of Racial Equality (CORE),
  22, 142, 143
Congressional Black Caucus, 201, 203
Cooks, Carlos, 60
Cooperative Research Network in
  Black Studies, 3, 23
Cooptation and Repression, 135-138,
  140
Crane, Les, 89
Cuba, 9, 18
  position on Malcolm X, 102-103
Cuban Missile Crisis, 145
Cuomo, Mario, 11

D

Daniels, Ron, 3
Davis, Eddie "Pork Chop," 60, 121
Davis, Irving, 199
Davis, Ossie, 107
Dee, Ruby, 107
Delany, Martin R., 55-56
Democratic Party, 203
Deracialization, 11
Diggs, Charles, 203
Double consciousness, 135, 136
DuBois, W.E.B., 24, 101, 120, 135, 207
Duke, David, 12

E

Eisenhower, Dwight D., 103
Entralgo, Armando, 102
Epton, Bill, 23, 107, 155
Essien-Udom, E.U., 45, 60

L

Lawson, James, 60
League of Revolutionary Black Workers, 178, 180-181, 182, 198, 202-203
Leaks, Sylvester, 60
Lee, Spike, 4, 94
Levison, Stanley, 48
Lewis, John, 129, 130
Lincoln, C. Eric, 113, 118
Lipsitz, George, 191
Little, Earl, 30
Little, Louise, 30, 31
Locke, Alain, 29
Lowndes County Freedom Organization, 189-190
Lynn, Conrad, 107, 155

M

Malcolm X, 142
and Africa, 37, 82, 87-88, 90, 93, 142
and African American middle class, 80, 81-82, 91-92, 93
and African American nationalism, 69
and African American working class, 27, 31, 33, 36, 41, 44
on African socialism, 86
The Autobiography of Malcolm X, 27-28
"Ballot or the Bullet" speech, 77-78
and Black Liberation theology, 173-174
Black nationalism defined, 72, 75-76, 80
and Black Student Movement, 169-170
on Black unity, 81, 83
charisma, sources of, 207-208
and Civil Rights Movement, 36, 37, 42, 43, 125, 211-213
on class and nationalism, 79

criticism of civil rights leadership, 73-74
critique of Black nationalism, 88-89
critique of capitalism, 85
critique of nonviolence, 168-169
electoral politics, 68, 78, 90, 128,170, 214
impact on Martin Luther King, 172-173
impact on Nation of Islam, 148
integration, position on, 80
intellectual method, 53-59, 207
leadership, 57-59, 210-211
memorandum to OAU Cairo meeting, 122-123
"Message to the Grassroots" speech, 76-78, 81
Muhammad, Elijah, relationship with, 69-70
and Nation of Islam, 33, 36, 42, 43, 55, 66, 68-69, 157-158
on nationalism and culture, 79-80
Pan Africanism in the thinking of, 87-88
perceptions of whites, 83-84, 92-93, 132
personal attributes of, 209-210
political thought, periodization of, 60-61
position on African liberation movements, 104
position on Japan, 111
position on Vietnam War, 111
prison experiences, 33
rhetorical skills, 208-209
on role of women, 84, 92, 114
sources of nationalism, 72-73
and students, 127
and Sunni Islam, 37, 42, 68, 100, 146, 174
trips to Africa in 1964, 37, 100-101, 122, 131
on violence, 77, 79, 90
Malcolm X Committee, 101
Malcolm X Foundation, 3

About the Author and South End Press

William W. Sales, Jr. is a scholar-activist with thirty years of experience in the Civil Rights, Black Student, Black Studies, and African Liberation support struggles. He is the author of numerous articles and the book *Southern Africa/Black America: Same Struggle, Same Fight.* Presently, Sales is a professor at Seton Hall University, where he chairs the Department of African American Studies.

South End Press is a nonprofit, collectively-run book publisher with over 175 titles in print. Since our founding in 1977, we have tried to meet the needs of readers who are exploring, or are already committed to, the politics of radical social change.

Our goal is to publish books that encourage critical thinking and constructive action on the key political, cultural, social, economic, and ecological issues shaping life in the United States and in the world. In this way, we hope to give expression to a wide diversity of democratic social movements and to provide an alternative to the products of corporate publishing.

Through the Institute for Social and Cultural Change, South End Press works with other political media projects—*Z Magazine;* Speak Out!, a speakers bureau; the Publishers Support Project; and the New Liberation News Service—to expand access to information and critical analysis. If you would like a free catalog of South End Press books, please write to us at South End Press, 116 Saint Botolph Street, Boston, MA 02115. Also consider becoming a South End Press member: your $40 annual donation entitles you to two free books and a 40% discount on our entire list.

Other Titles Of Interest:

African Americans at the Crossroads:
The Restructuring of Black Leadership and the 1992 Elections
by Clarence Lusane

Confronting Environmental Racism: Voices from the Grassroots
by Robert Bullard

Black Looks: Race and Representation
by bell hooks

Breaking Bread: Insurgent Black Intellectual Life
by bell hooks and Cornel West

How Capitalism Underdeveloped Black America
by Manning Marable